PARTY, SOCIETY AND GOVERNMENT

Contemporary France
General Editor: Jolyon Howorth, University of Bath

PARTY, SOCIETY AND GOVERNMENT

Republican Democracy in France

David Hanley

Berghahn Books
New York • Oxford

First published in 2002 by Berghahn Books

www.berghahnbooks.com

© 2002 David Hanley

Library of Congress Cataloging-in-Publication Data

Hanley, D. L. (David L.), 1944–
    Party, society and government : republican democracy in France / David Hanley.
        p. cm. -- (Contemporary France ; v. 5)
    Includes bibliographical references and index.
    ISBN 1-57181-966-5 (alk. paper) -- ISBN 1-57181-337-3 (pbk.)
        1. Political parties--France. 2. Democracy--France. 3. Politics, Practical--France.
    4. Social choice--Political aspects--France. I. Title. II. Contemporary France; v. 5.

JN2997.H36 2002
320.944--dc21   200103445

British Library Cataloguing in Publication Data

A catalogue record for this book is available from the British Library.

ISBN 1-57181-966-5 hardback
ISBN 1-57181-337-3 paperback

For Barbara

Contents

LIST OF TABLES

FIGURES

❧

PREFACE

The idea for this book arose from the chapter that I contributed to David Broughton and Mark Donovan's Changing Party Systems in Western Europe (1999). Attempting to come to grips, in a relatively short space, with the complexities of the French party system brought home to me how deep-rooted and historically determined that system is. A fuller examination of that complexity was clearly required.

Immediate causes apart, the present book has allowed me to merge, in a way that I hope is fruitful, two of my abiding intellectual interests: French society on the one hand and political parties on the other.

Readers will doubtless not expect me to justify four decades of engagement with one of the most sophisticated of civilisations, but a fascination with parties does perhaps require some sort of apologia. Few writers in any language seem to have much time for these creatures; when a political system works tolerably well, they are taken for granted. However, as soon as problems occur, they are usually the first to be scapegoated. Perhaps this is because parties are often seen in a very mechanical way, especially when they are analysed in terms of party systems: invariably they appear as functional pieces of machinery, obeying a certain logic (often perverse), but nothing else. I have always found this strange. Much of the work I have done on parties has involved fieldwork, working from the bottom up, as it were. Such work obviously attempts to use existing theory, but it can only be done properly if carried out with a very open mind and a refusal to put the object of study into a theoretical strait-jacket from the outset.

It may be the case that years of interviewing devoted activists, attending meetings and congresses or snatching answers from hard-pressed and elusive deciders begins to affect researchers. Be that as it may, such an open approach makes it very hard to see parties in mechanical terms. On the contrary, the closer one comes, the more the parties take on animal or even human forms, showing distinct behavioural patterns. They can exhibit strong and positive behaviour but can also secrete their own contradictions and pathologies. Without subsiding into anthropomorphism, analysis has somehow to address this non-mechanical dimension; this task is even more urgent when one tries to analyse, as is the case here, parties as components of a system.

Beyond this methodological concern, I have also been concerned to rehabilitate party as a political phenomenon. The focus of this study is France, and I have made no serious attempt to use a comparative framework, choosing deliberately to deepen the analysis of one party system in the hope that it may serve as a basis for later works. One can either write a comparative study or a one-country work, but not two for the price of one. I have taken the latter option, as I believe that the French party system, mature and developed as it is, more than warrants examination in its own right. Many of the criticisms levelled at party in France are echoed elsewhere, however. Equally, a number of the defences of party which I offer could be used, mutatis mutandis, in other national contexts. To that extent I would hope that the present work may help to allay, in a modest way, the tirades regularly loosed against party. For one basic truth needs to be restated periodically: whatever its shortcomings, there has been no better vehicle through human history for giving political expression to the demands of social groups ; nor is that situation likely to change.

The writing of this book has taken a number of years, facilitated by a grant of study leave from Cardiff University. Many friends and colleagues have contributed to it in different ways, often without realising; in particular I would like to thank David Broughton, Gordon Cumming, Graeme Garrard, Steve Griggs and above all David Jackson, whose good sense and lucidity remain as acute as ever after 40 years of friendship. Barbara's contribution was also vital, and it is to her that the book is dedicated. None of them, of course, bears any responsibility for the book's shortcomings.

ABBREVIATIONS

ALP   Alliance Libérale Populaire
ARD   Alliance Républicaine Démocratique
ARS   Action Républicaine et Sociale
BN   Bloc National
CD   Centre Droit (Third Republic)
           Centre Démocrate (Fifth Republic)
CDS   Centre des Démocrates Sociaux
CERES   Centre d'Etudes, de Recherches et d'Education Socialistes
CG   Centre Gauche (Third Republic)
CGT   Confédération Générale du Travail
CNIP   Centre National des Indépendants et des Paysans
DL   Démocratie Libérale (formerly PR)
ERD   Entente Républicaine et Démocratique (rightwards tendency of BN, mainly based on FR)
FD   Force Démocrate (formerly CDS)
FLN   Front de Libération Nationale (Algerian nationalists)
FN   Front National
FN-MN   Front National-Mouvement National (Mégret)
FNC   Fédération Nationale Catholique
FR   Fédération Républicaine
GInd   Gauche Indépendante
GRad   Gauche Radicale
GRep   Gauche Républicaine
IAESP   Indépendants d'Action Economique, Sociale et Paysanne (Third Republic)
IOM   Indépendants d'Outre-Mer (Fourth Republic)
LCR   Ligue Communiste Révolutionnaire
LO   Lutte Ouvrière
MDC   Mouvement des Citoyens (formerly CERES)
MRG   Mouvement des Radicaux de Gauche
MRP   Mouvement Républicain Populaire
PCF   Parti Communiste Français
PDP   Parti Démocrate Populaire
PPF   Parti Populaire Français
PR   Parti Républicain

PRS	Parti Radical-Socialiste (formerly MRG)
PSF	Parti Social Français (formerly Croix de Feu)
PS	Parti Socialiste
PSU	Parti Socialiste Unifié
PUP	Parti de l'Unité Prolétarienne
RepG	Républicains de Gauche
RGR	Rassemblement des Gauches Républicaines
RPF	Rassemblement du Peuple Français (1947)
	Rassemblement pour la France (1999)
RPR	Rassemblement pour la République
RS	Républicains Socialistes
SFIO	Section Française de l'Internationale Ouvrière
UDF	Union pour la Démocratie Française
UDR	Union des Démocrates pour la République
UDSR	Union Démocratique et Socialiste de la Résistance
UnG	Union de la Gauche (Third Republic)
UNR	Union pour la Nouvelle République
UR	Union Républicaine (Third Republic)

INTRODUCTION
Parties and Party Systems in the Political Development of France

All parties are fatal to the public good; it is in the national interest to crush them just as it is every citizen's duty to unmask them.[1]

Robespierre, quoted in Albertini (1961: 545)

Régimes based on parties are a shambles. We had one before the First World War, of course; for a long time it toddled along, and no-one took many risks...What did the parties do? They didn't do anything! They overthrew governments as usual...Between the wars you know what we had – a mediocre, impotent régime where disaster could be seen on the horizon and no-one really did anything to prevent it...That's party régimes for you. So of course we were beaten and crushed in 1940. We were totally unprepared, we were divided by the parties, we didn't have the weapons we needed.[2]

C. de Gaulle, broadcast of 15 December 1965

These highly critical views of parties are fairly typical of the dominant strain of opinion on this question during the past two centuries. It matters not that, ironically, the authors of our two quotations were both past masters at party management; their angry strictures have been replicated in innumerable places. They encapsulate what many politicians, voters and academic commentators feel about the rôle that parties have played in the political development of France. Parties tend to be blamed for the failures of the modern French state, whether it be the military defeat of 1940 and the subsequent burial of democracy by the Vichy régime, or the ignominious collapse of the Fourth Republic in 1958 at the hands of a soldier/settler lobby overseas (Williams, 1964; Julliard, 1967).

Continuing an ideological tradition which goes back to Rousseau, such critiques see parties as fundamentally illegitimate. Inevitably, it is alleged, they

1. 'Tout parti est funeste à la chose publique; il est de l'intérêt national de l'étouffer comme il est du devoir de chaque citoyen de le dévoiler'.

2. 'Le régime des partis, c'est la pagaille. Evidemment, on l'a vécu avant la Première Guerre mondiale; pendant longtemps cela allait cahin-caha...on ne risquait pas grand-chose...Qu'est-ce qu'ils avaient fait, les partis? Ils n'avaient rien fait! Ils renversaient les ministères comme à l'habitude...Entre les deux guerres...il y a eu alors ce qu'on sait, c'est à dire un régime de médiocrité, un régime d'impuissance, où le désastre se dessinait à l'horizon sans que l'on fit en réalité rien pour l'empêcher....Voilà le régime des partis. Alors naturellement on a été battu, écrasé en 1940. On n'avait rien préparé, on était divisé par les partis, on n'avait pas les armes nécessaires'.

represent narrow sectional interests and not the national or popular interest. Led by weak or incompetent politicians, they are said to be incapable of winning enough support for their own programmes or of making lasting compromises with others; one major source of such weakness would be the parties' basic lack of discipline. Contemporary critics saw them as perpetuating outmoded ideological struggles in their own interest (Tarde and de Jouvenel, 1924). At a low point in the Fourth Republic an exasperated commentator could even write that French parties did not represent real interests, just 'abstractions' (Lavau, 1953: 139). Latterly, parties are said to be in even greater trouble, in the shape of a 'crisis of representation', amplifying Daalder's concept (1992) of a 'crisis of party'. This refers to the general decline of voting of late and the fact that many who do vote give their support not to mainstream parties but to protest parties or new, untried forces. The mainstream parties seem to be struggling to draw in new members or activists (Perrineau, 1994).

Critics usually point out with relish that much of the disaffection with parties can be ascribed to their heavy and regular involvement in financial scandals or other types of corruption (Mény 1992; 1993; 1997a; 1997b) and refer to opinion polls which show very low ratings for career politicians (Mossuz-Lavau, 1994). Certainly, as Mair suggested (1995), the increasing involvement of parties at the heart of the state's operation is likely to increase their visiblity, hence vulnerability to criticism. The special dossier of Le Canard Enchaîné (1993) captured a widely-shared mood, making much play of the privileges enjoyed by the political class generally.

Given that parties have been heavily involved in the government of France since the 1870s, it might be wondered how France has achieved any sort of progress during this period if parties have been as destructive as is alleged. There are standard answers to this question. For earlier republics, it is customary to attribute the major rôle in devising and implementing policy to the civil service. In this version, beloved of English-language studies of France, the administration ruled while the elected politicians played party games[3]. Sometimes charismatic explanations are brought in. The argument is that the periodic crises engendered by parties' irresponsibility had to be defused by the intervention of a deus ex machina (Doumergue in 1934, Mendes-France in 1954, etc.). For the Fifth Republic, the champions of the administrative state and the 'Great man' theory of history can make common cause; critics of party are able to point to the development of presidential rule. This is easier for the earlier heroic period of gaullism, where the General and his team of technocrats addressed urgent problems with success, but becomes less plausible once the General's charisma had become routinised. We will show that the Fifth Republic, in either its presidential or cohabitationist variants, still allows huge scope for parties.

Parties remain at the heart of the French political process. It is generally agreed nowadays that France has developed a stable and efficient political system,

3. For a counter-view see Chagnollaud (1996).

widely accepted by its citizens, after long being regarded as the problem child of North Western Europe, capable only of running its politics in a fragmented and crisis-prone manner. Parties have been, and remain, central to the process. The parties have always been locked into a system, however. Unlike the Anglo-Saxon democracies which developed mainly two-party systems within which the major political conflicts could be resolved clearly (which does not necessarily mean in a non-antagonistic way), France produced very early on a complex multiparty system, in which the major cleavage lines within French society tended to throw up multiple organisations to represent those on either side of the division. Such multiplicity of parties is not necessarily a problem where the communities represented by the parties show cohesion and discipline and their élites can negotiate compromises with others in the political system; this is of course the basis of the 'consensual democracies' (Lijphart, 1968; 1977; 1997).

Unfortunately, France was, by the time mass democracy arrived, not remotely near to such a position. The violent social, ideological and political clashes, which recurred regularly between 1789 and the collapse of the Second Empire in 1870, guaranteed the existence of a badly split polity, with major, ostensibly irreconcilable, divisions on class and ideological questions (essentially the role of catholicism in French society), not to mention simple politics, which started with the very nature of the régime.

It is against this backdrop that the formation of the modern French party system needs to be understood. Since the 1870s (or even before, if one takes a generous definition of party) France has evolved a multi-party system of considerable sophistication, arguably, pace its critics, one of the most sophisticated in the modern world. The historical rôle of this system has been to manage the real and angry conflicts within French society through the political arena (which meant through parliament in the early stages, though, increasingly, parties have had to assume wider roles across society, as will be seen). In this way, parties have undoubtedly made a major contribution to the modernisation of France and to the loss of that 'exceptional status' which, it seems agreed, she enjoys less and less (Furet, Julliard and Rosanvallon, 1988; Duhamel, 1989; Hewlett, 1998).

In their task of representing and balancing different interests within a complex society, parties inevitably find ways of relating to each other. The more complex the society and the wider the range of parties expressing its demands, the more sophisticated such relationships are likely to become. Over time it becomes possible to discern distinct patterns in these relationships. At this point we may speak of a party system. A party system is much more than the sum total of the parties comprising it; it summates the relationships between these protagonists. Such relationships can be complex, subtle and at best semi-visible, but in complex polities they are what keeps the political system turning over.

Over 120 years ago France began to develop, with what seems in retrospect quite remarkable speed, a complex party system that would both give expression to the conflicting demands emerging from civil society and somehow balance and broker those demands. Previously, groups had sought satisfaction for their demands by attempting to overthrow the existing régime, sometimes successfully. Now the rules were to change (although not all players understood this immediately). In an era of parliamentary government resting on universal male suffrage, conflicts were to be settled by electoral and parliamentary means. Our contention is that the party system was highly efficient at brokering the claims of rival influences, but that the mechanisms of the party system have never been adequately explored. This process of brokering was often tense and dangerous; at other times it was low key, unexciting and possibly sordid. De Gaulle's diatribe quoted at the head of this chapter captures something of the anger and contempt which is widely felt for the underside of party politics. But whatever the reasons, academic studies have been reluctant to confront the rôle of parties acting within a party system in the development of modern French politics.

There are of course innumerable studies of individual parties and of the different republics, but it is comparatively rare for a study to bring together analysis of the régime and of the actual party system. François Goguel came instinctively close to this with his classic study of the Third Republic (1946). Nevertheless, while he conveys a sense of the dynamics of the régime, his use of the bipolar opposition between movement and order shifts conflicts to a higher plane; between two almost metaphysical principles rather than between parties – that is to say groups of men with an organisation, objectives, a strategy and common loyalties. Contemporary studies of the parties (Jacques, 1913; Carrère and Bourgin, 1924) were few in number and, while being informative, tended towards description or preaching. Very competent recent accounts of Third Republic politics such as Mayeur (1984) or Lévêque (1992) tend not to use the insights of recent work on party systems, stimulating as they can be on individual parties. The invaluable work done latterly by Paris-based historians associated with Jean-Marie Mayeur or René Rémond on significant yet little known aspects of partisan life in earlier republics (Billard, 1993; Harismendy, 1994; Sanson, 1992) testifies to the vigour of party scholarship; but again this work is heavily biased towards specific groups or forces at the expense of the partisan system per se. Nicolas Roussellier's studies of 1920s party politics (1992, 1997) combine political theory and historical technique adroitly and show awareness of systemic factors, however, the fact that they are confined to so short a period simply underlines the need for a longer-term study. Philip Williams' masterful study of the Fourth Republic (1964) comes nearest to seizing the logic of the party system, but it was written before political science became seriously interested in party systems in their own right and, in any case, it covers only the postwar period.

There is much work, some of it showing considerable acuity, on the party system of the present republic (Bartolini, 1984; Bell and Criddle, 1994a; Charlot, 1989; Cole, 1990; Ignazi and Ysmal, 1998; Machin, 1989). Such contributions make use of the more general or comparative corpus of work on party systems which has flourished latterly (Daalder and Mair, 1983; Wolinetz, 1988; Laver, 1989; Mair, 1989; Smith, 1989; Mair and Smith, 1990; Mair, 1997;

Pennings and Lane, 1998). Sophisticated political theory of this type can be very illuminating, and its influence will be seen at some points of this work. However, perhaps because of its generalising ambition and its wish to subsume as many different experiences as possible under broad comparative headings, it can on occasion be ahistorical, treating its subjects as if they existed in a timeless vacuum; parties have their own history, and so, by the same token, do the party systems of which they form part. This consideration is particularly relevant for a system as old as the French one, with deep roots plunging into a complex, slowly evolving society. Only an approach which combines diachronic elements with synchronic ones is likely to yield a proper understanding of such phenomena. Despite the vigour of recent scholarship, what is still lacking, in our view, is a longer term examination of the party system over three republics, from the 1870s to the present. We will attempt to provide such an analysis, marrying concepts from party systems theory with the insights provided by historical research. Political science and history do not always have to pull in opposing directions; it is our hope that a combination of both methods may yield some new understanding of an important political phenomenon.

Only such a *longue durée* approach will reveal the underlying logic of the French partisan system, while showing the changes which have occurred, for both continuity and change are present. It is hardly a caricature to say that if Ferry or Gambetta were to walk into the National Assembly today, they might be surprised to see strange bedfellows such as greens or communists; equally, it would not take them long to find out whether business could be done with such people, and if so, how.

Two preliminary points need to be made in conclusion. This book seeks to elucidate the way in which parties translated social demand into political forms. This meant, primarily, providing France with a viable government; the focus of the study is on how governments were formed and how they operated. It is not a study of public policy or government output, which have been amply analysed elsewhere; such outputs are not entirely absent from our account but they intervene only as a factor affecting the prime business – forming and maintaining governments. This focus on the prime task of the party system prompts a second consideration, to do with the nature of party. Much theoretical literature on party systems reads like an engineering or cybernetics manual, in that parties appear as pieces of machinery operating in accord with some overall external logic; even when 'endogenous' elements such as party strategies or internal conflicts are allowed to appear, then they are fed into the overall model like any other input. One appreciates the theoretical clarity which such a 'black box' approach can bring, but it does risk evacuating the human element. Parties are not simply machines, but teams of people led by élites, who analyse, predict and calculate on the full understanding that their competitors are doing the same. When a party 'takes a decision', it means that its leaders have adopted a policy and are trying to enforce it. These agents are trying to modify the structure, constraining as it always is, within which they operate; they are actually influencing what goes into the 'black box'. Without sacrificing to voluntarism, our account will try to restore the balance between agency and structure, which has become eroded to the latter's advantage.

The party system deserves a study in its own right as one of the factors contributing to the modernisation of French politics. We will begin by reviewing some of the basic assumptions about parties and how they represent interests within divided societies, focusing particularly on the rôle of party systems within this process. We shall then address the creation of a party system from the 1870s onwards, as France committed itself to a particular style of democracy. Thereafter, our framework will be mainly historical, as we attempt to seize the different periods in the development of French democracy and isolate their specific characteristics, showing always how the party system was at the core of this development, shaping it while in turn being modified by it. Our final chapter will draw together the overall threads of the period and suggest a tentative theoretical summation. In this way we hope to bring out the importance of a crucial but under-appreciated element of the modernisation of France.

1

THE PROBLEM OF REPRESENTATION
Party as Actor or Reflector?

The representative is the substitute for the group, which only exists through the actions of its representative.[1]

Gaxie, Economie des partis

This book has as its focus the contribution made by parties to French democracy; this contribution essentially consisted in the parties' ability, which they alone possessed to any significant degree, to represent the interests of the main groups of French society within the political process.

The notion of representation is full of pitfalls (Graham, 1994a). We need, first, to beware of the essentialist fallacy – in Sartrean terms, of putting essence before existence. Political analysts often write as if parties were mere reflections of perfectly defined social groups with an identity and clearly knowable demands; all that the parties do then is transmit such desiderata into the political process. It is as if parties are mirrors, albeit with a loud-speaker attached. This view of parties as essentially passive agents probably stems from marxist or sociological approaches, which tend to stress structure (usually social class) at the expense of agency.

This view of party has surprisingly deep roots across a wide range of literature. In their elegant essay on party, Donegani and Sadoun (1994) elaborate endlessly on the special function of party as a link between 'the one and the multiple'. They mean that party expresses some intermediary identity between the strong sense of individual identity characteristic of modern societies and the feeling of being part of a wider society; but these intermediary identities are simply assumed, in an abstract way, to exist already. Rosanvallon (1998: 182ff.), in his free-ranging review of representation within French democracy, also sees parties as providing some level of identity, replacing in a way the *corps intermédiaires* of pre-revolutionary France, beloved of his intellectual mentor Tocqueville. However, while he suggests that parties can to some extent help create social identities (p. 184), he does not follow up this insight, speaking, for instance, of working

1. 'le représentant est le substitut du groupe qui n'existe qu'à travers les actes de son représentant'.

class parties being 'une incarnation sociale' (p. 191). This is a very clear example of essentialism, taking the base of a party's support as something given.

Some recent writers, coming from a background which shows traces of marxism but owes most to the sociology of Max Weber and Pierre Bourdieu (1981), are much more ready to see parties as active agents (Offerlé, 1997; Gaxie, 1977; 1996). Despite its somewhat rigid vocabulary and its all-pervasive attachment to the notion of politics as a marketplace, this approach has the merit of refusing to see parties as mere incarnations of some immanent social reality. On the contrary, it stresses their creative functions. Parties actually identify and promote interests within society; they seek out issues around which support can be formed and they work hard to consolidate such support.[2] There is nothing spontaneous, then, about the formation of, say, working-class parties. These owe their existence not so much as to inevitable historical pressures (the class revolting against the weight of exploitation) as to the insight, organisational skills and hard work of a number of political élites. These élites identified class conflict as a fundamental issue on which large numbers of people could be mobilised (as voters and as activists); they then worked to organise such mobilisation through (their) party. In the last analysis, the party created the class rather than the reverse. In the business language beloved of this school of thought, a set of political entrepreneurs (the emergent social democratic élites) identified a new set of customers (the working class) and sold it a number of products (the various rewards that come from party activity both before and after winning office).

A second advantage of this approach is that it takes a sanguine view of the motivations of party leaders and activists. Much literature on parties (especially those of the left) tends to take at face value the parties' self-descriptions; these usually suggest an organisation pursuing large and quite noble objectives (either giving fair representation to groups in a context of pluralism or pursuing some more ambitious project of social transformation). The neo-weberian approach reminds us of the various rewards, both material and symbolic, which come with party activity; to pursue the market analogy further, the directors and workers of the party / firm are entitled to their profits or their career opportunities.

This type of approach is also valuable in that it stresses the tenuous and precarious means by which 'representation' takes place. Parties are constantly working to convince their social base (the interests which they are supposed to represent) that it exists and is entitled to certain goods. They also strive to convince this base (and themselves) that they are its sole competent representatives, and, by the same token, try to exclude rivals from any claim to repre-

---

2. Schattschneider (1975) is one of the best-known Anglo-Saxon exponents of this line. In his discussion of possible types of link between parties and individuals, Ware (1996: 197–202) tends to assume that ties of solidarity (typical of the phase of the mass party) are intrinsic and differ from the links between parties and more modern, 'detached' voters, who have to be won over by any number of strategies. Many might argue, however, that even solidarity is not spontaneous, but is worked at and developed by political entrepreneurs.

sent this base. Representation is thus a very inexact science, an 'ever-precari-
ous construction' (Offerlé, 1997: 107).[3] We will leave Offerlé the last word on
what representation by parties means in all its untidy reality (1997:109):[4]

> representing first and foremost themselves, their peers and the most active fraction
> of their voters, the representatives fit in, often unknowingly or reluctantly, with the
> expectations (contradictory, unstable, maybe even risky) of those who feel akin
> to them

Our approach will use the insights of this method, trying to lay stress on the
active, entrepreneurial rôle of party.[5] However, important as the efforts of
party entrepreneurs are, we have to recognise that parties are not called into
being on just any set of issues. We start, therefore, from the historical and
sociological approach to the problem of party formation associated with the
work of Rokkan and Lipset (1967) and developed by Seiler (1980).

From cleavage to family to party

The historical and sociological approach centres on the relationship between
deep-lying cleavages within a society and the eventual party system with
which that society endows itself so as to conduct its politics. Using an historical approach, such analyses usually identify four major types of cleavages
which emerge typically as modern societies develop. These are cleavages of
social class and religion, centre-periphery splits, often mediated through territorial or cultural differences, and the urban-rural divide[6]. The configuration
of parties in modern democracies can, according to this approach, always be
traced back somehow to this set of fundamental cleavages (Mair, 1990).

These cleavages arise historically as society undergoes a double process of
change, the complexity of which is only scantily rendered by a term such as
modernisation. On the one hand, nation-states are built. This process
involves cultural and ideological struggles against the hegemonic values of
the pre-modern or feudal order, often incarnated in the church; new loyalties
and values have to be imposed across the emergent nation as it is being built.

3. 'le résultat toujours précaire d'un travail de construction'.
4. 'représentatifs d'abord des représentants, de leurs pairs et de la fraction la plus mobilisé de
leur électorat, les représentants s'ajustent, bien souvent sans le savoir ni sans le vouloir, aux
atttentes contradictoires, erratiques, voire hasardeuses, de ceux qui se reconnaissent en eux'.
5. Kay Lawson's work based on the concept of linkage also allows us to see the process of representation in the dialectical way set out above, with perhaps a slightly different emphasis. In her
schema, citizens' demands are not merely fed into government by party; government can also
initiate within the process, setting agendas and stimulating support through use of the party.
Linkage is thus a two-way street, so to speak (Lawson, 1980).
6. This list is not fixed for all time, and active debate goes on as to whether it should be added
to. Are there, for instance, fundamental new cleavages between European-integrationists and
sovereignists? (Guyomarch, 1995). Or might age and educational differences now be attaining
the status of significant cleavages? (Budge, Newton et al., 1997: 218).

At the same time, the territorial consolidation of the new state means a lev-elling out of cultural, linguistic and even ethnic differences; people have to be made to feel part of the new unit. The imagined community, to use Ander-son's phrase, has to be made reality in peoples' minds by a conscious process of education and acculturation (Anderson, 1983). On the other hand, indus-trialisation is carried forward in a brutal process involving huge social dis-placement. A new class, the working class, is created, the peasantry is reconfigured, the older aristocracy is firmly marginalised and the bourgeoisie becomes clearly dominant.

As Seiler remarks, the bourgeoisie is at the heart of both these processes, which may overlap considerably in temporal terms. These socio-cultural changes carry an immense potential for violence, and violence usually breaks out early in the process. But as the societies develop culturally and politically, the conflicts become more manageable; the protagonists learn to conduct their struggles in the political arenas rather than on the street or the battlefield. This does not mean that the antagonisms disappear, but simply that both sides learn how to handle them; we could say that there was an agreement to disagree. At this stage it becomes appropriate to speak of cleavages rather than of conflicts.

Crucial in this evolution are parties. It is they who organise the protago-nists on either side of the stress line and attempt to protect their interests by fighting in the political arena. Historically, this is the stage when the suffrage begins to be widened and government becomes less oligarchical. The origi-nal social wounds remain, but they are memories rather than living realities; the parties remember where they came from and will use that memory to rally support. But they are now fighting political battles not physical ones.

Taking the four cleavages as starting points and assuming that each cleavage finds political expression in two opposed forces, we might expect then to find eight types of party (Seiler prefers the term 'family'). Thus, the class cleavage should produce worker and bourgeois parties;[7] the cultural or church/state clash should produce parties of religious defence and anti-clerical or secularist parties. The centre/periphery tension should produce nation-building, cen-tralising parties, set against regionalist or sub-national parties concerned to defend peripheral cultures, languages or ways of life. The urban/rural split should produce peasant parties and purely urban forces, but the latter type never materialises; on reflection this is logical enough in that the urban popu-lation are bourgeois, petty bourgeois and workers who are quite adequately represented by their own class-parties. The peasantry, victim of change, is a dif-ferent matter; it will often react by creating a party of its own. On this basis Seiler duly identifies seven classic families (1980: 126ff.).

Few analysts would quarrel with this method as a starting point, but one key

7. It might be asked why his model makes no mention of another type of class-party, namely the party of the petty bourgeoisie. Historically such parties have existed, and we would argue that the radical party in France was such a party (significantly it is absent from Seiler's model). It may well have begun life primarily as an anti-clerical party, but early on it assumed a number of features which clearly identify it as a defender of a certain stratum of the middle groups in French society.

point must be borne in mind, namely that the relationship between the social cleavages and the parties is not necessarily a simple, one-way connexion. Perhaps influenced by the apparent simplicity of mainly two-party systems like those of the UK and the US, studies often imply that a cleavage usually finds (or should find) expression in a straight opposition between two parties, one for the interests on either side of the cleavage. Thus, ideally, one bourgeois party should find itself confronted by a united workers' party; one religious party should be opposed by one party for rationalists, secularists, etc. Already this reductionist approach suggests a dangerously passive rôle for parties, stripping them of any rôle as active agents and threatening to reduce them to the status of social epiphenomena (the 'carriers' of pristine social interests). Historical reality is clearly more complex, and we may expect to find that in countries with long histories of sharp political conflict the relationship between social cleavages and the formation of parties was an untidy one, with cleavages overlapping and the party system thus being driven towards multiplicity and complexity rather than bipolar opposition. Such was evidently the case with France.

Certainly, in the French case the violence of the original conflicts and contradictions was archetypal. The Revolution ushered in several decades of frequent and direct class struggle, culminating in 1848–52; it is unsurprising that Marx used such empirical material to develop at first hand his methods of materialist historical analysis. Even after the Commune of 1871, social unrest was regular and acute enough to be used easily as a mobilising factor by party entrepreneurs. The church/state struggle was also brutal and prolonged. The assault on the status of the church contained in the Civil Constitution of the Clergy (1790) and in the dechristianising movements of 1792–94 was physical as well as juridical and economic.[8] Even after 1905, when radicalism had finally won its battle to separate church and state, clashes between catholics and soldiers or police over inventories of church property still resulted in riots, injuries and a few deaths, over and above the huge ideological polarisation caused by such measures (Mayeur, 1966: 111–46). These cleavages were deep and lasting and would require careful political management.

The two other cleavages appear less angry. The peasantry did not produce the sort of revolt that might have been expected from a class subject to the full pressure of economic development, nor did the French periphery, in all its diversity, produce lasting political mobilisation. These cases raise questions about the way in which the cleavages were translated into manageable terms by party entrepreneurs; why was it that some were easier to process

8. In rapid order, the church was stripped of its main income, the tithe, and saw its property (amounting to a tenth of the land-mass of France) confiscated and sold off. Many religious orders were banned. During the intense period of dechristianisation, over 1,000 religious were murdered and over 32,000 deported or forced into exile; most of the remainder were effectively forbidden to officiate (Gibson, 1989: 31–55). The Vendée region was the seat of a religiously inspired civil war against the Revolution for over two years. Although Napoleon I did much to restore working relations between church and state with the Concordat, the bitterness that the period left in popular memories in many areas can be imagined. It is no surprise that as Gibson says (p.53) 'the association of catholicism with the right … came to seem somehow natural'.

than others? It is to this translation of cleavage into party that we now turn.

If we examine the relationship between each of the cleavages in France and the party system which eventually emerged, we find mixed results. To take first the class cleavage, it is clear that the working class was able to produce partisan organisation to defend its interests. Unfortunately for theoretical tidiness, it produced not one durable party but two; one socialist, the other communist. Comparison with other countries suggests that there is nothing preordained about such an outcome, where a communist party escapes, so to speak, from the socialist shell. Clearly political explanations will have to be sought for this. Looking at the bourgeois parties, the picture is hazy in the extreme. In the year 2000 there is still no unified party to look after bourgeois interests in the way that the Conservative party does in the UK or the Republicans do in the US. In earlier epochs the picture was even more untidy, with a multiplicity of small, rather weak formations. Again the reasons for this are, we will argue, ultimately political, revolving around the strategies and calculations of party élites. Perhaps the best fit between class and party is, in its way, the radical party, which can be said to have defended a recognisable and numerous middle group within French society with great success. Even here, though, a large section of the middle class, namely Catholics, were ipso facto excluded from the party's embrace.

The most serious problem with the class/party relationship is the failure by the most numerous class to equip itself with anything resembling a partisan organisation (Lavau, 1953: 141). Marx's characterisation of the peasantry as 'a sack of potatoes' is well borne out by the political failures of this social group (still representing well over a quarter of the workforce after 1945). The Fourth Republic saw an ephemeral peasant party with a few deputies, and some of the groups in the interwar parliaments tacked the word paysan on to their title, usually as one of several adjectives. Yet pre-1939 Europe saw a wealth of peasant parties, and there is no reason to suppose that French farmers were any less clever politically than their counterparts in Hungary or Poland. Clearly other parties were able to persuade French farmers that they were appropriate representatives, be it on grounds of ideological proximity, ability to defend economic interests or whatever. The point is that active party entrepreneurs won a market by their efforts; there was nothing predetermined about this.

The radical case suggests strong interplay between social cleavages and ideological ones. Examination of the religious cleavage confirms this. Radicalism mobilised its troops on the basis of class interest certainly, and Birnbaum's vision of les petits contre les gros (1979) encapsulates this well. Berstein (in Lavau, 1983: 71–93) shows that the radical party became ever more conscious of its rôle as champion of the middle-groups at the expense of its previous rhetoric about an undifferentiated peuple. This class appeal was, however, inseparable from the radical party's anti-clericalism, an ideology which found expression both as a set of values, laïcité, (secularism), and a political programme (cutting the church out of public life). Such a programme was bound to exclude large sections of the middle class who were catholic, even if not fervently, but that was a deliberate choice by the entrepreneurs who founded the party.

The case of catholic political expression shows, from a different angle, how loose is the fit between ideological cleavage and party (Rémond, 1965: 57–88). Commentators long marvelled at the failure of the 'church's eldest daughter' to produce a viable christian democratic party before 1944, and then , having produced one, that the French party system dissipated it within a generation. Compared with the experience of neighbouring states, this failure does seem surprising, but perhaps only if one is subconsciously influenced by the reductionist approach described above. Once political factors are taken into account (strategies of key actors within and outside of France), explanations can be found, and the cleavage approach kept but modified.

The centre/periphery cleavage has had at best a muted expression in France. Daniel Seiler suggests that the real difference between today's RPR and UDF parties is that the former are diehard centralists, whereas the UDF is much more of a classical liberal party typical of parties of 'bourgeois defence' (1980: 352). The RPR is, from this viewpoint, the continuation of a long tradition of what Rémond (1968) calls the 'bonapartist right' – a party or parties dedicated to preserving national unity on the basis of strong government and concessions to the lower classes expressed in populist rhetoric. Implicitly the liberal or orleanist rivals to this current (to keep Rémond's terminology) would be decentralisers. Seiler was writing as debates on administrative decentralisation were coming to a climax prior to the socialist victory of 1981 and the implementation of a far-reaching programme. His thesis has some plausibility, but if the tension between jacobins and girondins has undoubtedly existed since the Revolution, it would be hard to claim that it has always found expression in tidy partisan form. When the orleanist right has been in power in its various partisan forms, it has behaved in a highly centralising fashion when it thought fit. Even since Seiler wrote, movement within today's two big parties suggests that UDF and RPR each have their girondins as well as their jacobins (Knapp and Le Galès, 1993); as in earlier periods, this antagonism tends to be subsumed by others. On the other side of the centre/periphery contradiction, regional parties have always existed, but have remained extremely marginal and never been a serious electoral threat factor on their own natural territory. Thus, regions like Alsace and Brittany tended between the wars to elect PDP representatives or deputies of similar christian-democratic hue, rather than regionalists or nationalists (Delbreil, 1990);[9] French Basques voted for conservative catholic deputies (and still tend to do so). Religious motivations proved stronger than (or became conflated with) regional ones. We would argue that the real reason for the failure of regional forces to emerge on a serious level has to do with a widespread consensus among mainstream parties. By the time of the mature Third Republic, all major protagonists were jacobins; the only serious regionalisers were the old, anti-republican hard right, whose power base lay precisely on the periphery. Mainstream party leaders all knew the potential fis-

9. An exception would be the small and short-lived group of Alsatian autonomist deputies (Républicains du centre) led by Michel Walter in the 1930s.

siparity of the French polity, composed as it was of gradual territorial and ethnic additions to the original core of Ile-de-France; they knew that the state had
made the nation and that unity needed maintenance and active sustenance.
These parties relied on active territorial management from Paris, via the prefects
and field services, as well as on the efforts of republican schoolteachers. They
were confident that this, along with the growth of a national market and modern communications systems, plus compulsory military service for young men,
could instil enough sense of a national community to keep the provinces loyal
(Weber, 1977). At the same time the cumul des mandats, the combination of
local and national office-holding, allowed provincial élites considerable access
to Parisian decision-makers and resources; this further tightened the bonds. In
these ways, the mainstream parties changed the market conditions to engineer
the exclusion of potential regionalist rivals. The absence of such forces in France
today, compared with the weight of, say, the Scottish National Party or Plaid
Cymru in the UK, suggest that their calculations were shrewd. Overall, it seems
clear that the centre/periphery antagonism has never been expressed cleanly in
partisan form and that to some extent it has been overlaid by other contradictions, partly because of the ability of parties to present it thus to the voters.

The urban/rural cleavage was, it can be seen, similarly subsumed. When this
cleavage does impact on party formation, it usually means the creation of some
sort of agrarian party. We have already suggested that, despite the huge potential for such a creation, it never happened because other parties reacted first.

Table 1.1 shows how the major party families can be derived from the main
cleavages. The number 1 shows the main origin of a given party; but with
time, parties also become subject to the influence of other cleavages. This
influence, which we might call secondary, is denoted by the number 2 on the

Table 1.1 Societal Cleavages and Party Families

Family	Working-class		Bourgeois	Anticler.	Relig. Defence	Centralisers
	Communists	Socialists	Republicans	Radicals	Christian	Democrats
Cleavage						
Class	1	1	1	2	2	2
State/ Church	2–3	2	1	1	1	2
Centre/ Periphery	3	2–3	2	2	2	1
Urban/ Rural	2–3	3	2	2	2–3	2

1: primary determinant
2: significant determinant, usually at a second stage
3: relatively unimportant

chart. In some cases it seems legitimate to postulate the effect of a further cleavage, 3. To give an example, the radical party derives originally from the church/state cleavage, but at a very early stage it could be seen as a defender of the middle classes (or the secularist parts thereof), combining a small-town, professional clientèle with strong swathes of support among the independent peasantry and enjoying clear superiority in certain geographical areas. It is factors such as the social structure of voters and activists, as well as party programmes, which may enable us to postulate the class character of such a party, beyond its initial ideologically based appeal.

The case of the socialist SFIO illustrates the problem in the opposite way. Conceived as a vehicle for working class revolution, the party exemplified proudly the central social cleavage between owners and propertyless. Soon it would increasingly espouse much of the mainstream republican ideology of anti-clericalism and laïcité. From the viewpoint of strict class analysis, such questions are at best irrelevant, at worst a bourgeois mystification, but with time such ideology became central to the party's identity, while its class character (measured by the social composition of voters and members, if not discourse) weakened.

There is nothing accidental about the influence of a second cleavage on the shape of a party. The party has usually made a distinct choice, identifying a new market of potential voters to add to its original core; in terms of Kirchheimer's ladder (1966), this is when a mass party might rise to the rank of a catch-all party. As for the effect of what we might call tertiary cleavages, the experience of the radicals and socialists is telling. Both were born of class or church/state tensions, the effects of which soon meshed, as we saw; but both also harboured, initially at least, decentralising notions. These did not last long, owing mainly to experience of government (local as well as national). Control of a well-oiled mechanism which allowed ample opportunity to reward supporters and consolidate an electoral base was something which came with the centralised state. Thus, beneath the class or secularist rhetoric which fuelled these parties, quiet conversion to jacobinism proceeded apace. Conversely, mainstream republicans were probably much more sensitive to this dimension from the start; their jacobinism went hand in hand with their secularism.

Looking back from the main party families towards the societal cleavages, we can now see how complex were the patterns of descent. Clearly, the working class parties, socialist and communist, stem from the primary contradiction of capital versus labour. However, this did not prevent them reflecting also, in a second phase, the church/state clash. They were drawn inevitably on to one side of the divide, the republican, and this became a source of electoral appeal. We have suggested that even a third cleavage, that of the centre/periphery, subsequently became important to the SFIO, which would show increasing symptoms of jacobinism as it absorbed other parts of republican culture. Its behaviour during the Algerian War (1954–62) probably marked the apex of this attitude. The bourgeois opponents of these parties, namely the groups of mainstream republicanism, reflect with equal intensity the class cleavage and the church/state one; rhetoric apart it is hard to assign more importance to one of these cleavages than the other in determining the rise of republican parties. Bourgeois republicanism talked more about church/state clashes, but it always acted as a conscious representative of clear social interests, the industrial, commercial and financial bourgeoisie as well as the broad swathe of petty bourgeois who followed its lead. If the republicans wanted to secure a secular democratic state, it was not simply out of idealism; such a vehicle seemed to them the most appropriate for the defence of the material interests which they represented.

The radicals and the christian democrats are derivations of the church/state tension; but neither was a disembodied classless formation. We saw that radicalism soon came to be identified with a certain type of provincial middle-class. By the same token, christian parties also tended to aggregate quite a broad class alliance, usually non-Parisian, under bourgeois leadership. This is why we have given such parties a relatively high score on the centre/periphery axis; they tended to become a focus for local identity as well as religious, thereby undoubtedly narrowing the space for more regionalist parties.

Probably the most difficult parties to place into this schema are what we have called centralisers. Most of the authoritarian right, from bonapartists through to the nationalists of 1900 and the Front National of today, has been driven by fears about the unity of France; it has never seen any kind of decentralisation as a recipe for strengthening that unity. This current stems clearly from the centre/periphery tension. Other cleavages are thus secondary in its genesis. This kind of politics was often considered clerical by definition; but there have been enough examples from the likes of Doriot to the FN to show that this is not always the case. Similarly, although the activist base of such movements may be petty bourgeois, the movements themselves are not classist in character. They are not intended primarily as a means of bourgeois defence. One particularly difficult subsection of this family to classify is gaullism. Seiler unhesitatingly derives it primarily from the centre/periphery tension, which fits well with analysts like Rémond who see it as a variant of the bonapartist tradition, but it is, at the same time, representative of a certain type of bourgeois interest that seeks a more nationally oriented economic policy. Its vote tends to come in normal times from the better-off, employers and independents. It has therefore a distinct class character, and this is why we have placed it among the mainstream republican parties rather than putting it with the pure centralisers.

Such then are the primary and subsequent derivations of the main party families in France from the main societal cleavages. Table 1.2 shows the different parties which belong to each family; they are listed roughly in chronological order of appearance within each family. In this way the link from cleavage to family to actual party can be seen.

In conclusion, what this survey of the cleavages in France shows is that the fit between cleavage and party formation is anything but automatic. The cleavages existed in France as sharply as they did anywhere else in Europe, but the way in which they were translated into partisan forces depended hugely

Table 1.2 Party Families and Parliamentary Groups / Parties

Working-class parties
Communists: PCF, PUP, Trotskyites (LO, LCR, etc.)
Socialists: SFIO and predecessors (POF, PSdeF, etc.), PS, PSU
Bourgeois parties: all mainstream republican parties – GRep, UR, Gauche radicale, Gauche démocratique, Républicains de gauche, Progressists / FR, ERD, ARS, CNIP, RI / PR / DL; Gaullism (RPF-UNR-UDR-RPR)
Secularist parties: Radical party, RS, MRG, PRS
Religious defence parties: Ralliés, ALP, Sillon / JR, PDP, MRP, CD, CDS, FD
Centralisers: Bonapartists, Boulangists, Nationalists, FN

Rural: Parti paysan
N.B. These are arranged in roughly chronological order for each family. For the full title of any group, see List of Abbreviations.

on the action of the party builders or political entrepreneurs. They constructed the identities of those they claimed to represent, in many cases shutting out prospective rivals with some skill. A crucial part of this exclusion process was due to the electoral system, that key component of all party systems.

Electoral Systems, Party and Localism

Universal manhood suffrage had been ushered in with the revolutionary advent of the Second Republic. This early gain was never reversed, although the conservatives who took over after 1849 sought to reduce the number of voters and the Second Empire used a combination of bribes and arm-twisting to influence outcomes. When the Third Republic was established, however, the consensus among élites was that the suffrage had to be respected; the main protagonists were now confident of being able to influence sufficient voters. The consensus also extended, less visibly, to keeping women off the electoral roll. Although socialists, and indeed the moderate right, would, in time, have women's suffrage as part of their programme, they seldom made it an overriding issue, leaving the senate (dominated by radicals and other republicans fearful of alleged clerical influences on women) to vote down bills in favour of women voting.

   If it was accepted that elections were necessary and desirable, this clearly left much scope for the management of the vote. Politicians never made the mistake of having one fixed electoral law written into the constitution. Each outgoing chamber remained the custodian of the mode of election; the deputies could and did change it as they saw fit (Table 1.3). That is, they chose the system most likely to secure their re-election. By the late 1880s, it was fairly clear what this was: le scrutin d'arrondissement (single member constituency) with two ballots. Earlier republican chambers had hesitated between this and its traditional opposite, proportional representation (PR), usually using the département, not the national territory as a whole, as the

Table 1.3 Electoral Systems used in Modern France

Date of Electoral Law	Type of constituency	No. of ballots	Method of attributing seats
1871	M*	1	Simple majority of votes cast
1873	M	2	At 1st ballot, absolute majority of votes cast; relative majority at 2nd
1875	S*	2	No change
1885	M	2	No change
1889	S	2	No change
1919	M	1	PR lists per department; absolute majority of votes cast; remaining seats allocated by quotient, then highest average
1927	S	2	As per 1875–1919
1945	M	1	PR lists per department; quotient, then highest average
1951	M	1	Paris region: PR lists with highest remainder. Elsewhere departmental PR; all seats to any list with absolute majority, otherwise by highest average.
1958	S	2	As per 1875–1919
1985	M	1	PR lists per department; highest average
1986	S	1	As per 1875–1919

M* = multi-member constituency
S* = single-member constituency
Source: Campbell (1966: 134–5); Le Monde, *Dossiers et Documents*.

basic electoral unit. Although the debate between single-member enthusiasts and PR supporters would rumble on throughout the Third Republic (Rosan-vallon, 1998: 154 ff.), peaking in the 1913 vote in favour of PR by the chamber, which the senate subsequently turned down, the prevailing preference stayed with the single-member system.[10]

There are understandable reasons for this preference. Third Republic chambers were very large by today's standards (Table 1.4). Constituencies were small, and often 5,000 votes on the second ballot could be a comfortable winning score. A deputy had to know his electorate well; he might know many of them personally. He had to be sensitive to their immediate needs (not

10. The work of Georges Lachapelle remains essential for Third Republic elections. An ARD supporter and lifelong lobbyist for PR, his regular electoral analyses (1914; 1920; 1924; 1928; 1932; 1936) drive home implacably the discrepancy between the actual results and what they would have been under his preferred system of integral PR. While his criticisms are repetitive and naïve (he seems surprised that voters actually vote against programmes or politicians and he postulates an automatic link between a PR system and the advent of disciplined mass-parties) his exposure of the mechanisms of electoral alliances and party shortcomings in this domain remains illuminating.

Table 1.4 Number of Deputies in Third Republic, 1871–1940

Legislature	Metropolitan Seats (N)	Overseas (N)	TOTAL
1871–76 (Assemblée Nationale)	753	15	768
I. 1876–77	526	7	533
II. 1877–81	526	7	533
III. 1881–85	541	16	557
IV. 1885–89	569	15	584
V. 1889–93	560	16	576
VI. 1893–98	565	16	581
VII. 1898–1902	570	16	586
VIII. 1902–06	575	16	591
IX. 1906–10	575	16	591
X. 1910–14	580	16	596
XI. 1914–19	586	16	602
XII. 1919–24	610	16	626
XIII. 1924–28	568	19	587
XIV. 1928–32	593	19	612
XV. 1932–36	596	19	615
XVI. 1936–40	598	20	618

Source: Campbell (1966: 72)

just to their general political preferences at election time) and know where to seek help with these in Paris. While the general political culture of an area or its sociology might determine voting to some extent, many deputies felt that it was on services rendered that a significant part of the voters judged them. The deputy thus became the hub of political activity; he would be supported by a committee, and he and they would decide about crucial matters such as second ballot deals. The first ballot would have multiple candidacies; to prevent these preliminary candidates from leaving their hats in the ring for the decisive second round, deals might have to be struck and awkward bedfellows made in order to maximise 'the republican vote' or 'keep out the atheists'. Clearly such situations might vary considerably between departments, but in the great majority of cases a deal was necessary. Lachapelle showed that, with the conspicuous exception of the Bloc National in 1919, the left was usually better than the right at désistement (standing down in favour of a candidate politically close but with a better chance of winning). In 1914, 1924 and 1928, the right could arguably have had a majority of deputies if it had made better deals on the second ballot, but missed out, whereas the 'cartel' of radicals, republican-socialists and republicans of GR type did proportionally much better, owing increasingly to their deals with the socialists.

The weight of the deputy in the party system can hardly be overestimated, and Dogan's exhaustive studies of deputies since 1870 bring it out clearly

(1953; 1961; 1967). Although the average tenure of seats was about ten years (a figure slightly superior to the UK during the same period), this figure conceals much underlying stability. It is true that narrow swings of the electoral pendulum could produce changes in the composition of a chamber, but this phenomenon worked only at the margins (Dogan, 1961: 63). In the centre was a core of deputies with fairly safe seats; four-fifths of those who served longer than two legislatures were re-elected continuously (1953: 323). Often such men went through on the first ballot, which suggests a high degree of voter stability in their area. Longevity in office tended to coexist with strong local implantation; an astonishing sixty-five percent of deputies were born in their department and a further fourteen percent nearby. Such affinities were usually translated into local office-holding; nearly all candidates were mayors or councillors, and two thirds of deputies continued to hold local office after election (Dogan 1967: 475). On the right and among moderate republicans, a deputy might owe his implantation to professional activity (landowner or farmer, doctor, lawyer or vet). On the left, a candidate would probably have had to work his way up by activism (militantisme) through the party machinery, such as it was. Whatever the network, the result would be similar. The eventual deputy would be a powerful local figure, with strong backing and a good hold over his supporters. If he was endorsed by a party organisation in Paris, the organisation would probably owe more to him than he to it.[11]

The proof of this situation can be seen in the fate of many leading personalities of the Third Republic, who struggled electorally (Dogan, 1953: 345). Usually Parisians with undoubted intellectual and political skills, such personalities often found the provincial seats into which they were 'parachuted' to be very marginal. Personalities as diverse as Jaurès, Blum, Reynaud, Ferry and Viviani all suffered defeat at times when they were national figures; it is hard to imagine a similar situation in the UK. Ministerial stability was, of course, high in the Third Republic (Estèbe, 1982); even if the cabinets themselves turned over quickly, the ministerial personnel showed high continuity. It is an irony of the system that ministers often had to struggle to get elected, only to find themselves dependent for a majority on much better implanted but mediocre local deputies. Dogan is quite clear about where the latters' loyalties lay (1953: 344):[12] 'in theory they were "representatives of the Nation"; in practice they represented their local district'. In short, the mode of election of deputies and their predominantly local character would always make it

11. Lachapelle (1924:37) accuses scrutin d'arrondissement of being responsible for 'intolerable electoral and political behaviour; official candidacies; arbitrary administrative interference; arbitrary application of the law; replacing justice with favours; creating disorder in the public services and budget deficits, where private and clientelistic interests prevail over the general interest'. Such strictures sum up the disappointment felt (mainly by academic commentators and would-be national party leaders) at a system which gave huge amounts of influence to elected notables and by the same token reduced the power of any central organisation (such as a party) to impose discipline on such men.

12. 'Théoriquement, ils étaient "représentants de la Nation"; pratiquement, ils l'étaient de leur arrondissement'.

hard for Parisian party élites to build any sort of disciplined machinery.

The consequences of this on party formation can easily be imagined. Ambitious national leaders from Gambetta to Waldeck Rousseau and leaders of the big left parties dreamed of a France of (two) large structured parties. They thought PR might be a way to this. They railed at a system where deputies represented mere 'committees', i.e., local interests, with little national perspective, but the single-member system, resting on the semi-visible system of local-national links and interest mediation, was never going to produce such parties, and was not intended to. At most, it could produce loose parliamentary alliances of deputies from a broadly similar ideological background with some convergent policy goals of a very general nature. There was no real chance of a top-down party, with centralised structures and a detailed programme, mobilising large segments of a distinct social group on an ongoing basis. Indeed, when such mass parties began to emerge after 1900, particularly the SFIO, they would have to integrate themselves into this mould of republican politics, which was well set by then. We know how soon the SFIO devolved real power to its departmental federations (controlled by deputies), showing how well it fitted into the system of local-national links (Bergounioux and Grunberg, 1992: 47–50).

Republican France arranged its elections in a way which meant that it could only be equipped with parties of a loose and flexible type. Local

Table 1.5 Turnout in Third Republic Elections

Year	Turnout
1876	76%
1877	80%
1881	69%
1885	78%
1889	76.6%
1893	71.1%
1898	72.3%
1902	80%
1906	79.9%
1910	77.5%
1914	77.3%
1919	70.7%
1924	83%
1928	83.7%
1932	83.5%
1936	84.3%

The size of the electorate grew from just under ten million in 1876 to just under twelve million by 1936.

Source: Lachapelle (1932; 1936)

activists (deputies and their committees) actively sought this outcome. Most importantly, voters regularly endorsed it in large numbers at the ballot box (Table 1.5).[13] The political entrepreneurs had invented a mode of partisan action that suited them and their clients, and to that extent there was a very strong fit between the party system and the society from which it derived. To question whether that system really served the society properly is another debate entirely, and one which is often contained in those analyses which dwell on the underdeveloped or weak nature of French parties. We will not seek at this point to enter that debate, other than to point out that weakness can be very much in the eye of the beholder. To take an analogy from the peasant world, any farmer knows that the best way to keep walkers off his land is not to erect robust fences but loose unstable ones which slip and slide when one tries to climb over them. We have simply tried to demonstrate here that if a system emerged based on a loose type of party, then this was so because the political élites agreed that this was what was required and because social interests did not disagree with their view.

Parties in the Third Republic: A Clarification

The discussion hitherto has assumed the existence of parties in the France of universal suffrage. A number of technical problems concerning the nature and status of party still need to be resolved, however, before we can begin our analysis. Officially, no parties existed until 1901, when the law on associations eased what had been an ambiguous situation concerning the creation of parties and other citizen groups, which had hitherto been restricted by a rigid set of legal curbs. Hence the reluctance of many writers to speak of parties or a party system during the Third Republic. Long before 1901, however, people spoke openly of the 'republican party', as if its existence were beyond dispute. Doubtless they felt that reality is no respecter of legal or constitutional formulae. Before 1900, the situation was in fact extremely untidy, and some methodological tidying-up is clearly necessary.

Raymond Huard has exhaustively chronicled the long march from the clubs of the French Revolution to the emergence of parties that would fit most modern definitions of the name (essentially, the radicals and socialists) early this century (Huard, 1994; 1996). His work reads at times, however, like a catalogue of failed attempts at party creation across different régimes by both left and right. Short-lived electoral committees could produce a reasonably coherent vote among their supporters (this opinion group or ideological family is really what was meant by the phrase 'republican party') and elect deputies of broadly similar views. Sympathetic newspapers directed by leading politicians might

13. Turnout varied between 76% and 84% during the Third Republic (Campbell, 1966: 69); the average for Fifth Republic elections is considerably lower. Lachapelle believed that with military service keeping many men away for long periods and administrative sloppiness over electoral rolls (e.g., failing to remove the names of the deceased) real turnout often topped 90% (1932: xiv).

keep political sympathies alive between elections, but that was as far as party organisation went most of the time. Periodically (usually after an election scare) a leading republican figure would discover the necessity for a more structured type of party, and even begin to organise. Steeg's national committee for republican organisation in the 1880s and Waldeck-Rousseau's Grand Cercle Républicain in the 1890s were seen ast he start of the republican party (Huard, 1996: 172–5; 226–45); but such initiatives invariably petered out.

The reasons for this are diverse. Restrictive legislation was the most visible one. Ever since the radical surges of the French Revolution, especially after 1792, the new ruling élites had had reservations about freedom of association, whether for political groups or trade unions. The liberalism of these élites found workers' combinations an unnatural distortion of the laws of the market, while freedom to organise politically might mean the triumph of jacobin or even socialist policies pushed through by the uneducated and vengeful lower orders, who were, according to the notables' world view, neither rich enough nor sufficiently qualified (capacitaires, in the jargon of the time) to deserve participation in the political process. Better then to restrict freedom of organisation to the committees formed just before the elections (open only to a small rich minority) which these régimes allowed ; after the vote the committees were expected to fade into nature. Even the press, the natural vehicle for informing and maintaining debate between elections, was regularly stifled by laws of varying severity. These restrictions were used by all types of régime, as the political entrepreneurs of the day sought monopolistic or oligarchic control of the political market. If they seem most natural to the authoritarian Second Empire, we should not forget that most of them have their origins in the liberal orleanist monarchy. Even when the Third Republic became established, the republicans were none too quick to lift the restrictions on association; why let the clericals benefit from such a liberty? Each side feared the other and thought that the best means of coping was to hamper the adversary by any means. Thus, a culture or mindset ensued which helped maximise the effect of the laws.

Cultural factors are also important in that early republicans undoubtedly believed, as idealists and historicists, that the triumph of their principles was inevitable and that it was enough to articulate these rhetorically; organisation was not necessary to ensure the victory of ideas (Huard, 1996). In some cases, organisational effort was not put into political parties, but into leagues (such as La Ligue de l'Enseignement), which were one-issue lobbies campaigning for particular segments of the republican agenda. Other republican élites put more effort into masonic lodges, which could act as think-tanks and loci of communication as well as mobilising élites in a discreet manner outside the purview of the law.[14]

The experience of the Second Empire was also important. Parliamentary politics grew in salience, and the (republican) opposition was forced to

14. The rôle of masonry in republican culture is a topic in itself, overlaid as it is by strong feelings of conspiracy, manipulation etc. from the non-republican side. Estèbe's conclusions about the rôle of republican ministers (1982: 210–26) are probably valid for republican personnel at large. Certainly the weight of masonry within the political class was considerable; Estèbe shows

organise itself, however sloppily. The government, however, made no attempt to create a formal bonapartist party of its own, but relied on the use of 'official candidates'; prefects would swing the influence of the state and its resources behind pro-government candidates, having done everything possible between elections to create loyal clientèles by distribution of various rewards, while intimidating opponents (Zeldin, 1958; 1973: 504–69). This use of the state apparatus as a surrogate party was to leave a long legacy in the mind of the French right; there would always be a temptation to shortcut the long labour of partisan organisation.

Thus, by the time the Third Republic arrived, France had a very stunted system of political expression through parties, despite being the first major European country to bring in universal male suffrage (1848). This underdevelopment was often compared by French politicians with the advanced state of US or British parties, despite the slower movement of the UK towards universal manhood suffrage (the organisation and density of the Tory party was a particular object of envy). However, mass parties with a solid base in civil society, independent resources and a serious organisation mark a step along the road of party development. Historically, they often develop from smaller organisations, 'cadre' or 'notable' parties as Duverger called them (1954); usually such organisations begin in parliamentary arenas before developing external structures within civil society, in contrast to the mass parties which are constituted in civil society before entering the parliamentary process. The France of the 1870s was adequately supplied with such cadre parties, legal curbs and conventions of nomenclature notwithstanding, and it is here that any account of the modern French party system must start. Certainly, the partisan forces which will be studied in the first part of this book qualify comfortably for Sartori's bottom-line definition of party as 'any political group identified by an official label that presents at elections and is capable of placing through elections ... candidates for public office' (1976: 63).

History and political science have tended to underrate the degree of cohesion and organisation of parliamentary groups in the early years of the Third Republic. Yet, even before the 16 May episode that is held to have consolidated the republic's existence, groups were playing an absolutely crucial role in the political system. Paradoxically, we are better informed on the work of parliamentary groups for the very beginnings of the republic than for its

---

that from 1877 to 1914, about 40% of ministers were on average masons, including some 15 premiers. Many of the ministers were second-raters, and many famous names were not 'brothers' (Waldeck-Rousseau, Poincaré, Barthou, Clemenceau), though at the same time many leading republicans were 'fellow-travellers', who often spoke at lodges (Caillaux, Briand, Paul-Boncour, etc.). This latter phenomenon perhaps gives the best clue to the place of masonry within republican culture. Rather than being a locus of conspiracy, it was a place of sociability, where networking took place, opinion was mobilised and élite support acquired. The lodges were good vehicles for this, because masonic ideology fitted so well with the bases of republican culture. Egalitarian, meritocratic and confident of possessing real knowledge, masonry was about progressing steadily under the guidance of proven élites – a metaphor for republican politics at large.

mature stage, approximately 1880 to 1914, thanks to the work of Rainer Hudemann. His combination of archival work and party theory sheds new light on the early republican system (essentially, the first legislature), although in the twenty years since he published his findings, noone seems to have undertaken work of similar depth on later periods (Hudemann, 1979). What emerges is a parliament run by very cohesive groups with distinct ideological and cultural identities and fairly clear policy goals. The groups had high internal discipline (probably much higher than that of some successor groups, more recognised as parties). They elected their own leaders, organised voting and debating tactics and carved up places on assembly committees via a system of formal and informal links between groups; account was taken of their weight when governments were composed (without ever being admitted publicly). Now, if these groups had taken the external appearance of parties as we have come to know them this century, we would say, unambiguously, that we were in the presence of a party system, which is, after all, the sum of those relationships, formal and informal, between protagonists. Obviously, these groups are not fully fledged parties. In terms of the classic curve of party development from cadre party to cartel (Mair and Katz, 1995) they are still at the bottom end of the scale, with fledgling structures outside parliament, few activists and little in the way of satellite or supporting organisations. Only after the First World War would France witness significant mass parties of integration which might, over time, turn into catch-all parties.

A recent French school of political sociology reminds us, however, that the label of party is not one which becomes attached spontaneously to an emergent organisation (Bourdieu, 1981; Gaxie, 1977, 1995; Offerlé, 1997). There is no 'natural' curve of progression from group of notables through mass party to catch-all party to cartel party and hence no point on such an imaginary scale at which an organisation qualifies objectively for the title of a 'real party'. To accept such a ladder of progression implicitly, as much writing about French parties often does, is perhaps to take the experience of the Anglo-Saxon democracies, where 'serious' parties emerged quite early, as a universal norm. The title of party is always ascribed, first by the politicians of the new organisation themselves (and possibly by their competitors) then by subsequent media or academic commentators. The important thing is to know who does the ascribing. Whoever does it, a decision must be taken at some point to award party status to such and such a group. We see no reason why the term 'party' cannot be used to describe the French parliamentary groups of the 1870s and after. They represented various interests within civil society adequately enough to be re-elected regularly and they had ideological and political cohesion and enough organisation to act in parliament in pursuit of their aims. Avril reminds us appositely that at any one moment a party is 'trinitarian', existing on three planes – as a set of voters, a political machine (operating essentially in civil society) and, crucially, as a set of office holders (1990: 72).[15] Pomper (1992) makes a similar point about the multilevel existence of parties. If one of the levels is weaker than others, this does not mean that we have to deny an organisation the title of party. If the extra-parliamentary infrastructure of Third Republic parties was weak (this is the main reason why they are often denied the status of real parties), then this may simply reflect the fact that at that period there was no need for anything more structured (Hoffmann, 1963). The groups could represent their supporters in civil society adequately without need of greater structuring. As new demands for representation emerged, new, more structured parties duly emerged, and the established ones adjusted their structures sufficiently to stay in business. That was to come later; at the beginning of the Third Republic, parliamentary groups were the adequate form of political party. To deny the groups party status is simply to commit an anachronism.

English terminology can help us here with its concept of parliamentary parties.[16] In our view this is exactly what these groups were; they existed mainly within the parliamentary arena (which is not to say that they were devoid of links with civil society – see below). Within that arena, however, they exhibited the coherence of a party and acted in a mainly unitary and purposeful way, as parties, pursuing distinct political goals. In so doing they inaugurated a party system, many of whose traits would persist well into the era when political groupings became the sort of parties with which we are more familiar – bigger, more visible, better rooted in society and able to communicate in other ways than merely through parliamentarians. The 1870s are thus the real beginning of the contemporary party system. Even after 1900 when purportedly nationwide parties like the ARD, FR or even the radical party existed, it makes more sense to see these organisations as emanations of parliamentary groups rather than the reverse. The ARD in particular was an empty shell; the candidates it sponsored (or who consented to sponsor it) belonged to a number of parliamentary parties. These were the loci in which they operated; the ARD was just a label. Even the radical party, much more structured in theory, included members of more than one parliamentary group (and of course not all deputies in the radical group were necessarily paid-up members of the party). What mattered in republican politics was the parliamentary group/party, and our focus will be firmly on this.

One further difficulty confronting analysts of the early parties is the shadowy nature of these groups. Legally, their existence was not admitted in the Chamber of Deputies before 1910, and deputies were, on one famous occasion, actually forbidden by the speaker to mention their existence in debate. In 1910, the rules were changed to allow groups to nominate members to parliamentary committees on a roughly proportional basis (Waline, 1961; Albertini, 1961). Before that, all chambers had been immediately upon their

15. Following King, Ware points out (1996: 6–7) that the dimension of the 'party-as-electorate' is not the same, qualitatively, as the party-as-organisation or the party in parliament. Whatever the truth of this assertion, if the party-as-electorate were not assembled regularly, albeit briefly, then neither of the other two dimensions of the party would exist for very long.

16. Avril indicates the utility of this term in his comparative discussion of US and UK experiences of party formation (1990: 74).

election divided into bureaux (usually eleven) on a purely random basis by drawing lots; the deputies then met in their bureaux to elect some of their number to committees and to carry out the most important task of any new chamber, la vérification des pouvoirs (validating the results of every constituency, with each bureau having to report on a number of seats). This process would occupy a large number of sessions of the new chamber, proving, if nothing else, that matters of legitimacy (and party advantage) came before policy.[17] Apart from carrying out these functional tasks, the bureaux had little meaningful existence; nor were they meant to, as the prevailing culture remained attached to the notion that deputies were individuals voting according to their conscience, not the carriers of demands for any sub-group (le mandat impératif). The bureaux were, at any rate, the only concession that the republic would officially make to collective organisation; but of course practice confounded official rules, and groups flourished, playing a rôle that was all the more important for being partly hidden.

Official records of the existence of these groups are sparse; Grévy even claims that there are National Assembly officials today who will still not accept that groups ever really existed (1996: 205). Certainly few group records survive (although they are known to have kept minutes of meetings). Fortunately, historians have been able to reconstruct the membership of the groups from parallel sources such as private archives or press reports and communiqués (which the groups used extensively) and to give us some idea of the way they functioned. That said, there remains some uncertainty about the exact membership of groups, and few subsequent attempts have gone much further than the pioneering work of Bomier-Landowski (1951). It is interesting to compare the various accounts of group membership in the Third Republic, for none of them coincide.[18] Often the discrepancies between numbers given for the groups are small and could be explained by counting up at different stages in the legislature (members sometimes shifted, particularly between sessions); but there are discrepancies, even if they do mostly concern one particular area of the party system (running from the so-called centre-right to the centre-left), which is the most sensitive one from the point of view of the workings of that system, as will be seen in later chapters. One should not however be carried away by minute detail; enough is known of the overall profile and activity of the groups for us to attempt a systemic analysis of their workings. More detailed knowledge of the groups would, we believe, refine our model rather than revising it

17. Lidderdale (1954) remains essential for understanding the procedural arcana of republican parliaments. Cf. also Mayeur (1984: 71–113).

18. The main sources are varied. After 1910 the Journal Officiel carried annual lists, which groups were obliged to submit to the Chamber and Senate administration. Before that the picture is less clear. L'Année Politique, edited annually by the moderate republican deputy André Daniel up to 1906, is very selective in its lists. For the period as a whole, a number of academic studies have their own eclectic syntheses, usually based on Bomier-Landowski, some combination of the above and archival material. Cf. notably Avril et al., 1989; Grévy, 1996; Harismendy, 1994. Jolly (1960–72) is helpful on individual politicians, but sometimes incomplete on their group membership.

out of recognition.

A final difficulty in identifying the groups/parties is their elastic character. Very often, a group of deputies in the chamber would take a different name from that of the party whose name they used in their election literature (this is less of a problem with the mass parties of the left). Invariably, deputies elected on the same party label would join different groups in the chamber. Sometimes, a deputy might shift to another group in the course of one legislature. Before the 1910 rule changes, membership of two groups (occasionally more) was not uncommon, and the mentality underlying this practice persisted in nonparliamentary arenas (candidates liked to secure as many electoral endorsements as they could). These technical problems are clearly impediments to a tidy conceptualisation. They do, however, relate to the developmental phase of parties before they acquire true mass structures and they certainly do not affect the workings of a party system significantly. Even if some of the individual components of the system are informal, the system itself functions; the informality becomes a variable in its own right within the functioning of the system and has simply to be incorporated into the analysis.

Parties and the Party System

So far we have addressed the question of representation by party and traced the derivation of the main party families from the classic cleavages. We have also shown that party was a historical reality before political and legal conventions deigned to recognise it. As we have implied, however, parties assume their function of representing citizens not in a vacuum but in competition with other parties, that is, within a system. Our investigation into the way in which French parties have contributed to the political development of their country will seek answers by looking at that party system.

We take as our starting point Sartori's definition of a party system: 'the system results from and consists of the patterned interactions of its component parts…a party system is precisely the system of interactions resulting from inter-party competition' (1976 : 43–4). Clearly the operative concept here is the system of interactions and how this is to be identified, classified and interpreted. The literature on this topic is immense and it is not our purpose to review it in detail here,[19] nor will we enunciate, at the start of our enquiry, a rigid conceptualisation of the French system into which all subsequent analysis must then be fed. We intend to work with the flexible concept of interaction between component parties, as we work through our historical analysis of how the French system developed. However, we will make two general theoretical points, which will inform this analysis.

---

19. For the most recent discussions see Broughton and Donovan (1999 : 1–7 and 255–74), Wolinetz (1997). Ware provides a readable overview of current debates (1996: 147–256), while Mair and Smith (1989) and Mair (1997) are more specialised.

The first concerns the notion of competition, said to fuel all party systems. From its original, descriptive preoccupation with the number of parties, party system theory has long since moved on to the dynamics of systems. Sartori has set the markers for most contemporary debate with his stress on the competitive aspects of party systems, seen typically in his concern with the problem of polarisation (the extent of ideological and political differences between parties). Much influenced by the climate of the Cold War and the weight of the Italian communist party, he bequeathed a dominant image of fierce competition between sometimes irreconcilable adversaries. Certainly, most analysts look first at the structure of competition between parties when they attempt to characterise the nature of any party system. Yet, the 'polarised pluralism' for which Sartori is best remembered sits alongside more subtle and ambiguous views of party systems in his work, particularly in countries with traditions of coalition. Here there can be as many elements of complicity as of conflict; competition exists, but it need not be untramelled. On the contrary, it can be filtered through numerous collaborative mechanisms, often the more effective for never being visible or avowed. One question which the analyst of party sytems must be prepared to ask, then, is whether such elements of collusion are present, even in apparently confrontational systems: does the adversarial language conceal accomodations between the competitors? In short, we must not forget that party systems can be as collusive as they are competitive.

Our second point is methodological. One constant danger stalks the analysis of party systems. This is the danger of emphasising structure at the expense of agency. Put more simply, it is very easy to see party systems as a piece of machinery, with a self-contained balance and logic: change one cog in the machine, and everything else adjusts automatically. Thus, if some new exogenous pressure is brought to bear on the party system (sharp changes in the economy, say, with a measurable social impact), it can be expected to adjust in consequence. The same is true if some endogenous factor intervenes (changes in the composition of existing parties, rise of new ones); the machine simply reprogrammes itself. Even historical approaches are no guarantee against this kind of reductionism; what happens here is that theory can simply be mobilised with hindsight to confirm the workings of the self-regulating machine.[20]

Such 'black box' approaches are present, with greater or lesser degrees of explicitness, in much contemporary writing about party systems. They are in our view too schematic. On one level, they certainly enable us to construct an account of how systems work; they isolate a process with inputs and an outcome. However, by doing so they risk oversimplifying some of the processes of that working, in particular the internal dynamics of party itself.

If we have to consider party in metaphorical terms, it makes more sense to see it, not as a piece of machinery, but as an animal. Parties are not passive,

---

20. Much of the argument about the 'freezing' of party systems (whether or not they have kept the basic shape that they had at their origins early in the last century) contains traces of this type of thinking. It can of course serve to justify either freezing or unfreezing with equal facility.

programmed devices, but living organisms with a capacity for reflexion and action. Their actions, once taken, mesh with the actions of other parties and produce effects which constitute the party system; but they are still actions. Parties are agents.[21] Even the false problem of whether or not parties are unified actors cannot detract from that fact. In truth, no party is ever a unified actor; parties are constant seats of struggle, as Poulantzas liked to put it, between contending interests. Nevertheless, at some point, one or more of these interests will prevail (for the time being at least) and will cause the party to act to its bidding.

Even the use of the word 'interests' makes too many concessions to the structuralist approach. Interests are mediated by groups of people; in parties this means recognisable élites and their followers. When we say that a party has acted, we mean that a team of leaders has decided to make certain move; probably the followers will accept this, but even if they do not, another team will emerge which will pursue a different course of action (very often the same, but under a different name). The point of all this is that when parties act and interact within a system, this action is the product of political élites. It is they who identify and evaluate the pressures on the party, devise strategies and tactics in consequence and persuade members to follow (or to challenge). This is a complex process; to reduce its outcomes a posteriori to the workings of a piece of machinery is not acceptable. Such reductionism fails to take into account the vital élite input, without which the 'machinery' could never work. Even when a system is well established and affects its component parties as a variable in its own right,[22] this does not change the fundamental situation; the relationship between the party system and individual parties is not a one-way relationship of dependency, but a dialectical one. The system as a set of constraints affects the actions of the parties; but by their actions they are at the same time modifying that structure. A dialectic does not imply passivity from one of its components but constant interaction. Therefore, our approach to the French party system will be aware of this dimension of agency. It is not intended to be overly voluntaristic, and it certainly will not subside into any 'Great man' theory of history, but it will seek to rehabilitate an active element of party systems too often lost sight of by systems engineers.

---

21. Mair proclaims his agreement with Sartori that 'parties and party systems are not simply objects, but also subjects. It is they who ultimately set the agenda and it is they who ultimately determine the terms of reference through which we, as voters and citizens, understand and interpret the political world' (1997: 9).

22. Or when, to use Mair's phrase (1997: 15), 'the party system is the creature of the parties, but at the same time they become its prisoners'.

2

THE THIRD REPUBLIC
Matrix of the Modern Party System

๛

In France we do not have properly united and disciplined parties, but groups
whose tendencies are not always very clear[1]

Lachapelle, Les Elections législatives

The modern French party system begins properly with the Third Republic. It
could be argued that this is either too early or too late as a historical starting
point; but neither of these arguments is valid in our view.

Those who believe that it is too late might follow Rémond (1969) in pointing
out that there was a party life of sorts in earlier régimes, particularly the Restoration and July Monarchy (1814–1848); even the Second Empire (1852–70) saw the
development of partisan organisation among the opposition. While recognising
that the parliamentary factions of notables in the monarchical chambers were
capable of quite sophisticated partisan manoeuvres, and that patterns of behaviour and political habits set in that would be seen again later, we would argue
that these systems suffered from severe limits if we are to talk of a party system.
We do not object to using the label 'party' to describe some of these formations;
indeed we mentioned in the previous chapter that analysts have always used
wide discretion in awarding it. However, given that these régimes were based on
restricted property-owners' suffrage (the advent of universal male suffrage in
1848 would multiply the electoral roll fortyfold), partisan expression within
them covered only a minute sector of society; the parliamentary groups reflected
tensions within a rich élite who were represented by an even richer micro-élite.
It is stretching terminology to call this a party system in the sense in which the
term is used today. Only with the advent of mass suffrage and a régime which
commanded widespread assent (measurable by high turnout of voters and the
absence of violent opposition) could other sectors of society be represented
within the political process, and only with the arrival of partisan groups to represent such interests can we speak meaningfully of a party system.

---

1. 'Nous n'avons point en France de véritables partis unis et disciplinés, mais des groupes
dont les tendances ne sont toujours pas très claires' (1932: VIII).

The other objection to our choice of starting point is found in most political science and contemporary history textbooks which deal with modern France; it is put forward with varying degrees of explicitness and was adumbrated in our discussion at the end of the preceding chapter. Briefly stated, it is that those partisan organisations which existed in France before at least 1900 do not deserve to be considered as parties. Even the best of such writing endorses this claim; Mayeur says that before 1900 France did not have proper (véritables) parties, except perhaps for the socialists and even they are doubtful (1984: 401). When it is felt necessary to support this claim (which is infrequently), appeals are made to formalism; only after the 1901 law on associations could official parties exist, therefore there were no parties before this date. Ritual mention is made of the poor extraparliamentary organisation of the right (involving implied comparisons with, say, UK conservatives or US republicans); alternatively, the SFIO (the only apparent claimant to mass-party status) will be compared disparagingly to the German SPD or the British Labour Party in terms of finance, members, etc. If the radical party warrants a mention, then its ramshackle organisation and indiscipline will be pilloried. In such ethnocentric, formalistic and size-obsessed perspectives, it becomes hard to know when France did acquire a serious party system; perhaps not before 1945?

Ultimately such views rest on a certain notion of party. Not content to accept a minimalist definition à la Sartori,[2] such writers imply that parties have to have attained a certain prominence (in terms of votes, organisation and insertion within civil society) before they really qualify for the label. They have to pass, as it were, a methodological means test; but, unlike social security claimants, access to the benefits (in this case the label) is reserved only for the well-off. Our perspective is more inclusive. We hold that parties take different forms according to the needs of their particular society or, more precisely, the way in which those needs are diagnosed and addressed by the party activists and entrepreneurs. Historical analysis of the Third Republic suggests that various needs for representation were identified and responded to by political forces. The years 1870–1940 saw the establishment of a number of parties who soon formed a series of relationships with their own laws and dynamics which, together, make up a party system. These parties were doubtless underdeveloped in comparison with the Anglo-Saxon states or Germany; but such considerations were of little interest either to the party entrepreneurs or the voters whom they sought a licence to represent. What emerged suited all concerned.

This system established itself deep within the French polity, surviving beyond the collapse of the Third Republic, a collapse for which it was inevitably blamed. If anything, the system incurred even more hatred for the failure of the Fourth Republic in 1958; there is a strong case for regarding the whole political motivation of the Fifth Republic as an attempt to reverse the

2. A party is any political group identified by an official label that presents at elections and is capable of placing, through elections, candidates for public office (Sartori, 1976: 63).

fundamental logic of the French party system as it has evolved historically. We would argue that this project has not been as successful as its founders hoped. Clearly, then, the party system shows remarkable powers of persistence, and one aim of this book will be to elucidate the reasons for this persistence.

The starting point of any investigation of a party system must, however, be the nature of the society that produces it. Having established that the France of the Third Republic was the matrix of the modern party system, it is to an examination of this society that we first turn.

Third Republic France: Society and Its Divisions

Le Béguec (1992:14) sees the years 1885–1939 as the 'key period for the acquisition of party culture in its most varied forms'.[3] This party-culture was acquired by a society with a number of distinct features, which must be understood.

In sociological terms, Third Republic France was a clearly hierarchical society (Mayeur, 1973: 55–94). At its base lay a massive peasant class; in 1876, 49.3 percent of the workforce worked on the land, and in 1896 the figure was still 45.3 percent (in absolute numbers there were, in fact, more peasants, since the workforce had grown during this period). During these twenty years the industrial workforce crept up from twenty three percent to twenty-five and a half percent. This peasantry was diversified in both its mode of tenure and its size, but there were high numbers of both small peasants and medium-sized owners, some seventy-six percent of farms being under 10 hectares. There was also among this a rural proletariat of non-owners, numbering perhaps 2.5 million out of a total rural population of some 8.5 million. The period down to 1900 was generally one of slow economic growth if not stagnation; hence the rural exodus was slow, as was the decline of farming. Governments would recognise and abet this phenomenon by adopting a series of protectionist measures culminating in the Méline tariffs of 1892.[4] Although agriculture obviously had its large units, and even traces of modernising agribusinesses, the rural world was generally more interested in stability and security rather than change and risk. This attitude extended to family life, where birth control was widely practised to avoid dividing land among heirs. This conservative mindset, applying to economic as well as social factors, is often caught by the epithet 'malthusian'.

The large and ponderous peasantry was to be a constant of Third Republic life. It coexisted with a much smaller, but diverse, working class. Numbering perhaps 5 million by 1900, this class was geographically scattered.

---

3. 'période-clé de l'apprentissage de la culture partisane dans ses formes les plus variées'.

4. These tariffs were not a monolithic, panic-stricken response to movements in world trade, but a clever, flexible compromise between the protectionist lobby (large sectors of agriculture, textiles, engineering) and free-traders (exporters, banks, transport and maritime interests). Such finely-worked deals are typical of the 'republican synthesis'. Magraw sees (1992: 229–30) 'a rational and nuanced compromise designed to conciliate divergent interests within French capitalism ... to minimise intra-class friction'. It was 'essential for the coherence and unity of the French élites'.

Apart from the heavy mining and metal working regions of the Nord or Paris, or the Lyon region and the South-East with its engineering and textiles, much industry was on a smallish scale in a wide range of provincial towns. Much of the intake of the factories was of recent peasant origin, and rural, rather than urban, attitudes persisted late into the day. Mayeur remarks that only towards the end of the century can one speak of a real proletariat. Social legislation lagged far behind that of Bismarckian Germany, reflecting the minority status that workers and industry generally enjoyed in the Republic.

The top of the social pyramid was constituted by a bourgeoisie with its own style and identity (Lhomme, 1960; Garrigues, 1997). Relatively small in numbers, its real weight was immense. Descended mostly from families which had profited especially from the Revolution, allied, in some cases, with older aristocracy, these notables had withstood the régime changes which had periodically rocked France across the century. Their grip on the main levers of finance and industry was tight; they were usually significant landowners as well, and amply represented at the top of the liberal professions and the state apparatus. They had usually been in control of the political process, though they had sometimes preferred to share political power (e.g., with bonapartism) the better to secure their social and economic base. Aware of its high specific gravity within the system, this group's attitude to the new republic would be absolutely crucial.

Beneath this top group, analysts sometimes distinguish a bonne bourgeoisie. Less wealthy and more provincial, this group included smaller industrialists and other capitalists, many of them rentiers, as well as the upper reaches of the professional classes, be they public or private sector. More numerically significant than the above are undoubtedly the middling and lower reaches of the median group, covered very loosely by the term petite-bourgeoisie; Gambetta's 'nouvelles couches sociales' is an attempt at a more flattering description. Non-manual workers essentially, the group comprised small employers, craftsmen, other independents and shopkeepers; to them should be added the small town provincial professionals, such as lawyers, doctors and solicitors. These categories would form the natural constituency of many republican groups, especially radicalism. Increasingly, their ranks would be supplemented by what might be called a new petty-bourgeoisie, the white-collar workers of the banks, insurance companies and other businesses. A significant part of this stratum would be found in the expanding public sector, with the advent of schoolteachers, transport and postal officials, local government officers and the like; no small part of the attraction of such careers was that they were safe jobs. Mayeur points out how desirable petty bourgeois status was to the children of the 'popular classes' (workers and peasants). A farmer's or miner's son might become a primary school teacher, whose own children might then rise up into the middle groups. Such social ascent was one good which the republic was expected to provide; its success would depend to some extent on its ability to do so.

Society was also divided in terms of its culture, both generally and with particular regard to the question of the political system. A major division remained between catholics and anti-clericals, reflecting fundamentally opposed world-views. The secularists, or laïcs, laid proud claim to the intellectual legacy of the Enlightenment and the Revolution, postulating a free human subject able to live solely in accord with his reason; any revealed truth of the type to which organised religions are by definition committed was unacceptable because logically undemonstrable. Such philosophical differences obviously had political ramifications; ever since the Revolution had launched its physical, legal and political attacks on catholicism (Gibson, 1989: 30–55), stigmatising it as an obsolete and harmful part of the pre-modern era, the quarrel between catholics and secularists had inevitably come to concern the nature of the régime and the nature of politics itself. Crucially the catholic/laïc split ran across social classes and geographical regions. There were (and still are) parts of France which could clearly be seen to bear a dominant catholic culture (i.e., Britanny, Vendée, Alsace-Lorraine, Savoie) just as there are other areas (South-West, Paris basin, Centre) which are clearly secularist. By the same token, each social group was split along such cultural lines. Even the working class had its catholic zones, where republican and socialist values would make little headway. The peasantry fragmented similarly; if the small farmers of the South-East found secular values a part of their political identity, their Breton or Alsacian equivalents found catholicism just as natural. The bourgeoisie had its secularists, Voltairean and proud of it; but it also had catholic elements whose faith coloured their politics profoundly.

It is hardly surprising that such diversity of world-view was replicated when it came to political opinion. By 1870, France had experimented with several types of political régime, and they all retained varying degrees of support. The notables probably favoured, in the main, the type of weak constitutional monarchy, long based on restricted suffrage, where they dominated a chamber which was the major locus of decision. However, the strange hybrid of bonapartism had shown that an authoritarian régime based on the personal power of a quite narrow élite could command high degrees of support, especially when it was economically innovative and quick-footed enough to shift the bases of its support (at different times the Second Empire used permutations of conservatives, clericals and modernisers, peasants and industrial workers). By the late 1860s such a régime could hold relatively free elections where its 'official candidates' did well (Zeldin, 1958; Plessis, 1973). Peripheral areas where the aristocracy still enjoyed deference from the lower orders could be relied on to deliver votes for unashamed apologists of absolute monarchy well into the twentieth century (Siegfried, 1913). As for republicanism, its past failures, especially 1848, cast doubt as to the extent of its true popularity, but its organisational skills were growing; it had high profile politicians and a steadily growing vote as the empire drew to a close. We should be wary of identifying republicanism exclusively with the popular classes. In many areas, peasants, and sometimes workers, would show deference to authoritarian élites of one sort or another. Also, the republican élites overwhelmingly consisted of bourgeois intellectuals.

One issue on which virtually all agreed however, at least publicly, was that any political system which emerged would have to rest ultimately on universal male suffrage. This had been won in 1848, well ahead of most of the rest of Europe (Therborn, 1977). The Second Empire had manipulated and tried to restrict the suffrage, but never dared challenge its existence; indeed, it learned to work it quite well. Some of the notables who had helped crush the Second Republic (1848–52) also learned to use the vote in opposition to the empire, abandoning their fear of 'mob rule'. Across the political spectrum, then, it was understood that universal suffrage was irreversible; this would be a powerful factor in the eventual institutional settlement.

Thus, when a pattern of modern republican politics did become established in France after 1870, we need to remember that this process took place in a stratified and slowly evolving society, where cultural and political divisions overlapped with social divisions in an extremely untidy fashion. We shall now analyse the process whereby republican politics became the norm.

Building the Republican Framework

The process of institution building after 1870 is well known, and we shall recall only those features necessary for our purposes. When the Second Empire plunged into a war with Prussia, its rapid military collapse, plus the capture of the emperor, created a power vacuum. Paris republicans promptly filled this vacuum by proclaiming the republic in classic revolutionary manner and constituting a provisional government. This latter continued the war against Prussia as the government of national defence, in which the two main republican leaders Ferry and Gambetta played important rôles. Elections took place in February 1871, so as to give the republic popular legitimacy, but they returned a huge majority of conservative and monarchist deputies, many of whom were in fact elected as peace candidates, wanting an armistice and a quick end to the war. Republican candidates were seen as intransigent and unrealistic, and suffered as a result. The new National Assembly secured a deal with the Prussians at the cost of heavy reparations, brokered mainly by the strong man of the new republic, the veteran orleanist liberal Adolphe Thiers, whom the Assembly had elected as provisional head of government and of state. Among the first acts of the new government was the repression of the Paris Commune – a bid for municipal autonomy which turned, rather incoherently, into an insurrection . Its defeat meant the political and in some cases physical liquidation of many of the cadres of the revolutionary left in French politics, but its legacy would colour the debates of the young republic in many ways.

With the war and the insurrection out of the way, the whole question of the régime and its institutions remained totally undecided. Monarchists felt encouraged by the vote of February to believe that the republic had little legitimacy with voters. Bonapartist supporters saw enough from by-elections to believe that the empire, maybe in a more parliamentary version, could make a comeback. Above all, republicans were divided as to what institutional forms the republic should adopt. The years 1871 to 1875, when the famous Wallon amendment led to the adoption of a constitution, are thus a period of transition, in which there emerged new political forms, and within which parties would contend. In reality the process of adjustment really went on until the end of the decade, by which time a recognisable type of republican politics, often described sarcastically as the 'Grévy constitution' (Burdeau, 1996) could be seen to hold sway.[5]

The 1870s saw an intense and sophisticated struggle between different groups with their own constitutional agendas, each trying to advance the interests they represented. The struggle was conducted with a pragmatism which speaks volumes for the realism and common sense of the political class, however, and a compromise resulted. The Third Republic was to pivot on three key institutions, supposed to counterbalance each other. Alongside the elected Chamber of Deputies (as the National Assembly became) would be a senate, whose composition was determined by an electoral college consisting mainly of local councillors. In its first version, it also contained some seventy-five life senators (elected by the deputies). A particular advocate of the senate was de Broglie, who, although typical of the orleanist notables who had reluctantly accepted the republic as inevitable (at least temporarily), wanted to limit the omnipotence of a single elected chamber, which was what most republicans wanted at this time. Supporters and opponents of the single chamber alike were influenced by memories of the revolutionary Convention of 1792–95. The original title given to the institution, le Sénat conservateur, betrays the agenda of those fearful of the consequences of universal suffrage. The senate was to enjoy the same legislative rights as the chamber, except that finance bills had to go through the lower house first. Unlike the lower house, the senate could not be dissolved, indeed, it had to give its approval to any dissolution of the lower house. Although the idea of a senate was anathema to the republicanism of the period, Gambetta was able to persuade his supporters to do some horse trading; the senate was thus voted on to the statute book, but so, by the same token, was the republic, with the three constitutional laws of 1875.

The third institution, the presidency, was more difficult. Again, traditional republican ideology had no use for such an office, seen as a surrogate monarchy; many of the conservatives who founded the Third Republic envisaged the president as keeping the seat warm, so to speak, for the eventual return of a monarch. Once the activist Thiers had been forced out of office by the conservatives (precisely because he had clearly come round to accepting the republic and a president as the best option for a political settlement), the weight of the office within the system became uncertain. In particular, it was nowhere specified how this office, elected indirectly by both houses of the parliament,

5. The best analyses of this process are Rudelle (1982) and Mayeur (1973; 1984). A succinct recent overview is Burdeau (1996). For a more classic detailed account see Chastenet (1952–63) or Mollier and George (1994).

related to the chamber of deputies, elected by universal suffrage and thus the ultimate repository of legitimacy. Neither was the position of the government clear within these parameters; if it was appointed by the president and responsible to him, this still begged the question of responsibility to parliament. The existence of the actual government leader, who began to be known as the président du conseil from 1876 onwards, was not even mentioned in any of the constitutional texts. These questions as to where real authority lay were answered by the crisis of the 16 mai (1877). President MacMahon, an avowed monarchist who hoped for a restoration, chose to ignore the election results of 1876, which returned a republican majority; twice he appointed governments which could not command the chamber's approval and were disavowed. Here was a clear clash between two conceptions of authority – parliamentary versus presidential. The chamber was then dissolved, and the new elections returned a bigger republican majority; MacMahon was obliged to form a government acceptable to the chamber, and, a year later, resigned to be replaced by Grévy. The conflict of authority had clearly been settled in favour of the deputies, with major consequences for the political system, as will be seen.

Grévy's style of presidency soon made it clear that, henceforth, political power lay firmly in parliament and mainly – though by no means exclusively – with the chamber (Lavergne, 1966). In this he was simply reflecting the consensus which had emerged within the political class after this period of turmoil, which could have been even more dangerous for the republic. One consequence was that demands for revision of the constitution now tended to be dropped by the republican left, who had previously been ready to vote with the antirepublican right in the hope of getting rid of the senate or presidency. From now on, realism prevailed, and only minor revisions would take place (essentially cleaning up the senate's mode of election by phasing out the life senators and giving urban areas more say in the electoral college). The main result of the 16 mai was to clarify the relationship of government and parliament. Grévy, elected by the clear republican majority of both houses, made it clear that the president's rôle was limited to seeking out a président du conseil and a team of ministers, but on the understanding that they would enjoy the support of a majority of the chamber. The president would not be a major policy-maker. Neither he nor his successors would ever again use the right to dissolve the chamber. In other words, it was up to the chamber to sustain or unmake governments; little help could be had from other institutions. Thus began a political system which has often been characterised as 'absolute parliamentarism'.

Political Parameters of the New Republic

The new political system emerged, not through any intrinsic merits, but because at bottom it suited the major interests within France better than any of the alternatives. As such, it represented a compromise between these interests. This is the real meaning of Thiers' remark that the republic was the régime which divided

Frenchmen least. The bourgeois notables, the middle classes and most of the peasantry could see enough use for the régime to back it with an electoral majority. This much had been evident from 1871, as a series of by-elections reversed the misleading results of the 'peace election' of February (Gouault, 1954). This gradual republicanisation of opinion can be traced back to the Second Republic, when elections showed that parts of rural as well as urban France had begun to believe that here was a régime which could serve their needs. After 1870, huge efforts would be made by the republican political class to 'sell' the republic to provincial France; this is when Gambetta characterised himself as the 'travelling salesman of the republic' (Grévy, 1996, 1998; Bury, 1973, 1982). By the time of the Grévy settlement, only parts of the old aristocracy on the periphery of France clung to the idea of a legitimist restoration; for generations to come some thirty of them would be elected as 'independent' deputies to a parliament where they provided some modest nuisance value. As to the other main group excluded from this 'republican synthesis' (Hoffmann, 1963), the emergent working class, it would be allowed to make its way into the political system, cautiously and grudgingly, via the channel of republican politics; for the time being it could be ignored, or regarded as a captive ally of republicanism.[6]

It is easy to see why this 'power bloc' (as Gramscian terminology might have it) covering perhaps three-quarters of French society, would be suited by the undynamic type of republic described above. The republic had shown after the 1877 conflicts that it could do what its supporters required: it could provide democratically elected governments with a reasonable degree of stability; it could guarantee a capitalist market economy, based on a large amount of small property owners; it could guarantee basic civic freedoms (though there would be bitter debate over which groups were entitled to which rights); it could provide a modest measure of local government after decades of administrative centralism (though the prefect remained, to show that jacobinism set limits to local autonomy); it could even provide a limited range of social reform, particularly in the field of education (widely seen as the key to social mobility), though here too there would be controversy and it could (and this was perhaps the area which it found most difficult) maintain a diplomatic and military posture which ensured that France was taken seriously.

Few supporters of the republic wanted more than the above, which is essentially a liberal agenda, not one of social transformation. Apart from the socialist current (much later) no major force demanded a sweeping style of economic or social intervention; deputies were expected to reduce expenditure, not multiply it. Social improvement was expected to come through education, voluntary action and the general 'trickle down' effects of a successful market economy, not through government legislation. Few republicans in the 1870s can have expected that in the two decades before 1900, France would acquire the second-biggest empire in the world. Once the republic had taken this action, it was accepted as another source of national pride and of

6. Elwitt (1975) sees the politics of republicanism as an alliance of the bourgeoisie, industrial, financial and commercial, with petty producers and peasants.

possible careers, provided it did not cost the treasury too much, but there had always been opposition to this type of initiative.

So far, we have discussed the republic in terms of national policy. This is only half the story, however. Deputies referred to themselves proudly as 'la représentation nationale', but as our discussion of electoral systems in the previous chapter showed, many of their constituents saw them as being at least as much of a 'représentation locale'. Thus, while voters might expect a deputy to sustain or criticise government on major issues, they would probably be more interested in extracting various public goods from him. A deputy seeking re-election spent most of his time neither debating nor even in committee, but in dealing with requests for job references, decorations, exemptions from military service, job postings in the public sector, or for a word in the ear of those who, in the public or private sector, could offer life chances of various sorts. Improbable as it sounds today, a vast amount of his time would be spent writing letters, usually by hand in these days before the typewriter and the secretarial allowance for members of parliament (Guérin, 1980; Guiral and Thuillier, 1980). In addition to dealing with individual requests, many deputies were local office holders – conseillers généraux or, increasingly, mayors, and were interested in obtaining larger, more collective benefits such as grants and the location of public enterprises, etc. This special link of locality and centre, where the representative cannot help but be seen to act as defender of local interests, predates the Third Republic, but the republic continued that style of politics with some aplomb. The main reason that Gambetta was able to persuade republicans of the need for a senate was that he marketed it as 'le grand conseil des communes de France' – an open admission of its status as a lobby for local interests. Such localism undoubtedly contributed to the consensus about the régime; a weak parliamentary system was seen as one in which representatives of all colours could hope to exert influence on behalf of their voters. Even the opposition was entitled, discreetly, to its share of influence. Certainly, the administration complained constantly about what it felt were undue pressures from parliamentarians pushing the claims of clients in the hope of re-election (Bruguière, 1982: 89–100; 119–27). Needless to say, despite making ever more demands of the civil service, deputies never ceased to complain about what they saw as its excessive numbers and high costs.

Widespread agreement existed, then, on the existence of a fairly mimimalist state. This did not exclude conflict, however, both between the (majority) republicans and their adversaries and also, arguably more significantly, within the republican camp. These conflicts structured the practice of politics within the maturing republic.

Republican Culture

Analysts have spoken of a 'republican model' of politics (Berstein and Rudelle, 1992). By this is understood a tight fit between the institutions, polit-

ical practice and the political culture of republican France. All of these elements are seen as being appropriate to the society of the period and the needs
of groups within it. In an appropriate metaphor, Berstein and Rudelle speak
of an 'ecosystem' (1992:7). This model, developed in the latter years of the last
century, enjoyed undoubted hegemony from about 1900 to 1930 and then
came under some stress. It is still legitimate to speak today of a republican
model of politics for the Fifth Republic, but this model is, in their view, qualitatively different. Having set out the main lines of institutional development
and practice, we attempt in this section to distil the main elements of republican culture as lived during the Third Republic.

Republican culture can be usefully apprehended as a value system. This
value system can be assumed to have been common to all nuances of the
republican family from opportunists through to radicals, and even socialists
and communists came under its sway to a large extent (Berstein and Rudelle,
1992: 159–71; Hazareesingh, 1994: 64–97; Nicolet, 1982). Clearly, different
parts of the family would stress some elements more than others, but the
fund of commonality was high. Republicans laid claim to the heritage of the
Revolution, particularly its stress on individual rights; liberal democracy was
the only proper form of régime which could guarantee such rights. Democracy primarily meant the primacy of the elected chamber; as the veteran Reynaud said in his famous 1962 speech to the lower house, the republic was
there and nowhere else. Ideologically, republicans believed in the primacy of
science and reason, destined to prevail in time, they thought, over the obscu-
rantism of revealed religion. Not all of them were atheists, or even agnostics,
but such was their intellectual and emotional hostility to catholicism that at
bottom most republicans thought it impossible to be a sincere catholic and a
true republican. Thus, the 'centre-right' type of party such as the Fédération
Républicaine would always bear the mark of Cain, as it were.[7]

Mainstream republicanism was often criticised for being obsessed with
political or ideological questions at the expense of social reality. It is undeniable
that the socio-economic conceptions of republicanism were those of market liberalism. Class based critiques of republicanism pointed out that its social programme consisted mainly of a reliance on education, seen as equipping the
lower classes with the skills necessary for a seamless ascent through society.
Left-wing critics thought that republicanism paid insufficient heed to the existing inequalities of Third Republic capitalism, citing its slow record of social
reform. Recent writing has tended to counter this view (Berstein and Rudelle,
1992: 173–208), but even republicanism's defenders agree that its social practice
did not stretch far beyond some modest measures of social protection, which
it would have preferred to see undertaken by voluntary organisations rather
than government. The radical end of the family was ready to sanction more

7. In one of the most lucid discussions of *laïcité*, Mayeur makes the point that far from being a
value-free and objective approach to matters of belief, it is as much a value-system and a militant
ideology as those religions which it seeks to oust from the public sphere (in Hamon, 1991: 108).

interventionist measures such as public ownership of infrastructure or utilities, and the radicals even came up with the doctrine of solidarisme to justify the introduction of a modest level of redistribution, financed through the daring innovation of income tax. Radicalism also talked of abolishing wage-earning. In fact the radicals, like their more moderate cousins, really thought in terms of creating a mass of small independent property owners (peasants and petty producers), buoyed up by public policy where necessary. The emphasis on education fitted in well with this aspiration, and, as Berstein has shown, public policy was used deliberately to try and engineer this sort of outcome, which was favourable to increasing the weight of the middle classes.[8] One inevitable product of these ideological thrusts was the obsession with les petits; a fearful, risk-avoiding economic culture was induced, reflecting the desire to protect situations acquises and to be content with stagnation. This mentality was as much a part of republican culture as anti-clericalism.

The final elements of republican culture are to do with patriotism. This involves not only a fairly uncritical love of the motherland, but a love of France for what she embodies. This is essentially a product of the political and ideological dimensions set out above: France is not France unless she is republican/democratic, secular and, one must add, jacobin. Republicanism fundamentally involves accepting that an enlightened Parisian élite is the best guarantor of national unity. With regards to overseas, this view of France as the 'lighthouse of humankind' could very usefully be adapted after 1880 to justify the acquisition and management of a huge colonial empire; it was France's moral duty to educate Asians and Africans as to the benefits of capitalist civilisation. This picking up of the 'white man's burden' became, in turn, a further source of national pride.

The above form the major pillars of the republican value system. They were shared, with greater or lesser emphasis on different aspects, by all the mainstream republican parties, from opportunists and their descendants through to radicals and republican-socialists. One point which needs to be stressed is that republican culture came, as Clemenceau once remarked about the Revolution, as a block; one could not pick and choose which bits of it one might espouse. Indeed if one were a republican at all, one had to espouse its values with a total warmth and commitment, to the active exclusion of all other belief systems, particularly religion.

This emotional attachment to republican principle has been baptised 'absolute republicanism' by Odile Rudelle (1982). By this she means that, for an important part of the republican family, it was not enough to accept the

8. A good example of this are the various laws (Berstein and Rudelle, 1992: 200) used to discriminate against larger commercial firms in favour of small. The use of the state school to create an upwardly mobile free-thinking public (hence more likely to vote for republican parties) also springs to mind. These are what Dunleavy would call, following the language of public choice theory, a 'preference-shaping strategy' (1991: 112–44). Instead of passively reacting to perceived interests or opinion, party entrepreneurs go out and try to expand or even create such interests by use of public policy.

minimal bases of a republic, that is, a freely elected parliament from which governments were derived plus a head of state elected either directly or indirectly. Core republicans believed that, in order to be a true republican, one had to adopt the whole of the republican culture or world-view, not just the mere political/juridical institution of the republic. Clearly, this meant signing up to the rationalist/secularist worldview outlined above; obviously such an engagement had both political implications in policy terms and social consequences in terms of people's lifestyle and their networks of sociability. Unless one entered this ideological community of enthusiasts, one's commitment to democracy was suspect in the eyes of republican believers. In other words, militant republicanism was an exclusive creed. It wanted committed partisans, not neutral allies with whom one might do business but no more. It was a highly ideological type of politics.

The consequences for the political system of this cultural/emotional syndrome are immense. Put quite simply, it meant that those who had tolerated or supported other types of régime and who might now have the same attitude of lukewarm loyalty to the republic, were unwelcome. This group included many from bourgeois strata who shared much of the republican socio-economic agenda, which was basically liberal. More particularly, it excluded quite deliberately any catholics who showed even loose attachment to their creed. The militant republicans were not interested in collaborating politically with catholics who might accept the parliamentary republic and its quite conservative socio-economic orientation, if the latter did not espouse their own particular metaphysic.

As it happens, evidence from elections suggests that in fact a comfortable majority of the French, including many catholics of moderate views, would have lived very happily with a minimum republic, where they could accept the form without necessarily sharing the metaphysics (Rudelle, 1982: 285).[9] Many republican politicians fell somewhat short of Rudelle's absolutism, being disposed, in varying degrees, to compromise with ideological adversaries. The outstanding republican leaders, from Thiers to Ferry and even Gambetta, certainly believed in the existence of this vast central bloc of moderate opinion, and felt embittered and frustrated at their failure to bring it together politically. The reason why they were unable to do so is that a significant part of the republican camp was not prepared to compromise in this way; eventually that part prevailed. The major question within republicanism was the *rapports de force* between consensualists and hardliners. Arguably a minority at the start, the radical hardliners eventually secured most of their demands.

The ways in which they prevailed tell us much about the partisan system of French parliamentarism. Given the fragmented nature of the groups and parties within parliament, there was always a choice for groups with a firm

9. J.-M. Mayeur makes a similar point, stressing that the early anti-clerical laws on education were digested easily enough by most catholics who 'accepted a secular society and the republican state' (Hamon, 1991: 123). Opinion does not, however, always remain passive, especially when parties have begun to work on it.

agenda. Either they built bridges to proximate groups, at the price, perhaps, of moderating their agenda, or they played the game of risk, pushing their agenda ruthlessly to the point of putting the system in danger, in the hope that the resulting polarisation would force more moderate allies to follow their line. Once a group had secured most of what it wanted it could well become more amenable to compromise, as newer, farther-reaching demands emerged, carried by freshly created groups, but that was for another day. In the short term, polarisation was the way to push an agenda, and this kind of logic lies at the heart of the party system of the Third Republic. Polarisation usually took place by politicians' deliberate stressing of their attachment to left or right. These loaded terms must now be discussed in depth, as they continue to structure French debate even today.

Left, Right and Centre

The notions of left, right and centre are as indispensable to French political discourse as they are imprecise. Unfortunately, one is compelled to use them, as all the political class did and continues to do (Imbert and Julliard, 1995; Winock, 1995). What follows is an attempt to locate these categories in terms of the parliamentary parties; there are limits to the precision that one can obtain, simply because politicians found it useful to play on the ambiguity inherent in the terms. Some theorists have followed Goguel in substituting movement and order for left and right. This may sometimes provide a slightly better empirical fit between party discourse and practice, but it avoids the emotional, hence political, use to be made of the latter two terms. Retrospectively, it seems hard to imagine that mere spatial descriptions should have taken on such huge sentimental and ideological overtones; but they did and still do.

By the 1870s, to be on the left was to stand for the republic. This meant, almost by definition, being anti-clerical and subscribing to a rationalist world-view. It probably also meant – and here the imprecision sets in seriously – some kind of commitment to human rights and social justice and to les petits against les gros (though how one defined these terms and how justice was to be secured left room for a wide range of interpretations). Moderate republicans like Ferry or Grévy were thus clearly men of the left for their period, even if their socio-economic agenda was one of capitalist conservatism. The right was about as easy to define: it meant opposing the republic, hence standing for some variant of monarchy. This was usually taken to imply some sympathy for clericalism as well, though the Voltairean bourgeois nostalgic for the July Monarchy might well have disagreed. There was also a tendency to equate being on the right with being rich and powerful locally, although again, this leaves aside the masses of deferential peasants and petty bourgeois who voted monarchist.

Contemporary analysts often saw the left/right polarity in terms of 'temperaments', an imprecise concept which probably comes near to what today would be called a political sub-culture. Siegfried spoke of 'deep-lying tendencies, a way of thinking about state and society, a way of approaching things or feeling them, of reacting or not reacting to circumstances' (1913: 496).[10] For Siegfried (1913: 457) the right meant, above all, hostility to the spirit of the revolution, which he equated with egalitarianism and opposition to hierarchy for its own sake. Thus, right-wingers were essentially deferential; even religion came second to this as a defining category. Berl (1932: 145) made a similar point.

These semi-coherent definitions were put under increasing strain. Already the presence of radicals within the republican camp necessitated some modification. These men who wanted to go further than the left (separation of church and state, democratisation of the civil service, even some measure of redistribution) could only be parked in a corner known as 'the extreme left'. In due course, as socialists and then communists appeared, each with a more far-reaching set of social demands, the extreme left space was taken up. Its previous occupants could only be shifted further towards the right, but the right meant antirepublicans. Political discourse coped with this dilemma by inventing the centre, which was defined negatively. It included those republicans who were not radicals or socialists or communists; Briand used to joke about being in the 'extreme centre'. It was a narrow space, however, as Siegfried remarked, for many of the centre deputies depended on second ballot votes from either right or left. Radicals still insisted that they were men of the left; communists were seen as the extreme left, though as marxists they rejected received republican categories totally, and the location of socialism was somewhere in between the two, especially once the SFIO started participating in governing majorities.

This essentially pragmatic approach to the definitional dilemma still does not exhaust the terminological richness of French discourse. Within the republican block, it became customary, after 1919 at any rate, to distinguish between centre right and centre left. The latter was comprised mainly of the *gauche radicale* or the *indépendants de gauche*; those deputies who positioned themselves between the radicals and the moderates (as the one-time opportunists and progressists now tended to be called). It probably also included the *républicains de gauche*, men like Flandin or Tardieu, though given the personalities involved, the definitions became broad here. Tardieu might well have been classed as centre-right, an important nuance, because this label primarily covered the (heavily catholic) Fédération Républicaine, generally considered to be a tardy and sometimes lukewarm convert to the republic. Only to the right of the FR lay what remained of the real republic-hating right, a few dozen deputies from the periphery, usually sitting in the independent group. However, it was not as simple as that; some of the FR (Vallat, Henriot) were really seen as being men of the right, despite their location in the FR.

10. 'les tendances de fond, une certaine manière de concevoir la société et l'état, de prendre les choses, de les sentir, de réagir ou de ne pas réagir sous l'action de telles ou telles circonstances'.

Many republicans felt that the FR was really part of la droite; if it claimed to be republican, then there were doubts about its sincerity, and in any case, it was clerical.

The picture so far is not a simple one, and at the risk of momentarily complicating it further, it is instructive to see how Siegfried classifies actual parliamentary parties on the left/right axis. The son of a leading opportunist, he certainly shared his father's republican convictions. His early work (1913: 496ff.) makes the following distinctions:

Pure right:	legitimists, other non-liberal royalists and the clerical right even if called progressists – in other words the FR
Pure left:	Second Empire revolutionaries, 1871 or 16 mai republicans, opportunists who stuck with Waldeck-Rousseau and Combes, radicals and independent socialists
Far left:	intransigeants of the 1870s, radicals who vote with the socialists and socialists
Moderate left or centre-left:	orleanists-turned-republicans, that is the Centre Gauche, progressists (until most of them split over Dreyfus) and *républicains de gauche*

By 1930 he had slimmed this down to a broad left/right/centre split, as seen in his analysis of the 1928 elections (1930: 234):

Left:	socialists, radicals, republican socialists and *indépendants de gauche*
Centre:	*gauche radicale* and its splits, *républicains de gauche* and ARS (Reynaud's group)
Right:	independents, FR and PDP

We may note that as a mainstream republican, Siegfried unhesitatingly puts the FR and PDP on the right, because of their clericalism; only 4 out of 18 PDP deputies are elected by left-wing votes on the second ballot, so that puts them on the right. (It also demonstrates the rough-and-ready nature of these ideological classifications, as one wonders how sincere left-wing voters could possibly support these 'reactionaries'.) Here too, the PCF is admitted to membership of the left, whereas previously Siegfried, uncertain how to treat a new genus of party, had simply parked it in a space on its own. By now he feels comfortable enough to assimiliate it into republican spatial logic.[11] The placing of the *gauche radicale* in the centre is interesting too. In the cartel election of

---

11. Lachapelle had similar difficulty in putting the PCF clearly on the left, doubtless because it proclaimed so noisily its break with 'bourgeois' republicanism in the name of marxism. Equally he had no qualms about putting FR or PDP firmly on the right, usually lumping them together with the old independents as one rightist bloc (1914: 15; 1924: 28–9).

1924, Siegfried had put it with the left, albeit with a caveat to the effect that the real demarcation line between left and non-left (or centre?) ran somewhere through the middle of this formation (1930: 238–9).

This view is offered not to create confusion for readers (though that is probably quite inevitable, unfortunately), but to show the approximate and unscientific nature of these left/right classifications. We can perhaps apprehend their real significance. They were emotional constructs that expressed fairly crudely how people broadly related to politics.[12] This is why labels were seen as important; a businessman or lawyer following say Poincaré or Barthou would have sought election as a *républicain de gauche* and would have been angry if spoken of as a man of the right simply because of his conservative views on economic or social questions. By the same token, a catholic deputy running for the Jeune République (the most socially conscious tendency within the christian-democratic spectrum) would probably share some of the SFIO's views on redistribution or international relations, but he would be careful to avoid being seen as a man of the left (because that meant anticatholicism). The labels betokened allegiance to ideological communities and were worn to impress fellow members of the tribe. It was not an exact science, but voters and politicians understood what the symbols meant, especially at the second ballot when each camp tried to gather in its own people. In Berl's phrase (1932: 180) they were 'myths that worked' (*mythes efficaces*). The neo-Weberians might prefer to speak of branding particular goods (parties) so as to identify them to potential customers (voters) and trigger reflexes of consumer loyalty. The vocabulary is not important, but the underlying reality is. When analysts use these categories as a sort of shorthand, if only because everyone has done so, we need to remember that they are dealing with ideological constructs that are politically manipulable.

Today the stereotypes of 'clericals versus republicans' from the politics of the late nineteenth century have become part of the folk memory of the different ideological communities within France (Braud, 1998). The same is true of the left/right polarity. There is nothing preordained or 'natural' about such oppositions and the ideological representations of them, which are fed into mass consciousness. On the contrary, they were developed and promoted by groups in aid of their political agendas. As was remarked above, political groups do not simply reflect or transmit demands which are somehow immanent in civil society, they identify issues and work on them, developing them into a programme of which the political groups themselves will

12. The dangers of cavalier use of sensitive vocabulary are illustrated by Adamthwaite's unhesitating description of the radical party as 'essentially a centre-right party' (1995:183). Written with the benefit of hindsight and using a political vocabulary commonly accepted in the Anglo-Saxon democracies of the late twentieth century, such a description seems uncontroversial. To a French person of the 1930s, whether an ordinary citizen or a member of the political class, it would of course have seemed totally bizarre.

naturally be the vehicle. Such work never stops, for if it does, the party goes out of business.

This active type of representation by parties was particularly evident in the France of the late 1800s. We now turn to an analysis of the party system of the period.

3

THE NATIONAL ASSEMBLY AND THE
BEGINNINGS OF A PARTY SYSTEM
Political Forces After 1870

෨෨

The first phase of the Third Republic was crucial for the construction of the régime and also for the crystallisation of a recognisable party system. After 1875, as the new institutions settled down and the assembly moved to Paris and became the chamber of deputies, a second phase of the system can be distinguished. In this first phase, our focus is very much on parliamentary politics, as this is the arena where the parties played a crucial rôle in the building of the régime. The starting point of our analysis is the illuminating work of Hudemann (1979).

Although, as Hudemann remarks (1979: 26), contemporary terminology was imprecise, with *parti, fraction and réunion* used indiscriminately to describe the parliamentary parties, the reality of the parliamentary parties is beyond doubt.[1] We may usefully distinguish seven parliamentary parties in this first assembly (Figure 3.1) running from left to right; cognisant of the nuances of French political culture, at the first sitting, the deputies occupied the seats in the semi-circle, quite spontaneously, as follows.[2]

On the far left sat the Union républicaine (often referred to early on as the radicals or *l'extrême-gauche*, though soon this title would be reserved for an intransigent subset of the UR group). It was led, though not formally chaired, by Léon Gambetta, and began with some 72 deputies. Generally, it was perceived as standing for the maximalist type of republicanism, as exemplified in the Belleville package (the seat which Gambetta had won in the 1869 election under the empire). This meant: a commitment to a freely elected parliament; guarantee of the classic freedoms under the rule of law; firm anticlericalism, including the separation of church and state; the thorough purging of the civil service to ensure that it was staffed with republican loyalists (even to the point of public employees being elected by popular vote);

---

1. Most of the groups evolved out of large, fairly open meetings for deputies, which often came to be known by name of the place where the meetings were held; thus, one of the right-wing groups that met in the Colbert rooms was soon baptised as the *réunion Colbert*.
2. Hudemann reproduces as appendices a number of key texts from each group that characterise their political positions very succinctly (1979: 367–95).

Figure 3.1 Party Groups in the National Assembly, 1871–5

Union Républicaine Feb. 1871	Gauche Républicaine Feb. 1871	Réunion Rampon Réunion Ferray	Cercle des Réservoirs		
		Centre Gauche Jul. 1871	Centre Droit Apr. 1871	Chevau Légers Aug. 1871	
					Appel au Peuple Feb.1872
			Réunion Colbert Mar. 1872		
		Républicains conservateurs Jan. 1873			
		Groupe Target May 1873			
		Groupe Lavergne Feb. 1875	Groupe Clercq Feb. 1875		

Groups in italics persisted throughout the legislature

Source: adapted from Hudemann (1979).

free and compulsory primary schooling; abolition of standing armies and a generous-sounding but rather unspecific commitment to social justice (Rémond, 1969: 212–3; Barral, 1968: 65–76). The style of this type of republicanism was polemical, emotional, frequently moralising and replete with appeals to history, a feature enhanced by the presence within its ranks of venerable quarant'huitard intellectuals such as Hugo, Quinet and Louis Blanc. Gambetta would try to tone down their image (and practice) beginning with his outlawing of the word 'radical' to describe his group. The bills put forward by the UR tended to be fairly unspecific beyond their demand to firm up the provisional status of the republic viz. their frequent demands for dissolution of the assembly and new elections (Hudemann, 1979: 41). By the end of 1871, the group would have two powerful newspapers to spread its message; the République Française acted as a national organ while the Petite République Française addressed a more rural and provincial public. The papers would act as a sort of electoral agent, publishing UR platforms and giving investitures to agreed local figures. The UR press appears to have been on a secure financial footing thanks mainly to liberal industrialists from Alsace enrolled by

Scheurer-Kestner, a leading Gambettist (Grévy, 1997: 112–29). As well as meeting regularly, the group had subcommittees to prepare tactics and interventions in debates. It also saw the very tentative beginnings of a sort of whips' system, with two deputies keeping attendance records, though the only sanction for the slothful was for their names to be published in the party press.

If the UR was formed of 'advanced republicans', some of whom began their career under the empire or even in 1848, the Gauche républicaine (GRep) stemmed mostly from another informal group in the Corps Législatif (lower house of the old imperial parliament) known as the *gauche ouverte*.[3] Its main leaders had formed the backbone of the government of national defence (alongside the reputedly more radical Gambetta) during the Prussian war, and it was dominated very much by the 4 Jules – Simon, Favre, Grévy and especially Ferry. The refusal of GRep deputies to join Gambetta's men in a single republican group speaks volumes. While personal enmities and leadership rivalries can never be underestimated in such circumstances, the autonomous stance of the GRep clearly displayed a more moderate, consensual style of republican politics. It sought to be a bridge to forces rather further to the right and not to be imprisoned in a hard-line republican lager. Like most of the other groups, the GRep met regularly (twice weekly) and had a presidium or steering committee, whose membership was supposed to rotate (although as tends to happen often, certain people found themselves in post almost permanently). The GRep gave regular briefings to the national press and had its own information outlets (known as *correspondance républicaine*) for the provincial newssheets. It was among the first groups to table legislation (e.g., appointing Thiers as head of government and state). It condemned the Paris Commune unambiguously (a sure sign of demarcation from the UR) and was, initially at least, coy about early dissolution of the assembly, preferring to build incrementally on the provisional arrangements for the republic. It was strong on civic freedoms and firmly jacobin. Unsurprisingly, in view of the above, it boasted a high proportion of freemasons (Hudemann, 1979: 48). Hudemann characterises it as standing for 'a republic of liberal-bourgeois and secularist stamp, based on order, rule of law and respect for the individual' (1979: 52).[4] With 102 deputies at the outset, and its pivotal position in the system, it was bound to play a key rôle.

If the left of the system is relatively straightforward, then its centre (these terms were used by all protagonists) was an area of fine nuances. The usual distinction is between centre gauche (CG) and centre droit (CD). Like their leader Thiers, many of the CG men had, during the Corps Législatif, joined the Union libérale, which grouped both moderate republicans and liberal monarchists of July Monarchy leanings; by July 1871 these two categories of liberal, for, essentially, that is what they were, had abandoned their separate meetings to merge

3. As Hudemann remarks (1979: 48), we still know very little of how this group and its fellows operated in the Corps Législatif.
4. 'eine liberal-bürgerliche, laïzistisch geprägte Republik, gegründet auf Ordnung und Gesetz und auf Achtung des Individuums'.

within the CG. They had tried to push the empire in a more liberal direction, towards voting reform, some decentralisation, more freedom for press and universites, etc. These men were economic and political liberals and they spoke for the pragmatic majority of the grande bourgeoisie, ready to accept the republic that they now saw as less of a threat to their social and economic hegemony (Lhomme, 1960; Garrigues, 1997).[5] They were happy to describe themselves as 'républicains de raison' standing for 'la république conservatrice'. A trivial detail, which attests to the high social status of this group, is that it met in the Jockey Club, where its members could, if they wished, play chess. The CG had parliamentary structures similar to those of the other groups, including a press service run by Joseph Bardoux, great grandfather of a more recent orleanist notable, Valéry Giscard d'Estaing. Under the chairmanship of Rivet (whose bill on the provisional powers of the president in 1871 gave the republic a breathing space) its acceptance of the republic was made clear. In 1873, some of the CG split off to form the Républicains conservateurs, as they were worried about the CG being drawn into an alliance with the leftists of the UR. These dissidents were mostly followers of Casimir-Périer, but they would remain close to the CG anyway, as the possibility of collaboration with the Gambettists became less daunting (see below). The CG had started the legislature wth 173 deputies and its weight would be crucial in any parliamentary dealings. Significantly, there was considerable overlap with the GR in terms of membership at this time when multiple membership of groups was still allowed. Thus, a third of the CG was also registered with the GR. At the same time, two-thirds of the UR were also members of the GR. This phenomenon of overlapping membership is clearly crucial. Unkind commentators have spoken of deputies with multiple membership as practising political tourism or political espionage; there may be some residual truth in such charges, but in our view the phenomenon is a political one in its own right and we shall return to it.

It may be thought that the centre droit (CD) founded by Saint Marc-Girardin and led, after his death, by the duke Audiffret-Pasquier was virtually indistinguishable from the CG. In fact, the real dividing line of the party system ran between the two, and there was very little cross-membership or transfers between one group and the other. The CD boasted some 180 members, mainly of orleanist origins and representing a blend of high finance, nobility and establishment intellectuals (Hudemann, 1979: 75). Its acceptance of the republic was lukewarm and provisional, and the main plank in its programme was to respect the provisional arrangement of the republic for a number of years, with the option of re-opening the whole question of the régime later on. It hesitated for a long time between an alliance with the (non-republican) right, i.e., a gamble on a restoration, and a partnership with the centre left, in the hope of promoting a conservative republic. However, it was

5. Garrigues speaks of the CG as 'la grande bourgeoisie des décideurs' (1997: 52) or (ibid.: 69) as a 'microcosme parlementaire de la bourgeoisie d'affaires'. His work generally stresses the homogeneity of this orleanist élite, linked by a high degree of endogamy and sophisticated networks spanning industry, finance, law, the media and intellectual life.

fearful that this would inevitably involve it in bargains with more extreme republicans. Although it had the usual group structures, the CD appears to have been more fissiparous than the rest. Thus CD dissidents (the forty-odd deputies of the so-called Lavergne group) would play a key role in the vote of the 1875 constitution. Conversely, the Clerq group would use this occasion to vote against the republic and drop into the monarchist camp.

The undisputed right of the system was the territory of the Cercle des réservoirs, which had begun as an intended forum for all monarchists. Although the réservoirs continued to exist as a kind of broad church where the different factions of the right could still meet, these factions had soon affirmed an independent existence. The most unflinching were the appropriately named *chevau-légers* (the nearest English translation would be 'household cavalry', although they owed their name to the street in which they met rather than to any martial skills), loyalists of the legitimist pretender the comte de Chambord, with a hard core of mainly aristocratic Bretons among their eighty or so deputies. With much less formal structures than the other groups, the CL acted as an entirely negative force, referring every issue back to Chambord for a decision. This explains why, as Hudemann remarks, the group did not bother to keep minutes (1979: 64). Some were ready to vote with the left against the 1875 constitution in a fine example of *politique du pire*. They followed their leader in all his blind stubbornness, including the insistence on doing away with the tricolour flag, which ruled out whatever slim chances he had of being recalled to the throne.

More moderate was another legitimist faction, the Colbert group, which numbered up to one hundred and twenty. Basically liberals, but also monarchists, they sought unsuccessfully to pull the CL and the CD into a broad moderate right formation. They accepted the constitution once voted.

Finally came the bonapartists of the Appel au Peuple. With some thirty deputies, elected mainly in by-elections, they pushed for a constitutional referendum, hoping that it would result in an endorsement of the empire against the republic or the monarchy. Such a lapidary programme concealed all the contradictions between progressive and conservative politics that had always been at the heart of this member of the family of the right.

These, then, were the main parliamentary parties. All were much stronger in parliament than outside, though we saw that on the left particularly, efforts were made to establish lines of communication with civil society. All had recognisable working structures of the type that parliamentary groups have possessed in most countries ever since. These were certainly efficient enough to enable the groups to influence the choice of the chamber's steering committee (speaker, secretaries, treasurer, etc.) and even, despite the system of bureaux, the composition of committees (Hudemann, 1979: 215). Importantly, the groups also had very high degrees of internal cohesion on votes; Hudemann measures an average of eighty-three percent, which is, as he rightly says, much higher than in most succeeding chambers. When a group voted for one of its own bills, a vote of one hundred percent was not unknown.

The one qualification which needs to be made about voting discipline paradoxically confirms the cohesion of the groups. On economic issues, as opposed to the political ones that have been our focus hitherto, there is a much looser pattern of voting, with local and regional loyalties visibly coming into play. Membership of the two main cross-party lobbies or intergroups (as they would nowadays be called), the farmers and the freetraders, had clearly very little to do with political/ideological loyalties; left and right both had their peasant lobbyists and protectionists, as well as their defenders of urban interests and their free traders.[6] What counted here were local rapports de force and how the deputy perceived them. However, defending economic interests was a different matter from the real business of the day, viz. determining the shape that politics was to take in future, and here, as Hudemann remarks, the identity of the parties in parliament remained highly coherent.

This founding period of the republic saw, then, the emergence of recognisable parliamentary parties. These combined in a system whose major features were soon apparent and would mark much of the succeeding period.

The Nature of the Early Party System

It is clear that from the start the system was one of pluralised polarism, to use Sartori's term. There were at least seven viable units, as we saw; and the ideological distance between extremes was sharp. The *chevau-légers* stood for traditional monarchy, deference and catholic values; the sharp end of the republican spectrum wanted a powerful single chamber, elected by the popular vote, to propagate values and policies based on reason and individualism. Compromise was not a notion that came easily to either pole, but within this general description, the system had subtleties of its own.

The first of these is undoubtedly the dividing line which went through the system; it lay between centre right and centre left. The subject of this division was not the political régime; we saw that the CD did not exclude the republican form of government. Crucially, several dozen of them (the Lavergne group) moved positively to endorse it; without their intervention the outcome could not have been guaranteed. In ideological terms it would prove difficult to separate the CD and CG. Both were liberal conservatives whose main concern was for a political stability that would guarantee their supporters a continuation of their economic comfort and social authority. The social origins of the deputies in the two groups were, moreover, indistinguishable.

It is hard, however, to avoid agreeing with Hudemann's view that the difference is sociological in a way. Or rather, it is at once sociological, cultural and political. The CG were ready to ally with republicans from both the moderate GRep and the UR, which contained more extreme views and people from a

---

6. Hudemann gives the names of members of these lobbies after his lists of group memberships (1979: 425–9).

wider range of backgrounds. In sociological terms this meant sharing power with the rising elements of the middle class, famously subsumed by Gambetta under the heading of 'les nouvelles couches' (Barral, 1968: 227–44; Grévy, 1997: 64ff.). This deliberately imprecise concept designated a broad swathe of French society that was beginning to prosper – small businessmen and professionals, craftsmen, the more successful peasants and public employees (a growing category) – and which might want its representatives to pay more heed to it than the traditional notables did. To co-opt 'les nouvelles couches' into the political élite was unacceptable to the CD, which would not see social authority watered down; hence its failure to rally fully to the republican camp.

The perceived existence of a sort of invisible barrier between the two centres affected the overall dynamics of the party system. It meant that the long-held dream of a 'meeting of the centres' could never be realised. By this term was meant the establishment of a conservative republic, possibly more presidential in style, and where the senate would weigh heavier, but at any rate based on parliamentary support from the CD and CG, plus allies from either side of this central bloc. Already, the parliamentary arithmetic made such a combination unlikely, but the sociological cut-off described above sealed the fate of the centre alliance. It was awareness of this that enabled Gambetta to secure a more open type of republic by combining his own UR, the GRep and crucially the CG into a type of majority that the professionals would soon call a 'republican concentration'. If the union of the first two members of the 'republican family' seems natural (already a major assumption, given the personalities and strategies involved, not to mention the way in which republican factions had neutralised each other during the Second Republic), then the addition of the CG to the republican majority speaks volumes for the skill of the UR leadership. Gambetta effectively disciplined his group, toned down its demands and, above all, its image. The years after 1870 were largely devoted to presenting the UR as a modern but sensible force that could govern France in accord with the conditions of universal suffrage and mass democracy. Much of the negotiating which resulted in the eventual votes in favour of the republic was conducted at private dinners between key leaders of the three main groups,[7] and much work was put in to ensure voting discipline (eventually, only a small handful of ultra-radicals voted against the 1875 compromise). In systemic terms, thus, a left majority was assembled and its dynamic attracted enough support from the right (the Lavergne group) to secure the immediate objective of consolidating republican institutions. The system remained polarised, even though its centre of gravity had been moved slightly to the left, as the losers in the 1875 votes remained mostly in the monarchist camp.

The system had proven that it could be used to secure political change. There was nothing inevitable about this. To ascribe the change of heart of some CG members solely to their fear of an authoritarian monarchist restoration is to ignore the way in which the republican parties, particularly the UR,

---

7. The diners were known sarcastically as the twelve apostles (Hudemann, 1979: 43–4).

used this situation to put together a functional majority. Parties were not passive actors in a process determined from outside; they took the lead, set the agenda and won their goal.

A more profound change was that these years saw the realisation by party élites that they would have to work in a plural system for the foreseeable future. Multiple membership of groups is a clear sign that this had been understood. Cross-membership brought an understanding of how politicians of similar, but not identical, mindset might behave; it was a prelude to other negotiations that would be undertaken sooner or later. Few politicians seem to have objected to this ecumenical practice. Politicians on the extremes might have dreamt of the sudden coming of a 'republicans' republic' or the equally brusque return of the monarchy, but the main protagonists knew that neither camp would win decisively, and that even within camps, especially among republicans, differences of ideology, strategy and tactics – not to mention personal and material rivalries – would ensure that their political family would remain divided. Politics would then be a question of making alliances, choosing friends and trying to exclude rivals (until one needed them). Noone was ever going to enjoy the types of majority which their colleagues in the US or the UK won regularly and which were the object of envious comment in republican literature; the sharper politicians knew this perfectly. Already it had been demonstrated that parties could not act without taking account of the effect of their actions on the other forces in the system. Furthermore, it was already clear that complicity could extend, productively, across lines of real or imagined division. Pluralism brought a mindset of its own. The founding years of the republic showed that this culture was beginning to spread.

In some ways, however, this situation remained unique. The party system had shown that it could produce an institutional settlement. Once this was in place, it remained to be seen how it would operate and how the parties would develop within it. After 1875 the nascent party system would enter a second phase.

4

THE MATURING OF THE
PARTY SYSTEM, 1876–1914

Thanks to its leaders…the régime was marvellously adaptable, in a way that
none of its predecessors had been since 1789

Estèbe, Les Ministres de la République[1]

The four decades before the First World War saw the party system settle into
a clear pattern. During this time the republic came to be accepted as the natural régime, even if it did not inspire universal affection.[2] In addition to the
consolidation of parliamentary democracy, the purging of the administration
and an extension of the rights of subnational government, important social
changes were implemented. Free, universal and compulsory primary education was introduced; trade unions were legalised and some very modest steps
were taken in the field of health and safety, insurance and pension provision;
the range of civic freedoms was cautiously extended through devices such as
the 1901 law on associations. Most of all, in the cultural field, the secular struggle of church and state saw a victory for the latter with the separation law of
1905, bringing to an end the Concordat which had ensured state finance for
the church in return for a measure of administrative supervision. In the economic sphere the main event was undoubtedly the adopting of protectionist
tariffs after 1890 which confirmed the republic's lack of economic dynamism
and its readiness to protect situations acquises in agriculture and industry.

Parliament, particularly the lower house, remained the hub of political
activity. As the workings of the Grévy constitution became fully apparent to
the politicians, distinct patterns of party behaviour could be identified. First
we identify the party groupings in the chamber, before presenting a systemic
analysis of their actions.

A number of general features can be singled out, running through most of
the period. First is the relative decline of the forces of the right. The rule-of-

1 'Par l'intermédiaire de ses dirigeants…le régime possède une souplesce extraordinaire
qu'aucun de ses prédécesseurs n'a connue depuis 1789'.

2. For Burdeau (1996: 90) the republic had, by 1914, tended to become identified with the
nation as a whole. Mayeur (1984: 402) sees 'intense popular support, bringing together men
from different classes and groups around the republic, which was by now indistinguishable
from the motherland'.

Table 4.1 Composition of Lower Chamber in Third Republic by Tendency (%): Selected Years

Chamber	Right	Republicans	Radicals	Socialists/ Communists
1871	60	31	9	
1876	36	53	11	
1877	40	48	12	
1881	17	69	14	
1885	36	44	20	
1889	37	45	16	2
1893	18	54	20	8
1898	18	48	25	9
		Modérés + Centre Gauche		
1914	13.6	25.3 + 1.5	28.6	17.3
1936	16.2	22.1 + 8.7	17.4	35.6

Source: Kayser (1962: 306–7).

thumb figures presented by Kayser in Table 4.1 show that the right (defined as basically anti-republican) averaged about a third of the seats, dropping from a peak of sixty percent in 1871 to around seventeen percent by 1914. Obviously the workings of the electoral system played a part here. In addition, the right's share of the 1871 poll had clearly been exaggerated by the peculiar wartime circumstances. It also seems that the republic actually gained ground among previously sceptical voters. Arguably, the forces of the right which remained lacked the organisational cohesion of their predecessors in the first parliament described above. Moreover, with time, parts of the right abandoned their anti-republicanism and sought (without lasting success) to become integrated into republican politics. In parliamentary terms this decline meant the swift disappearance of most of the Reservoir groups (CL, Colbert and, later, CD), a trend partly compensated for by the maintenance of a semi-viable bonapartist current for a decade or so. From the late 1880s onwards, the right would increasingly look to extraparliamentary opportunities to challenge the republicans. It always retained a parliamentary presence, however, even if government participation was kept strictly out of bounds. Yet, despite its purely oppositional rôle, the right was able to play a key part in the evolution of the party system, even if it could obtain very little leverage on policy.

A second feature is a series of changes within the republican bloc, beginning with the relatively swift decline of the centre gauche. Although providing government leaders at the start of the 'republicans' republic' (as the left liked to call the post-MacMahon era), the CG lost seats to the point where it was wound up as a separate formation by 1886, at least in the chamber. Its senatorial group continued to function, leading the struggle against income tax and other social legislation (Garrigues, 1997: 261). Much of its mantle fell to the 'government republicans' of the GRep and UR who would provide the core of the so-called opportunist governments of the 1880s.[3]

Increasingly apparent too was the emergence within the republican camp of the radical family as a force within its own right. The early chambers boasted a collection of brilliant individuals (*intransigeants* such as Blanc, Clemenceau or Pelletan), who occupied a smallish space on the left of the mainstream republicans (*l'extrême gauche*) and who could be seen as having to follow their more moderate cousins as a rule. By the mid-1880s the numbers and sense of autonomy of the radicals were clearly on the increase. It also seemed that their demands were increasingly incompatible with those of the mainstream government republicans. Increasingly, radicalism would make the running in the republican camp, reversing the previous situation.

A final twist was provided with the emergence of a viable socialist current. By the early 1890s this had escaped from within radicalism, so to speak, rather as radicalism itself had escaped from within mainstream republicanism. The united socialist party would wait until 1905 for its official birth, but long before that organised socialism was playing a rôle in the party system. This *sinistrisme* (the repeated emergence of new forces to the left of what was previously seen as the extreme) is a striking feature of the pre-1914 system.

One further trend is certainly the greater organisational visiblity of party during this period. The chamber itself would reluctantly register this fact by officially allowing groups to designate members of committees in 1910 (cf. Chapter 1). The years after 1900 saw the official registration of the radical party (1901), followed by the Alliance Républicaine Démocratique (1901), the Alliance Libérale Populaire (1902), the Fédération Républicaine (1903) and the socialist party SFIO (1905). While these developments undoubtedly mark a greater public awareness of party, a readiness to take party out of the chamber and into the electorate and (at least in the socialist case) a genuine attempt to address new social demand, it must, nonetheless, be questioned whether these new organisations, by no means as solid as their outer trappings suggested, really changed very much of the underlying logic of the party system, which was well set by then.

So far as systemic analysis goes, we begin with government formation and support or opposition, as this was the parliamentary parties' main task. It is worth recalling, briefly, the difficult conditions in which governments operated in the 'Grévy constitution'. Given that the president of the republic had opted for a weak rôle and that the right to dissolve the chamber was considered unrepublican after the MacMahon episode, the *président du conseil* faced a hard task. Dependent on a coalition for support (inevitably, given the plural nature of the chamber), he was vulnerable to any shift in his majority. His opponents (including notional members of his majority who might be thinking of changing sides) had at their disposal a major weapon, the interpellation. This was a question to the government which led to debate and ended

---

3. In the 1885 chamber, the two groups merged as the Union des Gauches.

with a vote for or against a proposed agenda for that day (the cabinet did not of course control the chamber's agenda); if the chamber refused the government's agenda, then it resigned. Some fifteen governments were dismissed in this way before 1914. Unable to call new elections, cabinets could only brandish the vote of confidence in reply to threats, but if a new coalition of deputies had formed against them, then the outcome of such votes was predictable. The senate, too, soon learned how to lever governments out by rejecting their bills on strategic occasions. The institutional mechanisms did not favour government.

Most crucially though, governments and deputies became used to this way of behaving. Often a government would go if it felt opinion turning against it (Méline, Combes) before any formal vote or if one or two of its members had resigned individually or perhaps on a trivial matter not really warranting resignation. The pre-eminence of the deputies came to be accepted; leaders with ideas about building disciplined majorities to put through far-reaching programmes (Ferry, Gambetta, and, later, Tardieu) were resented and duly taught a lesson when they had outlived their usefulness. Politicians thought in terms of short-lived cabinets, and so, in time, did voters. There were rules to the parliamentary game, which the bold forgot at their peril, and the main players in that game were the parties.

Such mental and institutional structures visibly affected governments. If we count some forty-two cabinets from the start of the 1876 legislature to the 1914 elections just before the outbreak of war, this means an average lifespan of barely ten months; many were in office for much less. This alleged instability needs to be understood properly. Commentators have often remarked on the high continuity of ministerial personnel even if the name of the *président du conseil* changed regularly.[4] There is a case for regarding some of these changes more as reshuffles than real changes of government. When the system had to produce a longer-lived cabinet, usually to address a particular set of problems, it invariably did so. In this way, a number enjoyed spans of two years or more: Ferry to build an overseas empire from 1883–85; Méline to preside over a period of economic consolidation after 1896; Waldeck Rousseau to lead the 'defence of the republic' after the turmoil of the Dreyfus case; Combes to push through anti-clerical policy immediately after; Clemenceau to manage a series of social tensions in the prewar period. Less visibly, certain ministers remained in place across a series of governments, carrying through reforms of a largely technical nature. Burdeau cites the examples of Freycinet at Defence and Rouvier at Finance (1996: 80).

4. Dogan (1953) insists on the general stability of the régime. Majorities and cabinets may have fluctuated, but this was more than compensated for by the stability of institutions, party leaders, voting behaviour, candidates and deputies, senior civil servants and, last but not least, ministers. Estèbe agrees, underlining the social homogeneity of the new republican élites from the 'nouvelles couches'. In his view (1982: 226) this helped them in their essential task of consolidating and maintaining the socio-political system. They enabled the state to perform its prime function of maintaining national coherence and preventing social classes from eliminating each other.

Table 4.2 Party Strengths in Third Republic Legislatures, 1871–1919

	Extr. Gauche	UR	GR	CG	CD	Droite Mod	Extr. D'te[a]	Bonapartist	Non-Group
1871–75		100 (115	100	173	185	200	200		
1876–77	98	194 (incls GR)	200	48	55(+22)[c]	109	83	34)[b]	
1877–81	35	130	130	30	30		25	75	
1881–85	46	204	168	39			70	105	
1885–89	60 Ouv/Rad[d]	GRad 40–100	UnG 200				45 — Union des Droites 200 (incls Bonaps)	45	80
1889–93	100	200+	Rép de gouvernement c300	40			165 (+44 Boulangists)[e]		
1893–98	Socs 50	Rad 140				Ralliés 35	60		
1898–1902	37	RadSoc 104	GDem+UnProg+RépProg 126	+95	+238		58 (+23 antisemites)[e]		
1902–06	29 (+ IndSoc13)	117	GRad+UnDem+RépProg 116	+102	+135	ALP 75	RépNationalistes 54		
1906–10	52 (+ IndSoc22)	139	134[f]	66	80	64	26		
1910–14	75 (+RepSoc31)	150	113	72 GD +	75Prog	34	19 (Droites)		
1914–19	101 (+RepSoc23)	172 (+23)	66 (+23)	34GD (+RepG54)	37FR	23	15		46

For full party names see List of Abbreviations.
a: For this period, extrême droite covers intransigent monarchists
b: Hudemann's figures, which include overlapping membership
c: The so-called constitutionnels, who eventually voted for the republic
d: The workers' and radical group predated the formation of separate party groups (radical party and SFIO)
e: These groups are classed together as expressions of the nationalist family
f, plus 53 GDem and 48 UR
Source: Bomier-Landowski (1951); Hudemann (1979); Avril et al. (1989)

By the same token, the party system could break awkward governments quickly and subtly when it was felt that they were overstepping certain lines in the sand. The shortlived ministry of Gambetta in 1881–82 is typical. Highly popular in the country and perceived as the republican leader, he was only allowed a few weeks in office before being parked in the honorary position of speaker. He had, as will be seen, transgressed party logic (mainly by his obdurate pursuit of proportional representation). The all-radical cabinet of Léon Bourgeois lasted only a few months in 1895–96, before being overthrown on a technical financial question by the senate. In reality, rather like Gambetta, he was perceived as standing for far too bold an agenda (of which proposals for a graduated income tax formed the core). Again, he had gone against a tacit consensus of the parties and so had to go. As the party system developed its sophistication, this practice of putting in 'dangerous' cabinets simply in order to show that they were unviable became known as lever l'hypothèque (probably best translated by a term from medicine rather than law – lancing the abscess).

These general considerations about the influence of parties invite a deeper exploration of some of the rules of the game. By taking an overview of the relationship between chamber and cabinets over the pre-1914 period, it is possible to deduce the working of some systemic laws. What follows is not an examination of individual governments, parties or legislatures, and certainly not an assessment of policy outputs, but an attempt to elicit underlying processes at work across a lengthy period. The focus is long-term, not conjunctural.[5]

Natural Partners, Dangerous Games

Tables 4.3a, 4.3b and 4.3c assess membership of government by party group for the pre-1914 period. The left-hand column contains the dates of a cabinet and the name of its *président du conseil*, plus the number of full ministers (under-secretaries of state in brackets). The remaining columns list the numbers of ministers and secretaries by group, with the group of the premier identified by an asterisk. For easier access, the material is presented in three tables rather than in a single very large one. This corresponds to some extent to greater availability of information; the further one advances in history, the more precisely one can denominate government members in terms of the party groups, as set out in Table 4.2 above.

The usual caveats are in order. The party provenance of a small number of ministers proved impossible to identify precisely; some sources, notably L'Année politique, give very loose descriptions of the party / group status of ministers (e.g., 'nuance radicale' or 'ex-majorité'). Such doubtful cases were assigned to the non-party category. Table 4.3b uses the broad category of républicains de gouvernement; in terms of our discussion, this refers gener-

5. For detailed accounts see Chastenet (1952–67); Bonnefous (1956–67); Mayeur (1973); Rébérioux (1975).

Table 4.3a: Party Composition of Governments in First Period of Third Republic, 1876–86

(Junior ministers in brackets)

	Nonparty	Centre Gauche	GRep	Constituti onnels	UnionRep/ ExtGche
Dufaure I					
9.3.1876–12.12.76; 9	2	5*	1	1	
Simon					
12.12.76–17.5.77; 10	2	4	3*	1	
Broglie					
17.5–23.11.77					
	Non-representative governments imposed by President MacMahon				
Rochebouët					
26.11–13.12.87					
Dufaure II					
13.12.1877–4.2.79; 9	2	4*	3		
Waddington					
4.2.79–28.12.79; 9(+6)	2	2	5*(+5)		1(+1)
Freycinet I					
28.12.79–23.9.80; 9(+6)	2		5*(+5)		2(+1)
Ferry I					
25.9.80–13.11.81; 9(+6)	2		5*(+5)		2(+1)
Gambetta					
14.11.81–30.1.82; 12(+9)	2		3(+6)		7*(+3)
Freycinet II					
30.1.82–7.8.82; 11(+5)	2	1	7*(+4)		1(+1)
Duclerc					
7.8.82–29.1.83; 11(+5)	2		8*(+4)		1(+1)
Fallières					
29.1.83–21.2.83	Terminated by illness				
Ferry II					
21.2.83–6.4.85; 11(+5)	2		8*(+ 4)		1(+1)
Brisson I	Caretaker government of *concentration républicaine* formed				
6.4.85–7.1.86	by Speaker until elections				

Source: *L'Année Politique*

ally to the moderates known as opportunists, then progressists. In terms of Table 4.2 above, it subsumes groups such as UR or GRep, then UnG or Gauche Démocratique. The crucial dividing line, so far as the dynamics of the party system go, lies between such groups and radicalism.

Despite the unavoidable generality of some of these categories, a number of trends clearly emerge. Governments were small affairs, rarely exceeding eleven full ministers, with the prime minister usually taking over a full department (only in 1936 would a separate civil service department be created for the prime minister). A small number of under-secretaries came to be added, usually less than four. Eventually, one of these, Colonies, became a

Table 4.3b: Party Composition of Governments, 1886–1905

(Junior ministers in brackets)	Nonparty	Réps. de gouvernement	Rads	Extr.gauche/ rad.soc.	Soc.
Freycinet III 7.1–11.12.86; 11(+4)	2	5*	2(+4)	2	
Goblet 11.12.86–30.5.87; 11(+4)	2	5*	2(+4)	2	
Rouvier I 30.5–12.12.87; 10(+1)	2	8*(+1)			
Tirard I 12.12.87–3.4.88; 10	1	7*	2		
Floquet 3.4.88–22.2.89; 10(+2)	3	2	5*	(+2)	
Tirard II 22.2.89–17.3.90; 10(+1)	1	9*(+1)			
Freycinet IV 17.3.90–27.2.92; 10(+1)	1	8(+1)*	1		
Loubet 23.2–16.12.92; 10		6*	4		
Ribot I 6.12.92–4.4.93; 10		7*	3		
Dupuy I 4.4–3.12.93; 10(+1)	3	4(+1)*	3		
Casimir-Périer 3.12.93–30.5.94; 10(+1)	3	7(+1)*			
Dupuy II 30.5.94–26.1.95; 11	4	7*			
Ribot II 26.1–1.11.95; 11	5	5*	1		
Bourgeois 1.11.95–29.4.96; 11	1	2	7*	1	
Méline 29.4.96–28.6.98; 11	3	7*	1		
Brisson II 28.6–1.11.98; 11	1	3	7*		
Dupuy III 1.11.98–22.6.99; 11(+2)		8(+1)*	3(+1)		
Waldeck-Rousseau 22.6.99–7.6.1902; 11	1	7*	1	1	1
Combes 7.6.02–24.2.05; 11	1	4	4*	2	

Source: L'Année Politique

Table 4.3c: Party Composition of Governments after 1905

(Junior ministers in brackets)	Rt	Non party	Rep/ GRep	RepG	GDem	Rep.rad Rad.dem GRad	RadSoc	RS	Soc/ SFIO[a]
Rouvier II and III 24.2.05–14.3.06; 11(+2)			4*			5(+2)	2		
Sarrien 14.3–25.10.06; 11(+3)			1			6*(+2)	4		1
Clemenceau I 25.10.06–24.7.09; 12(+5)		1		(+1)	(+1)	4(+1)	5*(+2)		2
Briand I 24.7.09–3.11.10; 12(+4)		2	1	(+1)		4(+2)	1(+1)		3*
Briand II 3.11.10–2.3.11; 12(+4)		2	1		1	4(+2)	3(+2)		1*
Monis 2.3–27.6.11; 12(+4)			(+2)			6*(+1)	5(+1)	1	
Caillaux 27.611–14.1.12; 12(+4)			1		2(+1)	4(+1)	4*(+2)	1	
Poincaré I 14.1.12–21.1.13; 12(+3)					1(+2)	6*(+1)	3		2
Briand III 21.1–22.3.13; 12(+4)					4(+2)	3(+1)	5		1*
Barthou 22.3–9.12.13; 12(+4)			3		3(+1)	4*(+1)	2(+1)	(+1)	
Doumergue I 9.12.13–9.6.14; 12(+4)					4*(+2)	3(+2)	4		1
Ribot II 9.6–12.6.14; 12(+3)			1*			3(+1)	8(+1)		1
Viviani I 13.6–26.8.14; 12(+5)					5(+1)	2(+3)	3(+1)	2*	
Viviani II 26.8–29.10.14; 14(+3)		2		3	2(+2)	2(+1)	3*		2
Briand V 29.10.15–12.12.16; 16(+6)	1	3	2(+1)	3	2(+4)	3*	2(+1)		
Briand VI 12.1.216–20.3.17; 11(+9)	1	2(+2)	1	2	1(+1)	1(+5)	2*(+1)		1
Ribot III 20.3–7.9.17; 14(+11)		(+1)	1(+2)	2*	2	2(+1)	3(+6)	3(+1)	1
Painlevé I 13.9–13.10.17; 18(+11)		2		3	2	5(+1)	5(+8)	1*(+2)	

a: SFIO only from 26.8.1914. Independent socialists before then.
Source: Bonnefous (1956-67)

full ministry. Gambetta had no less than twelve full ministers and nine under-secretaries, plethoric proof of his megalomania in the eyes of his enemies. Frequently, the posts of army and navy minister would go to non-party professionals in a kind of tacit agreement not to politicise these areas, but some of the top military did have known political sympathies, and, in some cases, a civilian politician could be put in (usually a sign of some political tension).

In the first part of the period, government formation was clearly the preserve of the mainstream republicans, stemming essentially from the GRep and UR, after an initial input from the CG. This group is often referred to as the opportunists (not pejoratively, but because these gradualists believed that reforms should be effected only when the moment was opportune), though in the view of some analysts (Grévy, 1997) the tag should strictly be restricted to the Gambettist group from the UR (Spuller, Bert, etc.). It was in fact an alliance of the majority of Gambettists with the GRep, increasingly dominated by Ferry, which provided the nucleus of the governments on either side of 1880, which passed major laws on education, local government reform and trade union rights, as well as tidying up the constitution (doing away with the life senators).

The parliamentary arithmetic meant that these government republicans needed either allies or the non-belligerence of some opposition groups (see Table 4.2). The question of alliances (or the impossibility thereof) dominated the party system. Some government leaders would have liked a broad two-bloc system in the chamber. There is a long tradition of writing by republican leaders, from Gambetta to Ferry to Waldeck Rousseau, lamenting the fact that voters never had a clear choice at election time; neither did governments when it came to choosing partners. These leaders dreamt of a generally accepted republic in which the régime question had ceased to matter and where a sensible, moderately reforming tendency (led by themselves) was confronted by a bolder grouping seeking more and deeper changes (essentially the radicals). However, the Third Republic was never going to produce a French version of Whigs and Tories. Part of the potential moderate constituency (most of the catholic voters) were held outside the republican camp for the time being, by mechanisms which will be explored shortly. However much such voters may have agreed with the opportunists on broad social and economic policy, the régime question and its attendant ideological passions got in the way. There could thus be no 'union of the centres', as this dream of a broad moderate grouping was sometimes called. Equally, within the progressive camp, the differences between radicals and the fast growing socialists would prove serious enough to overcome any initial centripetal pressures between them.

The governmental republicans were thus the natural candidates for office, but they would always have to perform in a minority situation, squeezed between a right deemed out of bounds as an ally and a radical left that wanted to draw them towards itself, into a *concentration républicaine*. The opportunists saw this tactic as a means ultimately to supplant them; Ferry in particular knew exactly what was happening and did everything to exclude radicalism from office. However, if the radicals were to vote with the right against moderate types of executive, then the latter could not survive. Needless to say, it did not take long for this to happen. Gambetta was an early victim of this conjuncture of opposites and so, eventually, was Ferry; the radical leader Clemenceau gained a reputation as a wrecker of ministries, but much of his firepower came from the votes of the right. The party system was thus one of tripolar instability.

There is little doubt that the radicals were the major protagonists in this system. Realistically, by the early 1880s the moderates had probably achieved as much as they wanted for the foreseeable future. Parliamentary democracy seemed safe, allowing places of choice for moderates both locally and nationally; the administration was being republicanised;[6] noticeable change had been achieved in education; an empire was being quietly built and social tension remained manageable. To these intensely pragmatic politicians, who in any case believed that history was working towards their long term goals (such as the end of organised religion and the advent of an enlightened citizenry), there seemed no reason to push any further. The radicals, more ideological, and feeling more pressure from voters, still had much unfinished business. The constitution needed reforming (that is, stripping of its president and senate): the church needed to be marginalised fully (school reform was acceptable for now, but only separation would complete the business) and urgent social reforms were required (which had to be addressed if only to stop the party from losing more ground to the socialists). Radicalism had a distinct agenda, a different personnel and its own electorate. To gain power it was prepared to play very dangerous games with the precariously balanced party system, and it did so in a cold-blooded way which belies the emotional, slightly caricatural vision which commentators often have of the party. Hence the readiness to vote with the enemy on the right. At times such behaviour came near to bringing the republic down, but, over time, these tactics would pay off.

A recognisable radical presence in government can first be seen after the fall of Ferry, when Freycinet, the archetypal moderate professional, brought in two radical ministers and four under-secretaries. He was succeeded by René Goblet, a man who occupied the space between radicalism and opportunism with some skill. By the end of the 1880s, Floquet had been sworn in as the first fully fledged radical head of government; the party was now, as the title of Kayser's book (1962) has it, at the gateway of power. This rise obviously reflects a growing electoral support in the country. More profoundly, it shows how a party starting from a minority position can impose

6. Wright stresses the nature and limits of civil service reform in France after 1870. The initial desire of the deputies to cut back a bureaucracy seen as costly, overpowerful and untrustworthy soon gave way to the realisation (especially by the opportunists after 1877) that governments needed an efficient civil service if only for electoral purposes and patronage. Hence, institutions tended to be kept intact, but filled with loyal placemen. In the purges after 1877, only one prefect survived; 1,763 magistrates out of 2,143 were sacked, as were 2,563 justices of the peace out of 2,941. This 'historic compromise' of liberal-minded deputies and professional jacobin administrators led to 'a complex, extensive, open and efficient system of political clientelism' (in Bruguière, 1982: 49–57). In terms of the party system, it reinforced the localism and deputy-centred nature of the system.

an agenda by single-mindedness and clever exploitation of the divisions within the system. For there was nothing inevitable about the radicals' rise to a position where, by the early 1900s, they seemed a natural party of government. Here was a party which understood how party systems work and how to get such systems to work in its interests. The radicals were past masters at political engineering.

The System under Test

We have suggested above what seems to us the normal logic of republican party politics. At regular intervals, however, this logic was put to the test by the onset of an exogenous crisis, to which the system had to react. These crises are the Boulangist threat of the late 1880s; the ralliement after 1894; and finally the Dreyfus case and its lengthy aftermath, effectively spanning the period from 1898 to 1906. Although these challenges were different in nature, they all put pressure on the underlying logic which we have identified.

The General Boulanger case is well known (Irvine, 1989a). He rose in the army by cultivating a distinctly republican profile (in a milieu still dominated by the old right) and associating with politicians such as Clemenceau, who is said to have been instrumental in having Boulanger made defence minister in the 1886 Freycinet cabinet, when he first entered formal politics. Here he flaunted both his revanchism, by making anti-German gestures, and his populism, by expelling members of the royal family from the army and claiming that troops on strike-breaking duty shared their food with strikers. When an embarrassed government retired him, he resurfaced as a campaigning politician who promptly began winning large by-election victories (the rules at that time allowed candidacies in more than one seat), on a ticket of vague constitutional reform. By now, a popular movement was under way, with demonstrations, songs and even the merchandising of Boulanger memorabilia. The republican general was, however, also being heavily financed by leading monarchist dignitaries, although this fact was never advertised. The political class was seriously worried and feared a coup by this new cult figure. Eventually, Boulanger was seen off by the threat of arrest and fled the country; the immediate danger was over, but he had by then given right wing politics a new direction, as well as perturbing the system of parties as a whole.

The politics of Boulangism remain subject to controversy. Rudelle (1982) saw, at least in the votes for the general, evidence of a popular, social type of republicanism, for which the moderate opportunists simply could not cater. Irvine (1989b) focuses more on the huge royalist backing for Boulanger (surely not given disinterestedly) and shows that candidates using his name did best in traditional areas of the right. Mayeur (1973: 167–80) stresses the paradox that Boulanger's entourage were all radicals or even socialists, but that this did not stop him bidding openly for catholic votes (albeit on the basis of integration into the republic and not its overthrow). Part of the confusion lies in the demagogic and irresponsible tactics of Boulanger, who was clearly ready to accept support from anywhere if it would help him to achieve political power; what he might have done with such power remains open to speculation. From our point of view, however, this latter question is less important. What Boulanger did was to send a seismic shock through a party system that, by then, was settling into a logic of its own.

Beneath the sound and fury of the Boulanger campaigns, the party system was testing out alternative majority combinations. When Boulanger was first sacked as a minister, the government of Goblet was overthrown by a combination of government republicans and the right. Previously, the right had tended to join with the radicals against the moderates. The immediate motive for this novel alliance was fear that Boulanger's posturing might lead to war with Germany, although some party chiefs clearly thought that the alliance might have more life in it. Mayeur (1973: 170) sees the advent of the Maurice Rouvier cabinet (a very typical Gambettist who moved further away from his radical youth as his associations with the world of banking deepened) as a tentative rapprochement of opportunism with the right, the more so as the bonapartist segment of the right under Duval was now proclaiming its readiness to work within the republic. Rouvier was canny enough to insist that he would not govern without a republican majority, but in fact his cabinet was based on the moderate republicans plus the benevolence of the right. The question then became: what could opportunism offer the right to keep it on board? Clearly the main demand, repeal of Ferry's educational laws, was more than they could offer, but compromise may have been possible (by granting, say, exemptions) if time had allowed, and a different sort of majority might have come on the agenda.

In the event, as Boulanger's momentum got stronger, majority opinion on the right tended to back him in the hope of harming or conceivably overthrowing the republic. Thus, once again, the 'union of the centres' was still born. Old instincts and ideologies reasserted their hold, party behaviour reverted to type, and Rouvier was duly dismissed by a combination of the right and radicalism. The factor that triggered the vote was a politico-financial scandal, when Wilson, a leading opportunist and Grévy's son-in-law, was found to be selling places on the honours list. The chance for the radicals to strike down the opportunist whom they hated most (apart from Ferry) was too strong; Grévy was duly forced to resign. This episode made it very difficult for those on the right who had been working towards a rapprochement with republicans. The radicals kept up the pressure by overthrowing another moderate cabinet with a vote in favour of constitutional revision, again allying with the right.

They were rewarded with the Floquet government, the first time one of their men had led an executive. The moderates were forced into accepting a number of places in this cabinet of *concentration républicaine*. Floquet did what was necessary by changing the electoral system from departmental PR back to single member constituencies, the best means of stopping the use of by-elections as plebiscites. There were limits to radical success, however. Soon afterwards, Floquet tried to push more of the radical agenda, with bills to bring in income tax and have the senate elected by universal suffrage. The moderates voted with the right and Floquet resigned, to be replaced by a cabinet of opportunist stamp which began the crackdown against Boulanger.

Retrospectively, then, it can be seen that this threat to democracy turned up some interesting possibilities within the party system. The possibility of an alternative majority of governmental republicans and pragmatic or resigned parts of the right had at least raised its head. Partly in reaction to that, radicalism had raised the stakes and won, at least in the short term, forcing its way into office and trying to frogmarch the opportunists with it. However, the opportunists were only ready to collaborate to the extent of saving parliamentary democracy. Once it came to implementation of the radical social and political agenda, they were quite ready to ally with the right, even though the latter was now deep in anti-democratic waters. Opportunism was linked to radicalism by its desire to preserve parliamentarism, but not much else. It was separated from the right by the right's hesitancy about the parliamentary régime (but how long might that last?), yet powerfully bound to it when it came to social and economic conservatism. The delicate balances and limitations of the party system could hardly be better illustrated than by this bizarre episode, and it is unfortunate that commentators have paid so much attention to the surface glitter and not to the reality of the underlying *rapports de force*.

One final development is deeply significant for the party system, with consequences extending far beyond 1914. This is the development of mass extra-parliamentary politics. Large pressure groups were not unknown (e.g., the Ligue de l'Enseignement), but the Ligue des Patriotes, led by Paul Déroulède, took matters further. Originally a group which aimed to foster patriotic values among the young, under Déroulède it turned into a mass movement, using petitions, demonstrations and marches as its preferred currency; increasingly, its nationalism became impatient with the parliamentary republic, which it saw as wasting resources on imperial expansion and not doing enough to prepare for the war of revenge against Germany. Radical coolness towards extending military service was a particular dislike. The Ligue des Patriotes invested heavily in Boulanger and helped to create a new style of right-wing politics where patriotism, previously seen as a property of the left, now became identified with an angry, authoritarian right (Girardet, 1983; Jenkins, 1990; Sternhell, 1978). Some traces of the league's influence could already be seen in the election of Boulangist deputies to the 1889 chamber, but more significant was that it set down a marker for the future with its politics-in-the-street style. Right and left would have to meet its pressures in different ways.

The *Ralliement*: Pressure of a Different Kind?

The *ralliement* is generally understood as a sustained attempt to integrate catholics into republican politics, that is, to detach them from their hitherto dominant attachment to the monarchist right (Sedgwick, 1965; McManners, 1972). This attempt spans the period from around 1890 to 1906. The impulse came from the catholic hierarchy, essentially Pope Leo XIII, who in a series of statements from the late 1880s, culminating in the encyclical Rerum Novarum, suggested that it should be possible for catholics to work within the framework of a democratic republic in order to defend their interests (Prelot and Gallouedec-Genuys, 1969: 245–310; Portier, 1993: 13 –61)). Temporal issues (politics) thus became separable from religious matters, and, in theory, the question of the régime could now lose its salience. This new line caused ripples on both the right and the left of the party system.

Implicit in the new line was the idea that catholic interests (the struggle to stem, if not reverse, the tide of anti-clerical measures) would have to be carried by some kind of party. Whereas such organisations existed in other European states by now (Belgium, Netherlands, Austria, Germany) where liberal or authoritarian governments were also imposing secularist policies, there was little sign of such a party in France. The best analysis of this situation is that of Stathis Kalyvas (1996: 114–66), which we follow here.

Before 1870, the church in France had benefited from authoritarian régimes, and even in 1875 still enjoyed much strength in the early Republic. It was state financed through the Concordat, it had its own schools and universities and even state schools provided space for prayers, religious instruction, attendance at mass and the presence of many members of religious orders as teachers. Religious observance across the country may have been in secular decline in terms of brute numbers, but the fervour of committed catholics was, if anything, increasing (Gibson, 1989: 230–31). Clearly, the hierarchy understood the ideological projects of the republicans and hated them as much as the republicans hated clericalism. However, surely misreading the strength of republican sentiment in the country, the hierarchy remained confident that it needed no political organisation of its own. Catholic voters were thus encouraged to vote for monarchists/conservatives.

When the republicans struck with the 1880s legislation, the church's reaction was weak.[7] Whereas in neighbouring countries the hierarchy had encouraged catholics in civil society to form various kinds of associations and pressure groups in order to raise consciousness and mobilise (and out of these civic groups would spring, in a later stage, actual political parties), this did not happen in France. On the contrary, the hierarchy went out of its way

7. From 1879 to 1888, religious orders were restricted, with the Jesuits being dissolved and others having to obtain government registration. Over 5,000 religious were expelled, their schools handed over to laymen or secular priests. The Ferry laws of 1882–83 brought in free, compulsory primary schooling and replaced religious instruction with civics. The Goblet law of 1886 replaced religious personnel in state schools with lay people.

to kill off such attempts as there were to mobilise catholics against the anti-clericals (e.g., de Mun's proposal for a catholic party in 1885). The main reason for this is that, as Kalyvas suggests, the hierarchy in France and in Rome were gambling on the end of the republic and the return of some type of authoritarianism better suited to their interests, hence the willingness to divert the catholic voter into an anti-régime vote. Hence also the interest in a loose cannon such as Boulanger, who might help topple la gueuse, as the hard-liners liked to call the republic.

Such calculations were probably optimistic at any time after the *16 mai* (at the latest), despite Kalyvas' generous attempts to find a rationale. The fact is that the church's leadership were poor strategists, who failed to see that the republic had taken firm root in most areas of urban and provincial France. Most analysts agree that the demise of Boulanger convinced church leaders that the republic was there to stay, hence the ralliement strategy. This change of tack meant that the mobilisation of catholics was beginning relatively late in the day. This lag would decisively affect the sort of party that eventually emerged and the way the party system was modified in its turn.

The first real attempt at organised political catholicism was the Droite républicaine, which began as a parliamentary group of monarchist deputies ready to embrace republican politics, around Jacques Piou, in 1890. It ran candidates in the 1893 election who scored around five percent and took thirty-five seats. This was short of what the instigators had hoped for, and they blamed the failure of moderate republican voters to help them out on the second ballot. In the 1898 poll, the catholic block, now under Etienne Lamy, put in more effort to coordinate the widely differing panoply of catholic organisations behind its candidates; it still only took 32 seats, and many of the organisations withdrew their support when Lamy declared the need for greater centralisation. By 1901, the radicals had raised the temperature of the ideological struggle once more (see below), and an Alliance Libérale was created to fight the 1902 campaign (Martin, 1976). It aspired to be more than a parliamentary clique or even a federation of organisa-tions like its predecessors, wanting to be a full party with a commensurate organisation across the country. It would at its peak lay claim to some 160,000 members (five times the socialist tally) and could show the beginnings of an institutional presence in civil society, with its own job placement bureaux, cheap credit facilities and legal aid for workers. It was able to draw in activists from parts of the older right and, to some extent, cartellise candidacies for parliamentary seats with them. The AL leaders were happy with the climate of polarisation created by radicalism, and looked forward to a straight fight between a united moderate right (in which they could aspire to hegemony) and the left, sectarian and collectivist at once (Martin, 1976: 676). Although in this polarised climate the right as a whole took forty-nine percent of the vote and came within a quarter of a million votes of victory, the Alliance only went up to seventy-eight seats. Soon after, the word 'Populaire' was added to the title; there was now 'a potential confessional party' on the scene (Kalyvas, 1996: 157). Certainly, catholic notables were generous with their money and their newspaper coverage.

Much rested on the 1906 campaign, but here the party fell back. The republicans had held it off, relatively few of their voters being tempted by the new formation. Soon, a third of the ALP vote would fall away, much of it (and not a few activists) going to the new, nationalistic politics of the right. Yet, in parts of France (Mayenne, Brittany), a solid local infrasructure remained where catholic republican deputies continue to be elected to this day. This suggests a huge missed opportunity to achieve a breakthrough and impose an important new force onto the party system. The reasons for this failure merit examination.

The root cause was the failure to mobilise catholics in a unified, centralised way. The monarchist leaders were sociologically and temperamentally incapable of organisation; they expected 'their people' to vote in accord with deference and possibly hints from the pulpit, but this was increasingly inadequate. Election evidence shows a steady seepage of 'natural' monarchist votes towards the republic, especially in rural areas. Some communes with ninety percent attendance at mass could still vote for radical candidates. As Kalyvas rightly suggests (1996: 143), fear that restoration might mean the return of feudal customs or dues only explains part of this swing to the republic. The key factor is the organisational effort put in by republicans to win votes. The years on either side of 1900 saw a major increase in electoral committees and similar bodies, especially in the radical camp (Baal, 1977). This may not have looked impressive in terms of durable, modern, disciplined mass-party structures, but it could turn out a vote.

The catholic camp could not do so to the same extent. There was no shortage of organisations in civil society, but many of these were local, and in any case, their political options could differ sharply. They encompassed christian-democrat views, with a strong social concern, as exemplified by the *abbés démocrates* of Brittany or the Nord, liberal/conservative perspectives (Piou's supporters) and a much more combative, authoritarian-tinged politics, which wanted to take the fight to the secularists, such as that practised by the Assumptionist monks who ran the newspaper *La Croix* and had a powerful network of electoral committees by the 1890s. To launch a party, though, the experience of other countries showed that it was first necessary to have a dense network of mass movements within civil society, which meant movements unified, centralised and directed by the hierarchy (even if laymen did most of the work). Once this consciousness-raising has been done and catholics know they have to fight for their rights, parties can then take root,. Church leaders in France never went through this stage, but attempted to create a top-down party, hoping that the party would radiate outwards from a parliamentary group. The results proved that there are no shortcuts. Ironically, only after the church had undergone the major defeat of Separation in 1905, did the movement to create a civil network begin. The interwar period would then show a serious success for the panoply of movements known as Action Catholique (Cholvy and Hilaire, 1988). In 1906, however, it was a question of picking up some very broken pieces and starting anew. The confessional party was a failure.

Even the advent of the weak ALP and its predecessors asked some serious questions of the party system, and it is to this that we now turn. The potential of the *ralliement* was finally revealed with the longlasting Méline government of 1896–98. This was composed, essentially, of moderate republicans, who by now preferred the term progressist to opportunist. This term was coined by Deschanel, one of a new generation of republican moderates who made their début under Méline (others included Poincaré, Leygues, Barthou and Jonnart). Constantly attacked by the radicals, Méline effectively owed his survival to a tacit pact with the right; Mayeur (1984: 166) quotes an occasion when all of the right bar twelve (therefore including a good portion of anti-republicans) voted with Méline against an *interpellation*. There were reasons for this understanding. Méline's protectionist policies suited farm and business supporters of both right and progessists. It is true that he dare not go back on the anti-clerical laws, as the *ralliés* hoped, but equally, he did not push their implementation very hard, turning a blind eye to numerous encroachments. The supreme advantage of such a pact for the progressists is that it kept them out of a *concentration* with the radicals. The deal rested on a narrow basis, however, as part of the right was still not fully won over to the republic, hence unavailable as serious members of a majority.

The radicals, for their part, were squeezed on their left by the rising socialist current (Ligou, 1962; Lefranc, 1963 and 1967; Willard, 1965). Although still scattered among a number of miniparties, socialism had fifty deputies by the early 1890s and was making inroads into radical territory. Partly as a result of this pressure, the radicals in the 1890s were split into three parliamentary groups more clearly than ever. The gauche radicale were nearest to the progressists, the *union progressiste* occupied a median stance, and the radical-socialists of Pelletan were quite happy to proclaim their proximity to the socialist current.[8] Significantly, there was overlapping membership between all the radical sub-groups. The radicals, thus, kept their options open.[9] Commitment to a full alliance with the socialists was not obvious for a party which basically represented small property-owners. The radicals' real aim remained to detach the moderates from the right, and to this end they kept up the merciless abuse of Méline. The Pope would draw up the right's lists at the

8. Lockroy, who belonged in the middle of the radical spectrum said that 'we're all socialists', but that the socialists should take out of their programme any attacks on property! Ths betrays not just a cavalier attitude to vocabulary but an instinctive belief that the socialists were, despite their economic theories, part of the same republican tribe (Kayser, 1962: 208).

9. Kayser (1962: 209) gives for the 1893 parliament: 105 members for the *gauche radicale,* soon to become gauche progressiste and then *gauche démocratique;* 38 of them had double membership of the radical-socialist group, while 14 also belonged to one of the moderate groups. The radical-socialists had 73 members; in addition to the 38 *gauche radicale,* 9 were also in the socialist group. It is hard to imagine a more eloquent image of the ambiguities of radicalism, which aimed to be a seamless web running across the whole of republicanism. For the 1898 legislature the more moderate tendency divided into two, spawning also a *union progressiste.*

next election, said Léon Bourgeois (Mayeur, 1984: 169); and the 'Black International' would take over France. The masonic lodges became more involved in radicalism during this period, and the organisational effort of the family was stepped up, peaking in the creation of the Parti républicain radical et radical socialiste in 1901.

Within parliament, the pact beween ralliés and progressists, both social and economic conservatives, but resolved to suspend their differences over the régime, worked quietly. Outside the chamber, radicals and socialists campaigned for anti-clerical and social advances, while the more militant side of the catholic camp, such as *La Croix*, retaliated in kind. The political temperature was steadily hiked up. Elite consensus seemed increasingly out of step with mass opinion, and it could be wondered how long the delicate balance might last. Once again, it would be an extraneous event that proved the catalyst for a further, brutal mutation of the party system. This was the Dreyfus case and its aftermath.

The Dreyfus Case and the Bloc: Towards Bipolarity?

The Dreyfus case is usually celebrated as the triumph of liberal and humanitarian values over prejudice and discrimination (Birnbaum, 1993; 1994). The final vindication of Captain Dreyfus, after 12 years, from false charges of espionage, crowned a lengthy campaign, particularly by the left, which claimed the victory as its own. In the left's ideological hall of fame, Dreyfus ranks alongside the Revolution, the Commune and the Popular Front. Justice is said to have triumphed over *raison d'état*; reason over anti-semitism; the efforts of concerned citizens and politicians over dishonest parts of the state, particularly the army and the courts. More prosaically, from the point of view of this study, the Dreyfus period saw some highly significant changes to the party system.

The first point to note is the rapid rise in political polarisation from 1898. Once it was clear that Dreyfus' original conviction rested on forged evidence, the intellectual and political left, hitherto unconvinced, began to campaign publicly for revision of the trial. In reaction, the right and a number of republican moderates pressed for the original verdict to stand. For many who shared this perspective, it was not a matter of guilt or innocence, but of whether a revision would undermine state institutions (this is what they meant by 'l'autorité de la chose jugée'); states are not supposed to make mistakes. In some cases, old anti-republicans simply saw blocking attempts at revision as another stick with which to beat the republic, and, increasingly, themes of anti-semitism surfaced on the anti-Dreyfus side. This ideology had surfaced in the 1880s in the anti-capitalist writings of Drumont. Now it received another, more religious bias as media like *La Croix* built it into their campaign. The political temperature rose sharply, dividing families and communities, and increasingly, the issue tended to polarise views; left versus right, republican against authoritarian. Although much of the polemic was carried on by the intellectuals of either side, it is clear that in terms of political forces, the running on the right was not made by the old parliamentary conservatives, but by a new right, especially the Ligue des Patriotes and similar style bodies which arose during this period, such as la Ligue anti-sémite and the Action Française (Weber, 1962). Although such bodies had friends in the chamber (some of them ex-boulangists elected on nationalist tickets after 1889, like the writer Barrès), their preferred politics were those of the street. Their aggressive rallies and demonstrations, including beating up the president of the republic at a racecourse, culminated in a farcical attempt by Déroulède to turn a demonstration into a coup d'état in February 1899. In addition to the hard right was the Ligue de la Patrie Française, which drew in a number of extraparliamentary activists, but its core was conservative, nationalist republicans. It may have had up to 200,000 members, most of them bourgeois and petty-bourgeois; these were not revolutionaries, but rather people who wanted the régime to stay firm and resist subversion. As Mayeur said (1984: 178), the main contribution of this body was, in the mid-term, to help pull a part of moderate republican opinion towards the hard nationalist right, which was less concerned with democracy than with the assertion of nationhood. The real influence of the leagues, mainly a Parisian phenomenon, should doubtless not be exaggerated, but given the fact that the upper reaches of the army and some parts of the judicial system seemed seriously insubordinate (as shown by their blatant attempts to pervert justice), and given that the public utterances of the right seemed to come increasingly from its authoritarian quarters while the *ralliés* remained fairly silent, republican leaders understandably felt that the institutions were under some threat. Hence the decision to form, in the aftermath of the 1898 elections, the government of republican defence under the respected former opportunist Waldeck Rousseau, summoned from the senate to head a cabinet clearly determined to take the fight to what it saw as a conspiracy of clericals and authoritarians. Certainly, the creeping rapprochement between moderate catholics and their republican equivalents had been dynamited; the 'clerical question' and its eternal partner 'defence of the régime' had now been placed firmly back at the head of the political agenda. The union of the centres was dead, but precisely because of this, the more extreme parts of the party system were back in business.

Waldeck moved swiftly against the perceived threat. The upper reaches of the army and magistracy were swiftly purged, and the 1901 law on associations signalled the first move against religious orders like the Assumptionists, requring them to seek registration. This anticlerical campaign would be cleverly escalated by Waldeck's successors into a full blown struggle after the 1902 election, culminating in the separation of 1905. The republic was certainly preserved in this way from any hypothetical danger, but what is noteworthy is the party politics of republican defence.

It is generally considered that republican moderates made the best showing in the 1898 elections, which would suggest that the policy of ralliement was gaining popular approval. However, the electoral committees of *La Croix* had actually campaigned against some of Méline's majority, making at least one minister lose his seat (Mayeur, 1984: 180). This upset a number of progressists who drifted out of the majority, causing Méline to resign, although technically he could still govern. In other words, the hard right of the catholic camp had been strong enough to thwart the efforts of the *ralliés*; once again, the extremes had polarised politics. Had the AL been set up earlier, it may have been in a position to deliver more voters along moderate lines. Here is eloquent proof of how the absence of an effective party can be a major stumbling block to any democratic reconciliation.

With Méline gone, it still proved impossible to maintain a moderate government based on the tacit support of the right, as the failure of Dupuy proved (he was voted down for trying to shift the Dreyfus case to a court reputedly more hostile to revision). The feeling that the right wanted too much for its support inspired the republican defence movement: a number of progressists, including the rising stars Poincaré and Barthou, split off from their colleagues to sign a protest, together with leading radicals and even a socialist Millerand. Here in embryo was the new majority. At its core lay about half the republican moderates (from the Gauche démocratique and Union progressiste groups), of whom Waldeck was an outstanding example, and who would, after 1902, form the Alliance Démocratique. Also central to it was the bulk of the radicals (though typically several dozen of them, strongly nationalistic, would remain in opposition). Finally, the new concentration was enriched by the addition – rather more than symbolic – of the socialist. The emergency of the hour had generated a new governing formula, spread further to the left than before. At the same time, those progressists not prepared to see Dreyfus as a question fundamental to the régime were now pushed back into opposition. The formal expression of this would come with the formation of the Fédération Républicaine in 1903. A new and durable split in the old moderate/opportunist family had taken root.

This recasting of alliances was not easy. The Waldeck government ran from General Gallifet, instrumental in repressing the Commune (and politically speaking, an opportunist of the Gambetta era) to the socialist Millerand. The senate accepted it much more easily than the chamber. There, Waldeck would not have survived if a dozen deputies had changed sides. As it was, the old right, the nationalists and Méline's share of progressists were joined in opposition by about thirty radicals. Thirteen more of these abstained, as did twenty socialists and twenty-nine more progressists. Waldeck's suporters thus included a crucial number of progressists (led, it is said, by Aynard, one of the rare catholic republicans), most of the radicals and most socialists. The presence of the latter was vital, and policy reflected this. The cabinet tried, via trade and labour minister Millerand, to develop arbitration to settle labour disputes and to extend labour legislation. Thus, Mayeur's comment (1984: 184) that the composition of the majority shows that ideological cleavages had overcome those of class, needs some qualification: bourgeois republicanism had to compromise and give something tangible to the representa-

tives of the growing working class if they were to help out with the ideological struggle. At any rate, given the cabinet's longevity, it seemed as if the
basis for a new party alignment might be there.

This seemed even truer after the 1902 election, which saw radicalism gain
at the expense of the moderates, proving again that a higher ideological temperature helps extremes. Waldeck recognised this by his resignation.[10] The
new Combes government would further shift the majoritarian axis to the left
by polarising politics even more.

The Combes government was one of the most energetic of the entire republic in terms of policy output, even if most of it tended to be in one direction.
There are good accounts of how this highly sectarian team pushed through
its programme of harassment of religious orders, closing of catholic schools
and seizure of property and breaking of diplomatic relations with the Vatican, all moves which set up the final act of separation for implementation by
the next cabinet (Mayeur, 1966; McManners, 1972; Larkin, 1974; 1995). The
style of government was confrontational and partisan, calculated to rally a
certain type of support; in this it succeeded.

The parliamentary arithmetic favoured the radicals in the 1902 chamber.[11]
Combes, therefore, took no socialists into government, relying mainly on his
own radicals with the support of pro-Waldeck moderates. In partisan terms,
though, he innovated strongly by his relationship with the *délégation des
gauches*; this was quite simply a steering committee of deputies from each of
the main groups supporting the cabinet – socialists, radicals, radical socialists
and Union Démocratique (moderates or progressists), in which each group
was represented according to its strength. It discussed policy issues with government and helped keep majority discipline. Within it, Jaurès, leader of the
pro-government socialists, was felt to be particularly influential and regarded
as a semi-official government spokesman. Clearly, such a body went much
further than traditional republican politics was used to, in that it seemed a
real harbinger of party government, with the cabinet as potentially a mere
mouthpiece for the shadowy parliamentary groups; complaints were heard
about government by committee. Certainly, the left/right polarity was
sharply maintained by this device, logically enough in that radicalism always
benefited from such a situation.

Combes innovated outside parliament also, with his famous system of committees (Baal, 1977). These rather amorphous bodies, which ranged from electoral committees to voluntary societies to masonic lodges, were seen as the
government's particular friends within civil society. Baal's survey reveals a
huge range of organisations sending messages of support to the government
(though it is hard to disentangle genuine enthusiasm from back-covering or

10. With characteristic bluntness he remarked : 'ils sont trop!' and recommended Combes as
his successor (Mayeur, 1984: 186).

11. Mayeur (1984: 185) conflates a number of sources to give 48 socialists, over 200 radicals
and less than 100 pro-Waldeck moderates against 127 progressists, 35 ralliés (now ALP), 43
nationalists and 41 old right monarchists.

simple obsequiousness in the hope of favours). In return, the government was open about favouring republican candidates for any kind of public post; and it relied on information from so-called 'republican delegates', mainly self-appointed, to determine the republican credentials of applicants. In other words, a system of part-time spies was called into being to support networks of clientelism, going beyond the unsavoury practices of the Second Empire. Distasteful though it seems, the system had support. Baal suggests plausibly, anticipating the opposition formulated by Birnbaum (1979), that combism in the provinces was an alliance of *les petits* – small farmers, petty bourgeois and workers – who looked to this new government to enhance their interests against *les gros* (priests, notables, capitalists and *grands bourgeois* generally). The mixture of anti-clericalism and talk of social reform – 'la République démocratique et sociale' – worked; the lower ranks saw sorting out the clericals as a prelude to wider social reform. This also helps account for socialist support. Certainly, Jaurès, who led the pro-government socialists, had an incremental 'ratchet' view of socialism, whereby any gain, cultural or material, could be banked, so to speak, as an unshiftable building block for the socialist future. Before he left office, Combes was canny enough to put bills on income tax and workers' pensions on to the agenda, reinforcing his social image. Successor governments would drag their feet, of course, but the radical/socialist alliance had shown its potential. Although Combes resigned over the files scandal (confidential reports, filed by private individuals who were often freemasons, were kept on officers' private lives, especially their religion or lack of it, with a view to determining their suitability for promotion) while still having a majority, the underlying cause of his departure was losing the support of a number of moderate radicals and mainstream republicans, worried that he was giving too much to the socialists. Ideological partnerships had some mileage in them, but class interests reasserted themselves in the end.

The left block would effectively run France till the 1910 elections. The remainder of the anti-clerical legislation was enforced with relative calm, thanks to the shrewd bargaining of the minister in charge, Briand, a new socialist from the independent end of that family (see below), who brokered agreement between church and government over the control of ecclesiastical property, the major problem of the new post-Concordat situation. Radicalism, particularly under the leadership of Clemenceau, would mostly control government in a period dominated by labour and agricultural disputes (sharply repressed by Clemenceau) and mounting international tension. Although one or two individuals (Briand, Viviani) began to figure regularly in governments, and although the independent socialists began to organise themselves as a party, the Republican Socialists (RS) from 1911 (Billard, 1993), the radical/socialist cartel (this was the name coming into usage) did not survive as a permanent arrangement beyond the republican defence period. In 1905, the socialist miniparties had joined into the Section Française de l'Internationale Ouvrière (SFIO) under the pressure of the Socialist International. One of the conditions of the merger was the banning of 'ministerialism' (sitting in governments led by bourgeois parties). Jaurès, effectively the leader of the new party, accepted this provision, although it ran contrary to the basic logic of his thinking. In reality, he counted on time and persuasion to make the SFIO a system party influencing policy and not a voice denouncing capitalism from the sidelines.[12]

This did not affect the stability of the partisan system. The test imposed on it by the Dreyfus case had shown that it could secrete all-left support when needed (for 'defence of the republic' and active anti-clerical legislation), but once the immediate problem was solved, the system was subtle enough to allow a return to the normal interplay of class interests, largely independent of the dominant ideological cleavage. The Clemenceau years, thus, saw limits set to the ambitions of the working class (repression of strikes, refusal of unions for state employees), but by 1914 a number of social laws (pensions, health and safety) had been voted in, as had, after a long parliamentary struggle, income tax (Elwitt, 1986; Stone, 1986). Democratic parliamentarism seemed to have found its rhythm, within which the demands of French society were being addressed, and the key regulator of this parliamentarism was the party system. The preceding pages have necessarily been of a descriptive character, as we gave a concise overview of the main movements of the system during the period under consideration. We propose now an analysis of the period that will identify the underlying recurrent patterns of the party system.

An Emergent Party Logic

From 1877 to 1914, a clear pattern emerged within the partisan system. It settled early into what we term tripolar instability, with a moderate or opportunist group of parties flanked by radicalism and a right that still did not fully accept the republic. During this period, the advent of a viable socialist party would further increase the potential for instability.

The opportunist groups were the natural axes of any majority, given their numerical strength, which reflected their embodiment of the minimalist, conservative republic that found the widest endorsement within French society, ut they could not govern comfortably alone. The right agreed with them on major economic and social questions, but was ideologically and politically unacceptable (in theory). Radicalism was a brother in the republican family, but a greedy one, insistent in its demands. Analysis of this *rapport de forces* suggests that the initiative always lay with radicalism, provided it were bold enough to use its muscle in order to force moderate republicans further along the path towards its goals. This it did ruthlessly, allying with the right to bring down opportunists when necessary and being generally ready to play

---

12. For discussion of the nature of SFIO see Portelli (1980), Kergoat (1983) and Bergounioux and Grunberg (1992). One of the best analyses of its action in parliament remains Fiechter (1965).

highly dangerous games in order to have its way. It played for high stakes but it won: increasingly the political agenda of France was set by radicalism.[13]

Even the crises to which the régime was subject were grist to the radical mill. Boulanger's rise put a stop to the creeping rapprochement between opportunism and the sensible elements of the right, which had been evolving rapidly towards a pragmatic acceptance of the republic. When the *ralliement* attempted the same strategy on a more serious scale with church backing, radicalism faced a real challenge to its leverage over the party system . In this sense, Dreyfus was a godsend, whatever short-term threats it might have posed. It enabled radicalism to re-polarise opinion along the classic left-right axis. It was able to do this all the more readily because the moderate catholic right was a late starter in party politics and not yet well enough established to keep a tight grip on catholic voters. Far too many of these were drawn towards the confrontational style of politics exemplified by *La Croix*, making the coming together of catholic and secular moderates even more difficult and so helping the radical cause. The poorly organised type of nationalist formations which would henceforth figure on the right provided a further source of instability, maintaining polarisation.

The governing formula which emerged out of the 'republican defence' cabinets was radical dominated; radicalism had succeeded in splitting moderate republicanism into two. One half it could work with (those parts of the progressist family like the *gauche radicale, gauche républicaine or gauche démocratique*), the other half (FR) was pushed into marginality with the right, now less acceptable than ever as a coalition partner and more fissiparous. Thus, radicalism remained the dominant force and was even preparing the gradual inclusion of the socialists as eventual partners. Overall, the system looked as unstable as ever, but within that instability, a core party, radicalism, remained in firm control. Its triumph showed the importance of organisation, as well as the ability to understand the partisan system and a willingness to seize the initiative from opponents who did not possess these attributes in sufficient quantity.

On these bases radicalism succeeded in carrying out most of its programme. As the party had judged, the majority of French society could live with the changes made by radicals (especially as some of the more ambitious parts of the programme had quietly disappeared). Once radicalism had become an establishment party, however, it remained to be seen whether the prevailing party-system logic analysed here could last indefinitely.

13. Ware (1996: 204) believes that only after 1958 was such voluntaristic agenda-setting possible, but this is to underestimate the dynamics of the pre-1914 system with its 'weak' parties.

5

FROM COMFORT TO CRISIS?
The Party System Between the Wars

❦

Any marginal or aspiring player is exposed to the attractions of a competitive
arena simply by occupying a place in it

Offerlé, Les Partis politiques[1]

The interwar period forms a distinct epoch in the life of the French party system. In barely twenty years, the system went from a position of apparently
comfortable stability to a crisis that saw the end of the régime.

The end of hostilities in 1918 saw the republic more firmly established
than ever before, having emerged on the winners' side after four years of
conflict, the outcome of which was unclear until well into 1918. During the
war, the party system had devised a new relationship with government
(Bock, 1998). Officially, until 1917 (when the SFIO opted out) all parties had
subscribed to what Poincaré termed *union sacrée*, that is, a multiparty support for the government with a view to maximising the French war effort.
The early war cabinets reflected this mood of consensus, including members
of the SFIO and even a leader of the catholic (still notionally anti-republican)
right in Denys Cochin, alongside men from the usual parties of government.
Such a presence would have been clearly unacceptable (on both sides of the
divide) in peacetime. While deputies and senators continued to scrutinise
the work of the executive, much of this took place behind closed doors in
committee (Bock, 1998: 372ff.). Significantly, none of the governments who
resigned before the spring of 1917 did so as a result of a parliamentary vote.
It took the failed French offensive of that year, and army mutinies, to bring
the deputies to emergency action; they duly dismissed the Painlevé government in favour of a Clemenceau cabinet. However, this was more the choice
of a particular war leader than a party-based move, and membership of the
Clemenceau government was based more on personal loyalty to *le tigre* than
on partisan grounds.

---

1. 'Tout joueur marginal ou prétendant, s'il a la possibilité de modifier les règles du champ
(de concurrence) n'en subit moins l'attraction par le seul fait d'y prendre position'.

These developments meant that when the first peacetime elections took place in December 1919, the political context was somewhat changed. Although old party patterns of behaviour were already reasserting themselves (cf. the ruthless exclusion of Clemenceau from the presidency of the republic, once he had served his purpose of helping France win the war and imposing the Versailles treaties), the party leaders nevertheless sought to profit from the perceived mood of wartime consensus and unity. With the exception of the SFIO and a part of the radical party (57 of the 86 deputies elected), the republican parties concocted joint lists under the loose heading of the Bloc National (BN). These alliances were facilitated by a change in the electoral system, which went back to departmental PR with the possibility for voters to adjust lists and even for there to be two ballots. Campbell (1966: 91) sees this as a hybrid of PR and the majority principle, with the latter effectively prevailing. Lachapelle (1920) had no doubt that the real aim of the new system was to reward mainstream parties capable of making a deal at departmental level so as to clean up all the seats at the expense of formations perceived as more extreme. Although the national formula concealed huge ambiguities in the nature and extent of departmental alliances between parties (Roussellier, 1992), the new legislature had, notionally, a large majoritarian bloc and a smallish left opposition (Table 5.1).

Before treating the development of the party system during this period, it is necessary to underline the changing context of that system. Whereas the period 1870–1914 was characterised by high socio-economic stability and, until late in the day, a non-threatening international environment, the 1920s and 1930s were more volatile. In social terms, while the peasantry still remained numerous and mainly inefficient, these years saw the beginnings of a rural exodus, determined more by the attraction of improved opportunities to be found in towns than by the pressures of economic need.[2] The working class was also changing, with the emergence of advanced sectors (electrical and engineering industries, petrochemicals, automobiles) employing workers concentrated in large units of production and often performing routinised tasks on the assembly line. These are the classic conditions for development of a distinct proletarian identity, though this advanced segment of the class coexisted alongside older strata of skilled workers employed in smaller workshops. The middle groups also grew in number, with public employees increasing by twenty percent during the period (Dubief, 1976: 36). Overall, in socio-economic terms, the picture is one of the largely premodern structures on which the republic was built undergoing slow but steady change; certainly these structures seemed to lag behind those of comparable countries.

Doubtless, the political system would have coped better with this in a more stable international environment, but the peace settlements of 1919–20 brought discontent both to the losers, saddled, as they saw it, with unfair reparations and a loss of national sovereignty, and to the winners, frustrated in their receipt of the fruits of victory. The period would be dominated by the

---

2. From 1919 to 1931 some 80,000 left the land annually (Bernard, 1975: 198).

question of how to handle Germany. The conciliatory approach favoured by Briand and radicalism (collective security agreements and disarmament under the auspices of the League of Nations) would alternate with more muscular attempts by the right to extract reparations (Poincaré's occupation of the Ruhr). As Germany recovered and the Nazis took power and rearmed, the debate between appeasers and proponents of a firm line (rearmers) became urgent. The equation was complicated by the rise of a powerful Italy under fascist leadership. Here too, conciliators clashed with opponents of dictatorship. Finally, the Bolshevik revolution of 1917 and the survival of the USSR through the civil war (where France and Britain had helped the counter-revolution) also cast a long shadow over French politics. The emergence of a viable and combative communist party was one effect of 1917, but so were the hesitations of French diplomacy, never sure about what rôle the USSR might play on the new European scene. Contained at first as a subversive enemy, it became a potential ally once fascism took hold. These basic facts are recalled here because of their major impact on the party system. Before 1914, foreign policy questions had mainly seemed reserved for specialists; now, however, these questions impacted directly upon domestic political life.[3]

Such pressure became particularly acute after 1930, when external considerations meshed with the growing effects of the interwar economic depression. As unemployment increased and prices and revenues fell with the general decline of economic activity, social unrest grew.[4] Peasants and the urban petty-bourgeois on fixed incomes perceived a worsening of their economic position, whatever the statistics said. Workers faced declining income and the prospect of unemployment. So did many of the public sector middle classes, as, until 1936, the government answer to depression was simply to pursue a deflationary policy involving job cuts and reductions in pay. Growing international tension also fuelled social unrest, as some groups became tempted by authoritarian formulae which were believed to be working in neighbouring countries, and others felt increasingly that war against such régimes was unavoidable. At the same time, the communists, a major force within France, were perceived as the willing ally of the USSR, a self-proclaimed revolutionary power. This inspired considerable fear among the bourgeois (and many socialists), in another example of how tensions that are, strictly speaking, external to the political system, can quickly be transferred inside it.

3. This is not to say that the prewar multipolar international system of similar sized powers engaged in fairly stable defensive alliances had been devoid of tension, especially when imperial rivalries erupted on the periphery. However, there is a qualitative difference between this type of stress, which could be brokered within the international system and the permanent fractures of the interwar period, expressed in the rise of fascism. This type of politics, fundamentally unstable, was not interested in making deals but in conquest by one means or another.

4. There is still dispute as to the extent of both unemployment and the fall in purchasing power. Following Lhomme, Dubief estimates (1976: 32) that by 1935 some 2 million out of a workforce of 12.5 million were out of work, and that purchasing power had gone down by 15% over the previous five years. Whatever the accuracy of such figures, the point is that perceptions of deprivation were widespread and found political expression in numerous ways.

Table 5.1 Party Strengths in Interwar Legislatures

	PCF	SFIO	RSoc	Rads	GRad/GRepDem	RepG/ADS	ARS/	ERD/FR	PDP	Indep	Nongroup
1919–24	15	68	26	86	93	61	46	183		-	29 21
1924–28	26	104	43	139	42+43 (+14 GIndep)a	38	29	104		14	28
1928–32	12	100	18+13	125	53+18b (+15 GIndep)	64		102		19	38
1932–36 (+9 Soc-Comm)b	10	131	28	160	48 (+35 CentreRep)c (+23+15 GIndep)	29		41 (+18 Pernot)d		16	14+6 autonomists (+7 IAESP)e
1936–40 (+26 Rainbow Left)f	72	148	29	108	39	44		49 (+33 Pernot)		13	12+16 autonomists

For full names of parties, see List of Abbreviations

a: Split from GRepDem and RepG; these 18 indépendants de gauche were new deputies
b: Ex-communists arguing for merger of PCF and SFIO (Parti unitaire prolétarien of Petrus Faure)
c: Short-lived attempt by Tardieu to draw moderates into one big centre group
d: Social-catholic split from FR (official group title was Groupe républicain et social)
e: Right-wing notables seeking a more social and agrarian gloss
f: Ad hoc grouping which broke up in 1937. Included pupistes (cf. note b), Parti Camille Pelletan (dissident radicals),some indépendants de gauche, Jeune République.

Source: Bomier-Landowski (1951); Avril et al. (1988)

In short, the tensions within French society, which had been managed with some success before 1914, became that much harder to regulate. Clearly, the party system would face greater challenges.

New Protagonists and Old Survivors

The interwar decade saw some modifications to the make-up of the party system. On the left, a significant new player emerged in December 1920. This was the communist party, PCF, born of a majoritarian split from the SFIO and eager to emulate the successful Bolshevik party and its revolution in Russia. It was mainly in Southern Europe that viable communist parties escaped, so to speak, from the shell of social-democracy, and in many ways the French case has more similarity to Mediterranean countries than to Northern Europe. There is a complex debate about the reasons for the PCF's successful take off, but paramount among them was the failure of the ruling élites in France (mainstream republicanism, that is) to address the urgent social demands arising from a working class that had suffered heavily in the war and was to be given little in return (Gallie, 1983). Relatively strong even at the start in terms of voters and office holders, the PCF would, by the mid-1930s, become an unavoidable factor of the party system, its revolutionary character notwithstanding. It also spawned in its early days a number of dissident groups such as the pupistes which would achieve modest representation in the chamber.

Further to the right (though its activists clung desperately to the notion of 'the centre' as their home on the political map), by 1924 a small christian-democrat party, the Parti Démocrate Populaire (PDP), had achieved a limited but consistent presence within the system (Delbreil, 1990). Picking up from the ALP in its concern to anchor catholics firmly to democratic institutions, this moderate formation usually drew between two and three percent of the vote and elected some fifteen deputies; its confessional character was clear if only from the geography of its vote (the traditional catholic regions in the West, North, North East and beneath the Massif Central, plus the protestant vote in Alsace). Appealing only to a part of the catholic vote (many voted for the moderate or hard-line right, and some of the more socially conscious for the Jeune République, a smaller more militant grouping), the PDP nevertheless retained a distinct identity and played a recognisable rôle.

Outside the framework of the parliamentary right, the phenomenon of the leagues would grow in importance. An early flowering of various leagues and pressure groups in the mid-1920s already showed some dissatisfaction with established political forces.[5] However, as the depression bit and fascism progressed abroad, various fascist imitations and epigones would arise to

5. On the early leagues see Plumyène and Lasierra (1963), Machefer (1974), Soucy (1986). Alongside the leagues should also be mentioned mass movements like the Fédération Nationale Catholique which, under General de Castelnau, campaigned for catholic civil rights (MacMillan, 1996).

complicate the picture further. The effect of such movements on the party system needs careful evaluation.

These three innovations stand alongside strong elements of continuity. On the left, the SFIO grew steadily, becoming a key party in the system – a destiny which it neither sought nor probably understood fully. Radicalism, at its apogee in 1914, clearly remained essential to the running of the system, and on the moderate right, the groups of bourgeois republicans in the chamber deriving loosely from the ARD (*gauche radicale, gauche démocratique, républicains de gauche*, etc.) continued to be the main material from which governments were formed, though the coherence of such groups became increasingly ragged. These groups of the centre and centre-right (this was the vocabulary which gradually became current), along with the socialists and radicals, provided the system with its fundamental dynamic. The newcomers would have to challenge them for influence. Such are the general party parameters of the period.

From *Bloc National* to *Cartel des Gauches*

Despite received images of the 1919 'sky-blue'chamber (so called because of the high number of ex-officers within it) as a replication of the 1871 *chambre introuvable*, it is clear that there was no possibility of sustained domination by a coherent right-oriented coalition. Even the electoral alliance of the BN was, to some extent, still-born (Roussellier, 1997: 24–48). Apart from the principled refusal of the SFIO, the radicals refused to sign up nationally, leaving local federations to make their own deals. Some of the right also preferred to stand independently. The Mascuraud committee, led by the senator of that name, which was the recognised parliamentary lobby for businessmen looking to influence radicalism and its friends, refused to endorse the BN. It had no national leader, as Clemenceau, the outgoing premier, continued the convention that outgoing leaders do not appear as partisan figures. In any case, the deputies had shown by their recent votes that his days as any kind of leader were strictly numbered. It would be hard to claim that the BN had much by way of a programme, other than determination to secure the fruits of victory (extract full reparations from Germany) and to fight vigorously against revolution; its propaganda made much of the alleged effects of bolshevism on the extensive social agitation within France. Certainly, candidates were long on the rhetoric of national unity and the need to preserve it during peacetime.

Under the rhetoric of politicians using 'feelgood' propaganda to secure re-election, partisan divisions remained as tenacious as ever. Roussellier has shown (1992) that there was not one straight left/right battle in each department, but a multiplicity of cases according to local circumstances. Given the subtleties of the new electoral system, which allowed voters to write in candidates' names on to existing lists and which awarded alliances winning over fifty percent with all the seats in that department, it could hardly be otherwise. Thus, some eight types of list denoting eight different sorts of alliance can be identi-

Table 5.2 Party Composition of Governments in Interwar Years
(Junior ministers in brackets)

	Nonparty	ERD/ FR	PDP	ARS^a	RepG.	GDem	GRep. GRad	UnRep (Senate)	Radsoc.	Rep Soc	Ind Gch	SFIO
Clemenceau II 17.11.1917– 18.1.20;14(+10)	1(+2)				1(+2)	3(+1)	2(+2)	1	5*(+3)	1		
Millerand 20.1.20–23.9.20 15(+10)	4*(+1)	1(+1)		1(+1)	2(+1)	1	3(+4)	1	1(+1)	1(+1)		
Leygues 25.9.20–12.1.21; 15(+10)	3(+1)	1(+1)		1(+1)	3*(+1)	1	3(+4)	1	1(+1)	1(+1)		
Briand VII 11.1.21–12.1.22; 16(+8)	1	4(+1)			2(+1)	2	4(+3)		2(+1)	1*(+2)		
Poincaré II 15.1.22–26.3.24; 13(+6)		3		1	1(+1)	1(+1)	4(+1)	2*	1(+1)	(+2)		
Poincaré III 29.3.24–1.6.24; 12(+1)		1(+1)		3	2	1	3	1*	1			
Francois Marsal 9–13.6.24; 13		4		2	1	3	3	3*				

Table 5.2 (Continued) Party Composition of Governments in Interwar Years (Junior ministers in brackets)

	Nonparty	ERD/ FR	PDP	ARS [a]	RepG.	GDem	GRep. GRad	UnRep (Senate)	Radsoc.	Rep Soc	Ind Gch	SFIO
Herriot I 15.4.24–10.4.25; 15(+3)	1				1		4		8*(+2)	1(+1))		
Painlevé II 17.4.–27.10.25; 12(+6)	2						4		3(+4)	3*(+2)		
Painlevé III 29.10–22.11.25; 15(+6)					1		4		7(+3)	3*(+3)		
Briand VIII 28.11.25–6.3.26; 14(+7)	1				2		4(+3)		3(+2)	4*(+2)		
Briand IX 9.3–15.6.26; 13(+8)	1				2(+1)		4(+4)		4(+1)	2*(+2)		
Briand X 24.6.26–17.7.27; 12(+9)	2				2(+3)	1	3(+2)		3(+2)	1*(+2)		
Herriot II 20.7–21.7.26; 13(+8)	1					2	3(+1)		6*(+5)	1(+2)		

Table 5.2 (Continued) Party Composition of Governments in Interwar Years (Junior ministers in brackets)

	Nonparty	ERD/ FR	PDP	ARS [a]	RepG.	GDem	GRep. GRad	UnRep (Senate)	Radsoc.	Rep Soc	Ind Gch	SFIO
Poincaré IV 23.7.26–6.11.28; 13	1	1		1	1		3	2*	2	2		
Poincaré V 11.11.28–27.7.29; 15(+4)	1	(+1)		(+1)	2	2	1(+1)	4*		5	(+1)	
Briand XI 29.7–22.10.29; 14(+4)		(+1)		(+1)	3	1	2(+1)	3		5*	(+1)	
Tardieu I 2.11.29–17.2.30; 16(+12)		1(+2)	(+1)	1(+1)	5*(+2)	3	4(+3)	1	1		(+3)	
Chautemps I 21–5.2.30; 19(+9)	1					7(+1)	2(+2)	1	7*(+5)	1(+1)	1	
Tardieu II 2.3–4.12.30; 17(+17)	2(+2)	1(+2)	1	2(+2)	4*(+4)	2(+1)	3(+4)		1(+1)	1	(+1)	
Steeg 13.1.2.30–22.1.31; 18(+13)	1	(+1)		3(+3)		1*(+1)	3(+3)	3	5(+3)	2	(+2)	

Table 5.2 (Continued) Party Composition of Governments in Interwar Years (Junior ministers in brackets)

	Nonparty	ERD/FR	PDP	ARS[a]	RepG.	GDem	GRep. GRad	UnRep (Senate)	Radsoc.	Rep Soc	Ind Gch	SFIO
Laval I and II 27.1.31–12.1.32; 18(+12)	1*(+2)	2(+1)	1	2(+2)	4(+2)	2	4(+4)			1(+1)	1	
Laval III 14.1–16.2.32; 18(+10)	1*(+2)	2	1	1(+2)	3(+2)	2	5(+4)	1		1	1	
Tardieu III 20.2–10.5.32; 13(+8)	1(+1)	1(+1)	1	1(+1)	4*(+2)	1	2(+3)	2				
Herriot III 3.6–14.12.32; 18(+11)	1				1	4(+1)	1(+2)		9*(+7)	2	(+1)	
Paul-Boncour 18.12.32–28.1.33; 17(+12)	1*				1	2(+1)	2(+1)	1	8(+7)	2(+1)	(+2)	
Daladier I 31.1–24.10.33; 19(+4)	3					2(+1)	2		9*(+3)	1	2	
Chautemps II 26.11.33–27.1.34; 19(+7)	1					2(+1)	1(+2)	1	11*(+3)	1(+1)	2	

Table 5.2 (Continued) Party Composition of Governments in Interwar Years
(Junior ministers in brackets)

	Nonparty	ERD/FR	PDP	ARS [a]	RepG.	GDem	GRep. GRad	UnRep (Senate)	Radsoc.	Rep Soc	Ind Gch	SFIO
Daladier II 30.1–7.2.34 17(+9)	1				2(+1)	3	1(+1)		8*(+5)	1(+1)	1(+1)	
Doumergue II 9.2–8.11.34; 20	5	1			3	2*	2	1	5	1		
Flandin 8.11.34–31.5.35; 20(+1)	4	2			3*(+1)	3	2		5		1	
Bouisson 1–4.6.35; 20	6*	2			2	2	1		5	1	1	
Laval IV 7.6.35–22.1.36 20(+1)	3*	1(+1)			4	2	2	1	5	1	1	
Sarraut II 24.1–4.6.36; 19(+4)	5			1	4	3		1	3*(+3)	1(+1)	1	
Blum I 4.6.36–22.6.37; 21(+13)	(+3)								8(+5)	1(+1)		12*(+4)
Chautemps III 22.6.37–18.1.38; 21(+14)									11*(+6)	1(+1)	(+1)	9(+6)

Table 5.2 (Continued) Party Composition of Governments in Interwar Years (Junior ministers in brackets)

	Nonparty	ERD/ FR	PDP	ARS [a]	RepG.	GDem	GRep. GRad	UnRep (Senate)	Radsoc.	Rep Soc	Ind Gch	SFIO
Chautemps IV 18.1–14.3.38;	20(+13)	(+1)							18*(+8)	2(+3)	(+1)	
Blum II 14.3–10.4.38;	23(+12)	(+1)							8(+7)	2(+1)		12*(+3)
Daladier III 10.4.38–21.3.40;	3(+2)b 1c	1(+1)	1						12*(+1)	3		
Reynaud 21.3–15.6.40;	2(+5)b	(+2)		4*(+1)		(+1)		3(+1)	7(+2)	3		3(+2)

a: basically, Paul Reynaud's followers, who tended to change their name in different legislatures
b: includes G. Mandel (independent right-winger) and followers
c: G. Pernot (leader of split from FR)

Source: Bonnefous (1956–67); *Journal Officiel*

fied. The simplest cases are those of straight SFIO, radical or hard right lists which stood against the BN. However, BN lists per se included 'grand alliances' (from radicals to right); alliances of centre and moderates; left and centre left; right and centre right; and finally very broad right wing lists which used the BN label. Each one of these would elect at least several dozen deputies.

Inevitably, then, the new chamber reflected the true fragmentation of French opinion as parliamentary-party logic took over from electoral deals. Far from being a 'broken mirror', the parliamentary groups were (Roussellier, 1997: 69) 'the reflection of an ancient electoral and cultural landscape', showing 'the diversity of voting temperaments'. Deputies elected on a BN ticket went to several different groups, thus the 'centrists' split among the RepG, RS, GRep or GRad and ARS. Equally, no group drew its membership exclusively from those elected as BN members. Even the rightish Entente Républicaine et Démocratique (ERD), of which the FR was the core, only had two-thirds of its men elected in this way, the others having fought against moderate republican lists. The radicals grouped their BN and non-BN members happily; the new leader Herriot made sure that they stayed as a separate identifiable entity, refusing to join up with moderate groups like the GRep or RepG. That said, a number of deputies elected using the radical label still ended up in the GRep rather than the radical group!

There was never a chance of a straight right majority facing a united left opposition, in a strict bipolarisation based on discipline and unity, actively desired by men like Tardieu on the right and Blum on the left. The majority would have to be constructed via argument in the chamber (and, less visibly, by deals cut elsewhere). In Roussellier's terms, factions would have to be transformed into partners by the government building a 'rhetorical diagonal' towards them. Three broad majority combinations were possible (Roussellier, 1997: 276): a continuation of the *union sacrée* going from the right (ERD) to the radicals; a republican concentration (omitting the ERD, but including the mainstream republican groups and the radicals); or a more rightward combination, starting from the ERD and stopping somewhere short of the radicals. None of these combinations was guaranteed stability or longevity at the outset; majorities would have to be worked at.

The composition of governments during this legislature suggests that the *union sacrée* formula comes nearest to describing the partisan reality. At any rate, all governments strove to be as inclusive as possible, taking in representatives from every major group from radicals to ERD. The best share of representation went to the groups in the republican centre like the RepG or GRep.[6] This would suggest a compromise approach to policy making instead of an

6. These central groups provided 51 out of 74 ministers during the period, 26 from the GR alone (Roussellier, 1992: 176). Yet these groups only covered one-third of the chamber. The ERD, biggest group with 183 out of 610, or nearly one-third of the chamber, only received one-sixth of the ministries. This shows that there were limits to the integration of the right into the majority; electoral results notwithstanding, mainstream republicanism still decided who were acceptable partners on its terms alone.

attempt to push through a rightish BN agenda. For Roussellier this is clearly the case; he sees governments making a trade-off between the different poles of their support. Thus, on religious affairs, favours were done to groups like ERD and ARS, with a high percentage of catholic deputies (Becker and Berstein, 1990: 200): the separation law was not enforced in the newly recovered departments of Alsace-Lorraine, a blind eye was turned to the return of teaching orders of monks and nuns and diplomatic relations were opened with the Vatican (in return for papal acceptance of the diocesan associations set up to run church property after the separation). This was not to the taste of radicalism, clearly, but this current was rewarded to some extent by the gradual trimming of successive governments over German reparations. During the legislature, French policy moved from absolute insistence that le Boche paiera, as the popular tag had it, to effective recognition that the sums required would never be forthcoming, hence the tendency to a more conciliatory approach under the auspices of Briand. This accorded well with radical preferences for disarmament and collective security rather than assertive foreign policy, but to the hawkish elements of the ERD, who thought in terms of occupying part of Germany or even splitting off the Rhineland into a separate state, it was a bitter pill to swallow. By such balancing acts, governments held majorities together; although, as Roussellier reminds us, support (or opposition) ran through the parties, especially those of the centre, rather than strictly between them.[7]

Thus, republican parliamentarism produced policy in certain areas, but arguably at the cost of neglecting others. Roussellier cites a raft of socio-economic issues, which were effectively sidelined by the overriding concentration on foreign affairs. These include modernisation of the state to cope with the reconstruction of devastated regions, the need to revise the tax system and the failure to devise a sensible system of running the railways. All these issues were linked to the failure to recognise that the post-1918 economic context was a new one, requiring new types of policy. It seemed as if the republican model could deliver on issues like constitutional stability, school reform or religious affairs, but that the new socio-economic questions forcing themselves on to the agenda were harder to handle. The failure of government to tackle the economic problems stemming from wartime (high domestic and foreign debt, rising inflation and a falling currency) until late in the day was typical. Faced with a run on the franc, the Poincaré government reacted with a knee-jerk policy of budget cuts, a twenty percent income tax rise and the securing of an American loan linked to acceptance of the Dawes plan (a clear downward revision of the amount of reparations which could be expected). The 1924 elections were, therefore, fought in the context of an austerity package linked to a foreign policy humiliation. Small wonder that the

---

7. A proof of the way in which consensus could prevail was the vote to open diplomatic relations with the Vatican by 390 to 179, with two-thirds of the *laïc* Gauche républicaine in favour (Roussellier, 1992: 299). The secularists talked up the diplomatic advantages and the need to reward catholics for their war efforts. Clearly there was no going back on the *laïc* laws; but the Vatican compromise showed that parties could meet half way if it suited them.

unanimist rhetoric of 1919 fell on deaf ears as voters moved away from the BN and gave a chance to the cartel.

The cartel no more represented a united left than the BN had stood for a united right. Herriot and the SFIO concluded a minimal alliance, with joint lists on which some RS and other republicans (GRep/GRad) also figured. As the BN groups were less united than in 1919, this formula proved successful, with 266 seats out of 568 (Lachapelle, 1924; Campbell, 1966: 97). There was no formal programme, but shared *laïc* values were stressed, as was faith in the League of Nations, defence of social legislation (such as it was) and opposition to Poincaré's austerity package (Becker and Berstein, 1990: 241). The SFIO had had great difficulty in persuading its members to accept the cartel; leaders referred to it as a 'one-minute alliance' (the time voters spent in the polling booth). The SFIO refused to join any government, offering only conditional support in the chamber. Herriot's cabinet was, therefore, mainly radical, with some members of centre-left groups. A mere glance at the parliamentary arithmetic showed that the cartel did not have a clear majority. Its ignominious failure in government has been well enough analysed to require only the briefest recall here (Jeanneney, 1977). While the cartel undoubtedly shifted foreign policy towards a more conciliatory line (incarnated by Briand) for several years, its attempts to revive anti-clericalism were a fiasco (Thibaudet, 1927), provoking massive opposition from catholics, who were at long last mobilised in mass civil organisations such as the FNC, which, as Kalyvas showed (1996: 114–66), had emerged a generation earlier in other parts of Europe. In France it was a case of better late than never, yet it was enough to see off the cartel's attempts to replay 1905. However, during a two-year agony, Herriot and his successors failed above all on financial matters. The vulnerability of the treasury to short-term loans, plus the readiness of the Bank of France (still a private institution) to reveal that it was breaching currency and loan limits in order to tide the government over, triggered a crisis of confidence among small holders of government stock (big capital had never trusted the cartel to begin with). The result was growing public debt and the collapse of the franc. The SFIO proposed bold measures such as a tax on capital and the forced conversion of short-term loans into long-term ones, both measures terrifying to large and small capital holders alike. The financial crisis persisted as battles raged within the cartel. It became clear that confidence would only return if the cartel stepped aside. This meant a republican concentration, but that was tantamount to denying the electoral results of 1924. By 1926, the radicals were ready to abandon the cartel, and Poincaré was called back to break the crisis with another austerity package. To help him, the radicals entered his government in a *union nationale* (Herriot sold this deal to his party with some difficulty). Soon, Poincaré had the budget in surplus with a mix of budget cuts and new taxes, aimed mainly to spare big capital and attract it back into France. In a shrewd move he set up a special fund to service the national debt and had it inscribed into the constitution. Psychological measures such as this reinforced the message that the sensible centre-right was back in charge, and after the 1928 election, Poincaré would be strong enough to devalue the franc to twenty percent of its prewar value, a measure rendered inevitable by international economic reality, but which would have been inadmissible under a left government. This much is known; what is of interest here are the implications for the parties and the party system.

The most obvious lesson of the cartel is the ease with which a left-wing majority was levered out of office thanks to the pressure of capitalist interests. If nothing else, the episode fed the left's fund of mythic resentment against the right. To the traditional images of the reactionary and the clerical could now be added the feeling that 'we were robbed', by 'the wall of money' or the malign influence of the 'two hundred families'. Rhetoric and emotion apart, however, the cartel's failure asked some hard questions of the left, starting with the very definition thereof. For several years after 1901, the bloc des gauches had cohered on the basis of republican defence and some (not very far reaching) gestures towards social reform (Stone, 1986). By the 1920s the world had changed; the republic was stronger than it had ever been, and it was not possible to mobilise ingrained reflexes of anti-clericalism much beyond polling day. Now the left had to face economic problems that went to the heart of the social system. To solve the financial crisis, decisions had to be taken which were bound to penalise some categories – big capital if the SFIO were listened to, but smaller rentiers and large swathes of the middle classes would suffer even with the conventional types of recipe associated with Poincaré. Radicalism hesitated uneasily between the two alternatives, knowing that its petty-bourgeois clientèle feared collectivism, but afraid to ally openly with the right, even if it felt reluctantly that sound money policies were probably inevitable. In short, the crisis revealed the growing incompatibility between the two families of the left. The SFIO stood for social transformation, not management of capitalism; radicalism had a large and threatened middle-class to defend, which was more frightened of a partnership with socialism than it was of the economic policy of the centre-right. In the absence of a serious republican/anti-clerical stake or some other external threat, it would henceforth be hard to keep the two parties allied firmly.

This division within the left becomes clearer when one realises that the notional cartel majority did not derive from radicals and SFIO alone but needed the votes of the GRad (Siegfried, 1930: 137). These centre-left republicans, descended from the opportunists, were liberal conservatives in economic terms, and it is they who eventually voted down the cartel and opened the way for Poincaré. The GRad were only being historically consistent. Before 1914, their rôle in the left bloc was to shore up the republic with anti-clerical measures, while putting the brakes on social reform (Wileman, 1994).

The political impact of the harsh facts of economic life showed that radicalism could no longer set an agenda within the party system. For a good decade before 1914 it had used 'republican defence' as an issue to assume hegemony within the party system. After 1919, with the republic strong and an ambience of national unity, there was a danger that it might be seen as having done its job and so lose influence. Herriot, well aware of this, worked hard to rebuild the party's base and above all to reaffirm its identity as the republican party (cf. his refusal to merge with others, as described above). While the 1924 vote confirmed that he had partly succeeded in his aim, subsequent experience showed that radicalism could no longer hope to head a governing left alliance as it had done before. It is precisely with this lesson in mind that Herriot was ready to take the party into the Poincaré government and ally with part of the right. He recognised that the party had to adopt a more pivotal, centrist position within the system if it was to survive. This effect on party logic is one of the deepest consequences of the cartel.

The rôle of the SFIO was also called into question (Judt, 1976). Without the influence of Jaurès, the party had tended to retreat into a position of revolutionary purism. Its version of marxism still postulated a revolution to end exploitation and usher in a classless society. Unlike the communists, it did not see revolution coming about under the aegis of a centralised, vertical party which would then install a dictatorship of soviet type. Rather, the revolution would occur when industrial capitalism had become the dominant social form and the working class formed the overwhelming majority.[8] In the meantime, the party still had to decide which rôle to play within the party system. This question became more pressing as the PCF began to make inroads into its natural support of workers and even the poorer peasantry. Two options were available: outright denunciation and imprecation (a space which the PCF was rapidly filling) or some kind of constructive relationship with the republican parties.How close could such a relationship be? While it was mostly acceptable to militants to defend the republican *acquis*, including a fairly unstinting endorsement of anti-clericalism, the republic was hardly under threat in 1924. Alternatively, collaboration with radicals and 'advanced republicans' could be justified on reformist grounds, it being possible to argue, with Jaurès, that each reform constituted a landmark on the road to socialism. However, if it was acceptable to vote with the bourgeois parties on some issues, did this collaboration extend to entering government? Only a minority of the SFIO was ready for this now. It had been hard enough for Blum to persuade the party to agree to a mere electoral alliance. In the event, then, SFIO refused to join the government, though its votes in the chamber were loyal. One can argue that, had the party gone into Herriot's cabinet, the effects could have been worse in that the small savers might have panicked even more than they did. Poincaré did not think so, however, as he offered the socialists places in his national unity government. What he was doing was inviting them to become an explicit system party at national level (they had long ago settled comfortably into town halls). For the sake of doctrine and internal unity the SFIO refused, but the problem of its place in the system had been put firmly on the agenda; a party with over a fifth of the deputies (and growing) would find it harder and harder to sit in the cold of unconditional opposition. Blum and his colleagues knew this and would writhe uncomfortably for some time yet as the party inched towards taking responsibility.

8. On the SFIO theory of revolution see Kergoat (1983); Portelli (1980); Ziebura (1967); Bergounioux and Grunberg (1992).

In terms of party culture, this legislature also witnessed a significant new trend, namely, the 'majority switch' or *majorité de reflux* (Delcros, 1970). By this is meant a change in the political complexion of a majority in mid-legislature, in this case a move from a left cartel to a government dominated by the centre-right, but including radicals. On the face of it, this seemed like a denial of voters' will. Put simply, the French had not voted for Poincaré in 1924, but ended up with him in charge of government. Whereas previous legislatures had seen subtle changes in the character of majorities (more or less of the republican family co-opted according to the needs of the moment) this marked a qualitative shift; in the pre-1914 parliaments the left *bloc des gauches* had modified its frontiers and allies, but never handed over to a cabinet of the right in mid-stream and then served in that cabinet. That this could happen now was due to the changing perspectives of the radical party, hitherto regarded as a stable part of the left. The magnitude of this trend should not be underestimated: it opened up new possibilities for the system (as well as for radicalism, of course). In a sense, however, it meant a further confiscation of power from voters towards party leaders. Defenders of radical strategy tend to think that the party was simply translating the contradictory impulses of its electorate into coalitional behaviour; radical voters were with the left on republican issues, but fearful of it on socio-economic questions.

A final feature of this period is the recrudescence of the league phenomenon, largely dormant since 1914 and the *union sacrée*. As the cartel came in, various leagues were revived or created. We shall deal with the nature and function of these (quite diverse) phenomena later in the chapter. For the present we may note the flowering of a significant mass movement with paramilitary trappings in the shape of the Jeunesses Patriotes (JP) and a short-lived attempt to imitate Mussolinian fascism in the shape of the Faisceau. Millerand's Ligue Nationale Républicaine was a somewhat different attempt to give, yet again, a durable national framework to the different components of the parliamentary right; it was as unsuccessful as its predecessors (cf. Chapter Four).[9] All of these movements tailed off sharply once the moderate right was back in office. It was as if fear of the 'socialism' of the cartel triggered a mobilisation which the existing weak forces of the right could not canalise; hence the angry, street-oriented style of these mass movements. The manner of their fading raises questions about their relationship to the parliamentary right, to which we shall return.

---

9. Maurras' Action Française is a case apart (Weber, 1959). Despite its elegant attempts to fuse authoritarianism, nationalism and pre-capitalist economics into a doctrinal synthesis, and despite its audience among parts of the intelligentsia and Parisian students, its impact on party politics was nugatory. It had a few friends among the deputies and its street gangs could cause disturbances (especially around 6 February 1934), but the republican right and centre-right mainly ignored it, especially after the papal condemnation of 1926. It is hard to avoid the impression that its intellectual chic has attracted more attention than its political impact warranted.

From the Reign of the Right to the Popular Front

The period on either side of 1930 was perhaps the best one for the right in the Third Republic. In an initially benign economic context, thanks to the confidence re-established by Poincaré, the right enjoyed effective dominance till 1936. In the five years and ten months from Poincaré's recall to the 1932 elections, the moderate right headed government for all but six weeks, which were simply used to demonstrate, via the abortive Chautemps and Steeg cabinets, that any return to cartel-type majorities was unfeasible. Briand's leadership of some cabinets is not a sign of their leftward leanings but a proof that this 'independent socialist' had become indispensable within the camp of mainstream republicanism. A conciliator and fixer of some skill, he could work with anyone and was a natural ally for moderate republicans. The lion's share of office during this golden period went to the moderate centre-right, in which rising politicians like Tardieu and Flandin emerged as leaders. The actual management of party groups proved difficult, as Tardieu's well-known observations attest, but Table 5.2 shows how carefully the rewards were distributed among the centre-right and its friends. The radical party shared in government for some of this period, until ordered to leave by its 1928 congress (which saw the rise of a left current under Daladier opposed to concentration-type politics).

The cartel alliance was kept going for the 1932 elections. By most counts the cartel won, enabling Herriot to form another ministry. Lachapelle attributed its success to better alliance discipline, which helped the radicals in particular (1932: XII). This time, the SFIO found a clever excuse for not joining government: it simply put forward a shopping list of demands which it knew perfectly well were unacceptable to radical voters.[10] One consequence of this was a split within the party. A number of deputies and federations who wanted to be in a reformist government were eventually expelled in 1933 (Marcus, 1958; Cointet, 1998). These so-called neo-socialists had other arguments with the SFIO beyond government membership,[11] but the split underlined the delicate position of the party, with an ever increasing vote that it seemed unable or unwilling to translate into action. Herriot, meanwhile, was seen off more easily than during the cartel, and office soon reverted to centre-right combinations dominated by Laval and Flandin. Radicals continued, of course, to serve in them. These cabinets had to deal with the full effects of the depression: economic activity declined, unemployment rose, exports sank, inflation persisted (Jackson, 1985). The main remedy offered was the classic one of more deflation: by reducing government expenditure it was hoped to decrease inflation and public debt, and restore

---

10. SFIO demands included slashing the defence budget, nationalising the railways and insurance industry, regulation of banks, a forty-hour week with no loss of pay and a wheat marketing board (Lévêque, 1994: 205).

11. In particular, the fascination of men like Marquet and Déat with what they perceived to be an operative synthesis of nationalism and social change realised by fascism, a concept summated by Marquet in his slogan Ordre-Autorité-Nation. During the Nazi occupation these two ex-socialists would end up among the most hard-bitten collaborators.

confidence and investment. Few counselled devaluation to help exports. The anger of the middle-classes, not just rentiers but public employees as well, grew and was seen in support for the leagues and groups like war veterans' associations campaigning to defend pensions. Discontent with the perceived corruption of deputies and the inability to solve the economic crisis fused in the riots of February 1934, when some of the leagues besieged the chamber and had to be driven off by the police at the cost of deaths and injuries. Two governments fell as a consequence of this, and the parties only defused the crisis by joining in a *union nationale* led by the GR veteran Doumergue, an ex-president of the republic. This calmed the anger momentarily, but the episode of the 6 February had laid the ground for a dramatic shift in the party balance.

This would take the form of the broad left alliance known as the Popular Front. The fear of a 'fascist coup' engendered by the 6 February combined with fears arising from the progress of fascism in Italy and Germany and its implications for peace in Europe.[12] The USSR promptly seized the implications of this trend by pushing the different national communist parties onto a new track, via the Comintern. Instead of causing revolutionary disruption, these parties were to work unstintingly to shore up democratic régimes in Western Europe, with a view to strengthening them against any fascist expansionary aims and thereby protecting the USSR. This meant readiness to ally with bourgeois parties, even in government, and ceasing attacks on the non-communist left. Communist tactics had hitherto mainly involved attacking 'social traitors' and 'social fascists' (meaning social-democratic parties) as a priority (Bell and Criddle, 1994b: 68–75; Claudin, 1975). In France, local SFIO and PCF activists began demonstrating together. The party leaderships went along with the movement, and the radical party, sensing the direction in which opinion was moving, remembered its left credentials. By mid-1935 the three had agreed an electoral platform together with the inevitable RS.

Table 5.3 Party Performance in 1930s Elections (Seats)

	PCF + far left	SFIO	RS	Radicals	Right
1932	12 + 11	129	37	158	259
1936	72	147	51	106	222

Source: Campbell (1966)

12. It is not proposed to enter here the debate as to whether the leagues were fascist or merely some variant of specifically French authoritarian traditions. Anglo-Saxon historians (Soucy, Passmore) tend to incline to the former view, while French, following Rémond's notion of a bonapartist right, lean more to the latter. To an extent the debate is irresolvable because there is no agreement on what exactly constitutes fascism. The point here is that contemporaries perceived a 'fascist threat' and mobilised in consequence, with important effects on the party system.

The Popular Front (PF) platform owed much to the radicals. Once it had decided to play the bourgeois card, the PCF was keen to tone down maximalism of the type which the SFIO had defended in 1932, and happy to reassure voters by following the lead of the oldest left party. The eventual programme promised to work for international peace: at home the PF would restore order by dissolving the leagues and protecting freedoms. In the economic sphere it promised to boost spending power and employment, without being too specific, though devaluation was ruled out. It also promised to nationalise defence industries and to take greater control over the Bank of France, destroyer of the previous cartel. Voters were clearly exasperated at the economic failures of the centre-right and worried about order and peace; the alliance won handsomely.

As the SFIO was the biggest party, Blum was asked to form a government. He had by now prepared an ideological justification for taking office: this was the famous 'exercise of power'.[13] His cabinet rewarded radicals and RS well; the PCF stayed out, unwilling to provoke fears among moderate voters. The mixed success of the Popular Front over two years has been well analysed elsewhere (Jackson, 1988; Bodin and Touchard, 1961; Renouvin and Rémond, 1967). If it secured real benefits for workers in the shape of paid holidays, union recognition, a forty-hour week and pay rises, and if it promptly neutralised the more dangerous leagues by dissolving them, it struggled generally over foreign policy. It was reduced to recommending non-intervention in the Spanish Civil War and had to preside over the humiliating Munich agreement in 1938. Above all, the Front was undone by the failure of its economic policy; its pre-keynesian demand-led measures resulted in inflation, loss of confidence and capital flight leading to devaluation, while failing to provoke a major economic revival. All this was fundamentally determined by the relationships of the Front's constituent parties.

Beneath the rhetoric of left unity, each partner was in the alliance for very different motives. On the face of it, all were interested in repressing the leagues and strengthening parliamentary rule (though the PCF's own war veterans had been stirring the pot outside the Palais Bourbon as recently as 6 February 1934). Radicalism was interested in survival. Sensing public mood move away from the deflationary policies put through by the governments in which it sat, it sought to attach itself to this movement and save as many seats as possible by second-ballot deals. It was also interested in hitting at the leagues, inimical to the type of parliamentarism which the party now exemplified better than anyone. This was as far as it went. Any bold strategy for economic revival would be judged

---

13. In Blum's system, the seizure (*prise*) of power would take place only when the material and subjective conditions for the move to socialism were fully present. In the (lengthy) meantime, socialists might help or join a (bourgeois) government in order to stave off an authoritarian threat ('occupation of power') or to promote serious reforms which might hasten the advent of *la prise du pouvoir*. This was the 'exercise of power'. By such devious logic, the party could be talked into assuming the governmental responsibility which, in the republican system, its vote inevitably connoted. Ziebura (1967: 283–90) has a succinct discussion of the theory.

on results, and if these were likely to hurt the party's middle-class clientèle, then the radicals would begin to distance themselves swiftly from their partners. The communists' aims were also relatively clear, unless one follows Kriegel in believing that the PCF still hoped instinctively to pull off some sort of putsch in the confusion of 1936 (in Renouvin and Rémond, 1967: 125–35). Once the Soviets had urged the 'turning' of 1934, then everything had to be subordinated to the strengthening of democracy and the rearming of France. Accordingly, the party would swallow some bitter pills (urging workers back to the factories after the spontaneous strike wave of 1936, non-intervention in Spain, the pause in reforms of spring 1937 and even readiness to join a national unity government). Shoring up republican France was the priority. Dupeux shows the high loyalty of PCF votes in the chamber (in Renouvin and Rémond, 1967: 109–24). It took the party's vote against Munich to seal the split with radicalism (Berstein, 1982: II, 550–52). Any gains that came with the new line (popularity from being associated with certain reforms; big surges in voters, members and deputies; deep penetration of the labour movement) were strictly secondary. They were banked for use later on, so to speak. Generally, the huge forward surge that the party made in 1936 surprised its leaders. The key point here is that the PCF's change was virtually entirely dictated by the Comintern, that is the CPSU. Here is one of the clearest instances of an extraneous pressure substantially modifying party behaviour.

Membership of the PF alliance posed most difficulties for the SFIO. At long last it was forced to assume office, against the will of most of its militants and not a few cadres. It would have to test out whether meaningful reforms could be prised out of capitalism (as the 'neos' had claimed), or whether the purists were right in claiming that only revolution could bring change. The party entered office in a mixture of fear and optimism.

If the partners' motives for alliance were mixed, the same is true of their experiences in coalition and the effects which it had on them. Office was particularly cruel to the SFIO. It was able to put some popular reforms on to the statute book, but its overall impact in terms of socio-economic transformation was modest. It also learned the bitter truth of the party system, that is, the controlling rôle of radicalism. It was the radicals who pressed for non-intervention in Spain, slowed down reform and eventually (via their senate group, for the deputies were too clever to disavow their partners openly) secured the overthrow of Blum in 1937 (Larmour, 1964). They then headed what were still notionally Popular Front governments until 1938, when Daladier ended the alliance and brought the centre-right into his government with Paul Reynaud as finance minister. The radicals then began to water down the social gains of 1936, while cracking down hard on the PCF-inspired general strike to protest against this and the Munich agreement. By the end of 1938, Berstein (1982: II, 565–90; also in Rémond and Bourdin, 1978: 275 -306) shows a party profiting from the climate of impending war to move rapidly to the right, and not afraid to use decree-laws (anathema to 'real republicans') to circumvent parliament. Its main aim was now defence of the beleaguered middle-groups, frightened

by the financial misadventures of Blum, and fear of socialism was as prominent as fear of Germany. Finance minister Georges Bonnet, fiscal conservative
and arch-appeaser, symbolised the new face of radicalism. Bridges to the left
were burned, and some deputies even talked of easing up on the laïc laws.
Under a popular decisive leader, believed to have kept France out of someone
else's war, the radicals seemed a hegemonic party again, in charge of a 'natural' concentration running quite far to the right. For a party which entered
the legislature on the coat tails of the left, this was no small feat of political
entrepreneurship, whatever one may think of the ethics of the operation. The
trick of the 'majority switch' had once again been masterfully pulled-off.

In terms of its own development, SFIO saw its contradictions exposed by
office (Greene, 1969). SFIO supporters of the alliance with radicalism learned
how limited was its value; such was their disillusion with their radical allies
that they and the rest of the party helped vote down the two Chautemps governments which preceded Daladier. The party had more trouble on its left.
Long accustomed to an open system of factional behaviour (Graham, 1994b;
Hanley, 1986: 30–44), which was arguably one of the better proofs of its
democratic credentials, the SFIO had seen the development of two major
groups, the Bataille socialiste and Pivert's Gauche révolutionnaire. The former, workerist and pro-rearmament, tried to push the party closer to the PCF,
while the latter, influenced by Trotskyism, urged rapid and more sweeping
social changes.[14] The two clashed hard on rearmament, as the Pivertists were
pacifists wanting to slash defence expenditure, not increase it. This weakened
the SFIO considerably, and the Pivertists were effectively expelled at the 1938
congress. This shows that factionalism is much easier to manage in opposition, when there are no policy consequences stemming from principled decisions taken at congress. In government there is no escape from awkward
decisions, however skilful the rhetoric. At any rate, the SFIO re-entered opposition weaker and more divided, but having undergone a steep learning
curve. Significantly now, it was also part of the pool of potential governing
parties, almost irrespective of its own volition. The system parties had made
it an offer which it accepted. There may well have been 'special circumstances', but in systemic terms, a threshold had been crossed, and SFIO was
now well on the way to becoming a system party.

The PCF was, in many ways, the winner. Its absence from the actual cabinet
(though it did offer to join the later Popular Front governments, only to be
refused, and called for a Front des Français, even more broadly based than the
Popular Front) enabled it to profit from the atmosphere of reform and even to
agitate for more, without being too closely associated with tough decisions
like non-intervention. (The PCF abstained on this issue, but actually voted for
devaluation). In this way it built up its strength. Already, the electoral gains

14. These demands were sloganised by Gauche révolutionnaire leader Pivert after the election win in his headline: 'Tout est possible!' The communist L' Humanité, reflecting the pragmatic line of the Comintern, was headlined: 'Non, Marceau Pivert: tout n'est pas possible!'. On
the left-socialist groups see Greene, 1969; Rioux, 1973; Rabaut, 1974.

were huge (from ten deputies to seventy-two); party membership swelled to over 300,000, and it is now that the party really began to colonise the main CGT trade union centre, swollen by the huge influx after the mass strikes of 1936 (Lavau, 1981: 64–78; Bell and Criddle, 1994b: 70–72). Obviously, the party's allies mistrusted it, never knowing how firm its commitment to the régime was or whether a change of Soviet foreign policy might reverse it again suddenly. They were also unhappy to see the growth in its strength, not knowing to what uses it might be put. This did not change the fundamental fact that the PCF had moved from peripheral status to the rank of a significant player. Henceforth, it would either have to be some kind of ally in a left majority, or, if it was to be marginalised as it was before 1936, then this would be a much harder task and would clearly have implications for the types of majority that could be constructed (probably moving their axis further to the right). In Sartori's terms, the PCF had achieved considerable blackmail potential. The Ribbentrop/Molotov pact of August 1939 and the PCF's endorsement of the subsequent carve-up of Poland (confirming its obedience to Soviet orientations) put the party in an impossible position when war was declared. Daladier duly banned it, solving at a stroke the question of its place in the system; by 1940 France was at war and there were more important issues at stake. This was a temporary reprieve, albeit dramatic, for the party system. With the return of democracy in 1944, the salience of the party and its effects on the system would loom larger than ever. Here was one direct result of the Popular Front experiment.

One modest component of the alliance found little change. The Republican Socialists remained a key group of the centre-left, taking their small share of posts in all cabinets from Blum to Daladier. Again, the party system demonstrated the utility of such a pivotal group. A small cog it may have been, but it helped to keep the machine in motion. More important in systemic terms, however, are developments on the right .

Forced into clear opposition by the election results, which also favoured the FR at the expense of more moderate groups, the right used all its parliamentary strength to fight Popular Front legislation. It was also associated with strident media campaigns, which sometimes attained a new low in personal abuse (Bodin and Touchard, 1961) as well as renewed mobilisation from the leagues. Commentators distinguish the total opposition of the FR, which refused the SFIO offer of a 'Thorez to Marin' government of national unity in 1938, from the more nuanced attitude of the groups deriving from the ARD, who still hoped to wean radicalism away from the marxist left and join it in a 'republican concentration' (Jeanneney and Sanson in Rémond and Bourdin, 1977: 341–57 and 324–40). The co-opting of Reynaud by Daladier, and the latter's policy shifts, showed this hope to be well founded. Wileman (1990) strains to show the ARD and its groups as evolving towards a more generous social programme, which actually endorsed some PF legislation and he talks up their democratic commitment. Nevertheless, as he admits, even the ARD refused the all-party formula proposed by Blum; it was obviously no keener than the FR to widen the circle of governing parties towards the left. Once the Popular Front was officially ended by Daladier, the FR felt able to vote him its confidence, even though it had previously shown interest in some of the more aggressive leagues. Some FR leaders like Henriot and Vallat, among the most vocal critics of republican parliamentarism, sat on the executive committee of leagues like the Jeunesses Patriotes or were in the Croix de Feu. This could only be interpreted as a nod and a wink from within the system towards its enemies. This tendency was compounded by the FR's rapprochement, for a time, with Doriot's Parti Populaire Français, until the PPF was suspected of being in receipt of finance from fascist Italy.[15]

This shadow cast by nonparliamentary forces deserves further comment. As usual following a defeat of the parliamentary right, league activity boomed, mainly via the JP and a new organisation, the Croix de Feu (Soucy, 1995; Passmore, 1997). Originally an ex-servicemen's association, the Croix soon came to be, under the slick and energetic management of de la Rocque, a vast repository of middle-class discontent, rallying a mass membership probably larger than that of the SFIO or PCF. While sharing the paramilitary structures, patriotic discourse and stress on active protest of the traditional leagues, it developed a programme which combined dislike of parliamentarism with anti-capitalist critiques (although retaining an unflinching hostility to marxism) and appeals to traditional family values which borrowed from social catholicism. For Berstein (in Sirinelli, 1992: II, 61–111) this force, which became the Parti Social Français (PSF) in 1935 in advance of its impending dissolution, was, by 1939, well set to become – for the (non-radical) middle classes – 'the first big political party of the modern, popular right, compared with the traditional, old exhausted cadre parties'.[16] Denied the right to fight the 1940 elections because of the wartime proroguing of parliament, the PSF had already won over a few deputies from the right. From by-elections it seems clear that its main enemy was the established moderate right. In 1940, it might well have made considerable inroads into the moderate right, putting further strain on the party system, but the parties of the right were saved by the bell.

The PSF apart, the function of the leagues in the 1930s seems to have been to provide an outlet for strongly held feelings and resentments that the weak parties of the right could not provide (and which, given their notable-dominated structures, they could only fear). The leagues could express this anger; it was as if there were a division of labour, with the bile being spent by the leagues and the everyday political work carried on by the parliamentary parties. This division was watched over carefully by those leaders like Taittinger

15. Jeanneney believes that the industrialist F. de Wendel, a leading light of the FR, was also financing the PPF (in Rémond and Bourdin, 1977: 349; Jeanneney, 1976: 589–90). Doriot, the ex-communist mayor and deputy of Saint-Denis, after being ousted as a possible PCF leader in favour of Thorez (the soviet preference), set up his own national communist movement, which soon moved towards open fascism and pro-Nazi sympathies. See Wolf, 1969.

16. 'la première grande force politique de la droite moderne et populaire, face aux formations traditionnelles de cadres vieillis et essouflés' (in Sirinelli, 1992: II, 101)

Table 5.4 The Fédération Républicaine in Interwar Governments[a]

No. of FR deputies	% of chamber	% of majority[b]	% of ministries[c]	Govt.
1926 104 (595)	17.5	24.6 (423)	7.7	Poincaré IV
1928 102 (606)	16.8	32.6 (312)	5.2	Poincaré V
		22 (464)	7.1	Tardieu I
		23.3 (431)	8.8	Tardieu II
		31.7 (321)	10	Laval I & II
		33.3 (306)	9.5	Tardieu III

a: selected governments
b: notional number of supporting deputies in brackets
c: full and junior ministries counted as equivalent

Source: Bonnefous (1956–67) ; *Journal Officiel*

with overlapping membership of league and party.[17] It was a delicate balance to maintain, and the case of the PSF shows how a new organisation could escape from the hands of the right's notables into those of new élites. How these latter would have behaved within the system which they had set out to oppose was never to be discovered, but perhaps the historian may speculate that the party system would have coped with the PSF at least as well as it had already done with the radicals, SFIO and PCF, to name but three.

This focus on extraparliamentary pressure should not divert attention from some recurrent features of the relationship within the right and centre, and between these poles and radicalism. If we take the years 1926–36 as a time of (briefly interrupted) right hegemony, then some very clear patterns emerge. First, whenever a rightish majority governed, the FR could expect a share of office, but a very small one – usually one ministry for the inevitable Marin. Such a share was invariably well below the FR's percentage of deputies in the chamber, and within the majority (Table 5.4). We touch here on one of the silent interdicts of republican culture; the right is accorded slightly more respect than before 1914, but it is still a barely tolerated junior partner of the 'real republicans'. One could make a similar observation about the peripheral presence of a PDP member, usually Champetier de Ribes, in concentration governments; here was the token catholic.

There are nuances within the republican family. Poincaré based his cabinets on *gauche radicale* or *gauche républicaine* men, with a fair number of *républicains de gauche* and a small presence from the Action républicaine et sociale

17. Berstein argues that Taittinger really wanted to unite all the right behind one recognised leader, preferably Tardieu, after 1934 (in Sirinelli, 1992: II, 97). His basic view, founded mainly on the Croix de Feu, is that the leagues were 'protoparties', preparing the ground for a real party of the right like the PSF.

(mainly Reynaud's followers). When he was denied use of radicals by the party congress, he filled up the spaces with republican socialists.[18] Senators were used extensively, reinforcing the loose party-character of his teams. Tardieu governed without radicals (not entirely from choice, admittedly), basing his teams less on the GRep and more on the *républicains de gauche* (what Wileman calls 'business conservatives'), logically enough for the most business-oriented and dynamic of the right's leaders. The Laval-Flandin combinations saw the return of radicals, especially after Doumergue, when, typically, five radicals would sit alongside two *Gauche républicaine* and three or four RepG. These are small nuances, which translate both the style of particular leaders and the pressures within the centre and the ability of its groups to bargain for influence. Radicalism also joined in the game, exacting its share (but no more) once it returned to coalition after the 6 February. There were no formal agreements, but everyone knew what to ask for and what to expect. Of such balances was republican party politics made. It is also noteworthy that this period of dominance saw a greater fragmentation of mainstream republicanism at group level than ever before. The 1932 chamber had six serious groups from what Wileman calls the 'assorted centres' , not counting Walter's Alsace-Lorraine group and a small peasant-oriented split. This was in addition to the right as such – FR, independents and the (very unfairly classified with them) PDP. Many of these groups could have joined forces; e.g., Georges Pernot's Groupe républicain et social could have joined the PDP, as the principal motive for its splitting from the FR was its attachment to social catholicism. However, it preferred to fight alone. Clearly deputies saw the advantages of small-to-medium formations as vehicles for influence and possibly advancement; in the scattered parliaments of the 1930s, small could indeed be beautiful.

The Party System Between the Wars: An Overview

Several new features of the system can be distinguished during this period. The first is the changing nature of representation, though the extent of change should not be exaggerated. We refer to attempts by parties to mobilise more massive support within civil society. The PCF is the leading exemplar here. Clearly it defined a new type of politics; there was a clear goal (revolution) and a distinct enemy to overcome (the bourgeoisie). The means of triumph was a new sort of revolutionary party, which demanded higher commitment and subordination from supporters. These the PCF obtained, thanks to the energy of its early élites (and some help from the Comintern). Lavau showed how the party made an aggressive bid to be the voice of the working-class,

---

18. In Siegfried's view (1930: 167) the RS did not exist in the country and represented nothing but the views of some deputies. They were a group whose function seemed to be to welcome deserters and ease them into government without making them into reactionaries. This harsh view encapsulates well the key rôle of pivotal groups (*groupes charnière*) within the party system.

striving to link its identity and aspirations to the party (1981: 69ff.). Through the CGT union in particular, the party brought politics to many workers previously untouched by it (it could even be argued that the SFIO's worker clientèle remained largely untouched by this movement), often among the semi-skilled and unskilled in the new industries. By 1936, the PCF had not won over all the working class by any means, but by its voluntarism it had imposed itself as the major spokesman for that group and was consolidating its culture widely within it. Here was a new relationship between a social group and its representatives.

The PCF example invites reflection about the status of the SFIO. It also claimed to be a mass workers' party, but it was qualitatively different from the PCF. SFIO had working-class voter heartlands and even significant worker membership in places (Nord, Pas-de-Calais), but its main activists were increasingly lower white-collar workers, often teachers or other public employees. Its leaders were Parisian intellectuals, sociologically nearer to those of the republican right than to the working class autodidacts of the PCF. Moreover, the party was heavily engaged in republican culture; secularism, defence of parliamentarism and even freemasonry mattered to SFIO activists, while to the PCF they were bourgeois mystifications. In other words, the values that SFIO espoused inclined it to a different type of representative function and a different way of relating to civil society than that adopted by the PCF. It did not seek to organise actively for a soviet-style revolution, but to manage and increase an already quite diverse electorate. It also presided over a growing municipal empire. So, although the SFIO might be seen as a mass party, in many ways its functioning was nearer to that of radicalism than the PCF.[19]

For the parties of the right, very little changed in their relationship with civil society. The FR and ARD had, notionally, the structures of modern parties, with branches, departmental federations and (invariably plethoric) national bodies, but they had had them before 1914. These formations remained notables' parties, dominated by the local chief and his backers. After 1933, Flandin made a serious attempt to make the ARD look like a proper party (Wileman, 1990). However, despite programmatic renewal, deputies elected on ARD tickets still joined whatever parliamentary party they chose and voted as they felt fit. Whether grassroots membership of the party really grew is a matter of speculation, and so far as its material foundations are concerned, it never got beyond the standard methods of the centre right, i.e., the begging letter to (fairly stingy) industrialists. The most that can be said is that if Flandin and some others felt that there was now a need for a more serious type of organi-

19. Lévêque points out (1992: 198–202) the generally weak implantation of SFIO in civil society, in particular its lack of associations to spread its culture and values. This was compounded by its divorce, from early days, with the principal such association, the CGT labour movement. Only in a few areas where it had a longstanding municipal presence could it penetrate society densely. Awareness of this factor could only help deputies to see themselves as local men, needing all the spectrum of republican votes, rather than carriers of a mass organisation.

sation, then this realisation came late in the day and little had been done to put it into practice by the time war came. Meanwhile, the PSF had developed from a genuine mass movement within society and was beginning to threaten the established right. Had the PSF won a significant number of seats in 1940, against the traditional notables, then the republicans might well have been forced to conclude that only better partisan organisation would preserve their chances, but war removed that dilemma. Generally, the right was concerned to manage existing assets with a minimum of innovation, as, increasingly, were radicalism and the SFIO. Only the PCF and PSF strove to mobilise new groups in a new way so as to disturb the still dominant republican consensus within society.

Perhaps this prevalence of traditional mentalities helps explain the increasing feeling after 1930 that politicians (and parties) were increasingly out of touch with society and therefore incapable of solving persistent problems, political or economic. The literature of the period is replete with critiques of the whole politico-economic system, coming from both left and right and more often from sources difficult to classify in these terms. These 'nonconformists of the 1930s' (Loubet del Bayle, 1969) usually focused on what they saw as dysfunctions of the political system – in particular the weakness of executives. Such weakness was often seen as partly explaining the inefficiency of economic policy. Most critiques of this type looked to the state to dynamise the economy in various ways, while complaining that it was unable to focus itself clearly for action. Proposals to achieve this usually involved strengthening the premier vis à vis the deputies (e.g., by making it easier to dissolve, or limiting the capacity of deputies to increase expenditure).[20] The electoral system was inevitably criticised for fragmenting opinion. Parties never rose to this bait, however. If the premier's logistical resources were strengthened by giving him his own cabinet office, his political base continued to be circumscribed by deputies. Even modest proposals to make dissolution easier led to the overthrow of Doumergue, hailed as the saviour of the republic months previously. The use of decree-laws, allowing government to act and to spend in defined areas before securing parliament's approval, was accepted reluctantly on grounds of pure expediency, but deputies resented it as unrepublican.

Not everything remained entirely static between the wars, however. The circle of acceptable republican partners was subtly widened. We have seen that the FR was effectively granted the status of a system party; the republican mainstream would now accept it into government, admittedly at discount rate, but this was the price one paid for membership of the republican club. The PDP, also used as a makeweight, is a different case, because, unlike the 'reactionary' FR, it was small. Republicans felt totally unthreatened by catholic democrats, so could offer them the occasional minor post in government. Had this current grown in strength, then a less generous attitude might

20. Burdeau (1996: 105–114) provides a succinct overview of these problems. The views of the radical 'Young Turks', typical of these critical movements, are analysed in Berstein (1980: II, 101–25).

have been taken. Even the SFIO was allowed to put half a foot in the door; its membership of a majority was followed by entry into government, then – for consecration must never come too easily – a return to opposition. The radicals and moderates had shown that the SFIO could be added to or subtracted from the pool of potential governing parties (rather like the FR). It is true that radicalism and its allies used the SFIO cleverly, but use of partners/allies was one of the fundamentals of the system; the new partners had to learn to do the same to their seniors. They had to learn the rules of the game as they went along, once invited to play in it.[21] Finally, if the previous combinations of parties could still be used to form majorities according to the established formulae – concentration républicaine, national union or cartel des gauches – the invention of the Popular Front added a further weapon to the armoury, namely the all-left majority. Moreover, movement from one type of majority to the other could be assured by use of the 'majority switch', a tool which could work wonders in the right hands. Those hands usually belonged to radicalism, which sat at the hub of nearly every majority, often flanked by the centre-right family of the RG, GR, etc. These were the forces which controlled the movement of the party system.

One can appreciate why most of the parties saw little real need to disturb arrangements which saw their men elected and enabled governments to rotate subtly. At bottom they remained confident of their ability to keep in step with opinion and remain competitive. This confidence appears justified when one considers the effortless 'rebadging' of radicalism under Daladier, its shift of partners and its recapture of the premiership. There was no talk then of a 'crisis of radicalism', as there had been prior to 1936. In 1940, Daladier speculated that the radicals might come back with two hundred and fifty deputies. Winning elections and keeping office were what mattered; the rest was ideology. The core parties of the system knew how to win, thus their mentality prevailed and ensured that the fundamental logic of the party system did not really change during this period.

The Third Republic Party System: A Long-Term Perspective

The defeat of France in 1940 and the subsequent imposition of the Vichy régime, voted in by panic-stricken parliamentarians in July 1940, brought a sudden end to a political system which had attracted much criticism, but whose brutal demise few would have predicted. Having seen the gradual evolution of the party system over several decades, we present now a synoptic view of it.

One could begin by describing the party system in conventional terms borrowed from Sartori. To that extent, it is clear that a pattern of strong multi-

---

21. One crucial step in the induction of new partners was their rôle in chamber committees. It is significant for instance that in the right-dominated 1928 chamber, the chairs of the general adminstration and foreign affairs comittees were given to socialists. This is hardly a mark of exclusion. The radicals, also election losers, took four other big committees (Avril et al., 1989: 89).

partism prevailed from the start. It is also clear that the multipartism was in some measure polarised, though care needs to be taken with this statement. Such descriptive cadres do little, however, in our view to seize the essence of the republican party system. This is because they are concerned to bring out its competitive elements. It should be apparent by now that elements of cooperation and complicity played a huge part in the workings of the party system. Offerlé remarks (1987: 91) that the field of party competition implies a minimum of tacit collusion between the players; the Third Republic certainly bears out his observation.

Republican parties and their opponents were deliberately weak organisations designed to operate in the 'Grévy constitution'. This institutional arrangement gave maximum opportunity for flexible groups with fairly weak policy demands to run government by agreement (not always public agreement, of course). The deputies had a high degree of common culture, being drawn from similar professional backgrounds and they were, above all, sensitive to the local needs of constituents. The system provided opportunities for advancement with its regular and subtle rotations of office. None of these factors bespeaks sharp conflict or polarisation within the party system.

Clearly, this remark needs qualification. Before the *16 mai*, the chambers were polarised sharply between monarchists and republicans, and there was a real political stake, namely the shape of the régime. Once the republicans had won this battle, which they did relatively quickly by giving electoral substance to what was a growing majority of opinion, the party system changed sharply. The rapid reduction of the antirepublican forces and their limited ability to influence outcomes was the best proof of this.

The hegemony of the opportunists gave a new shape to partisan conflict. Henceforth, moderate republican parties (or centre-left or whatever term one prefers) were now in control of government, and they now faced challenges on the left from the rising tide of radicalism, as well as from the established antirepublican right. From a two-bloc logic (all republicans together against their enemies) the system had become tripolar, with the new fissure growing inside the republican camp. The nature of the conflict would now change however. From about 1880, the republican form of government probably suited most politicians and their electors, arguably more than some ever admitted. The logic of confrontation between parties became more subtle, even though the rhetoric belied this. If we take the relationship between moderates and radicals for instance, it is clear that the common elements far outweigh the antagonisms. The matrix of republican culture produced both types of party, and both were happy with a deputy-centred democracy, which was seen as the best expression of the rationalist, secularist, liberal individualism stemming from the Revolution. The disputes between moderates and radicals were about the speed of change, not its direction. In practice, this amounted to arguments about whether to push for Separation more actively, or to limit active intervention to, say, school reform, in the confidence that reason would do its work in time. Even the class bases of these parties were not sharply distinct. The mainstream republican parties were led by a bourgeois professional stratum aware of the needs of their class, but they drew in voters on a cross-class basis from the peasantry and middle groups also, as did the radical party, that beacon of the middle-classes, itself led by articulate members of the bourgeois intellectual strata. Although radical economic policies might sound vaguely threatening to bourgeois interests, the 1930s showed that in the final analysis, radicalism was as much the party of sound money and liberal capitalism as its moderate cousins of the *républicains de gauche* or ARS. After all, it had sat in government with them often enough.

Even on the other side of the spectrum, the challenge to the republican mainstream was blunted. There always remained a hard core of antirepublicans, numbering maybe three dozen at most. Such groups had no blackmail potential and certainly no value as possible coalition allies. Strictly speaking, they were irrelevant to the party system, apart from the fact that their mere existence could be pointed to when it was necessary to rally wavering republican voters. They were simply bogeymen. Increasingly, in the place of what had been the old right, a new type of pragmatic politician came to be elected, accepting the republic (not as enthusiastically as the 'real' republicans), probably a catholic and mostly committed to the defence of bourgeois social and economic interests (except for a bold few advanced christian-democrats). Such men sat for the ALP and its successors and the FR. They were not liked by mainstream republicans who thought their loyalty to the régime conditional (though one should not use examples from hindsight such as the behaviour of Henriot or Vallat under Vichy to blacken such politicians collectively), but they were not a threat to the régime; they could be relied upon to provide opposition to the major secularist policies, but that was all. On general economic policy or foreign affairs, they might even be more reliable allies than some *gauche radicale* or radical party men. Inevitably, then, the question arose as to whether, and on what basis, such parties might be acceptable as coalition partners.

Once the mature Third Republic had established its existence, then, the majority of its parties were involved in a muted sort of conflict, where the antagonisms were not fundamental, but controlable. The stakes were now mainly holding office, not driving through dramatic new policies. All concerned were increasingly aware of this, and the logic of party relationships became highly subtle; phrases like *le jeu des partis* were used to capture the feel of this new logic. We attempt now to systematise some of its profound and largely invisible rules.

Mayeur remarked that republicans decided with whom they cooperated, not the reverse (1984: 400). This suggests a great deal of party control over government formation and policy implementation. We would agree with this, on condition that attention is paid to the internal dynamics of republicanism, for it is clear that after 1877, a centrifugal logic is employed. Radicalism wished to gain office in order to go beyond the opportunist programme. In order to do so it was prepared to vote with the right against opportunist cabinets, who were then forced to admit radicals into government. Voters seemed to approve of this concentration, so the radical vote increased, and instead of being junior partners the radicals began to head administrations and implement their ideas. The culmination of this process would be the Combes government. Radicalism played hard to win, usually against its own side. It also used political crisis as a tool to stop any rapprochement of the centres (moderate republicans and ex-rightists, *ralliés*, etc.) and keep the moderates roped into *concentration* formulae. Thus, events like the Dreyfus case, presented as threats to the republic, were also instruments of party strategy, enabling radicalism to continue tying in other republicans and setting the agenda. This type of centrifugal strategy predominated until 1914.

The radicals' very success in government changed this logic however. As the party became an established party of government, partly displacing older republican formations, and as it carried out much of its programme, it lost the ability (or the incentive) to continue the centrifugal, agenda-setting strategy. By 1919, the party stood much more for continuity than change. Hence it could be found increasingly in coalition alongside parties coming from the right of the republican spectrum, including even the FR on occasion. Radicalism still remained pivotal to the system, but now it was the natural centre of that system, not the leftwards-pulling force it had been before 1914. Increasingly, the centrifugal pull came from the SFIO, a socialist party that had arisen to carry the demands of growing social groups which could not recognise themselves in a radical party that had visibly lost any ambition to change. SFIO had entered parliament as an anti-system party (in the sense of wanting a transformation of the régime); ostensibly its 'otherness' was greater than that of the radical party when radicalism had first appeared on the left of the system. Hence its initial reluctance to accept office on any terms other than the totally unlikely one of a massive majority with a mandate to legislate capitalism out of existence. However, as the party grew and became a fixture on the left of the republican camp, so much of whose culture it shared, it was drawn irresistibly into party logic. Offerlé's remark, quoted at the head of this chapter, to the effect that mere proximity to a field of competition draws one inevitably into the game, is amply borne out. Initially used to shore up the system against 'reaction', SFIO gradually became aware of its muscle, which it began to use against what it saw as radical backsliding in the 1920s and 1930s. We saw that on occasions it could vote with the right against radical-led governments, exactly as radicalism had done against the opportunists decades before. The logical upshot of such behaviour was to force radicalism into an alliance with SFIO and such sections of mainstream republicanism as could be mobilised on a programme of republican defence plus some vague reforms (essentially the RS plus some *gauche radicale*, etc.). This was the cartel, successor to the *concentration*. In this leftwards slide, SFIO was the major force, not the radicals. Just like radicalism, it was transformed by the approach of office. Its more ideological elements expelled the *néos* for making explicit what many SFIO had only half realised, namely, that if a party keeps getting elected over a long period then, sooner or later, it is going to have to take a share of office. The party mainstream knew in fact that office was inevitable, hence Blum's elaborate theology of *exercice du pouvoir*.

The government experience of 1936 did enable SFIO to accomplish a number of policy objectives. This was not the revolution, to be sure, but it helped convince voters and members that the party could make a difference in government. SFIO thus became a possible partner in a system whose centre of gravity it had helped to shift leftwards. Its 'otherness' faded.

The rise of the PCF, partly explicable by perceptions of socialist failures and compromises, enhanced the leftwards drift of the system. At the outset the PCF had no more intention than had the original SFIO of working in a system which it was pledged to overthrow. Moreover, its republican/jacobin elements were fairly tenuous at the start. However, gradual settling in to the furthest-left space of the system created at least a potentiality. If ever the PCF was to change its discourse (judgements about whether it was 'sincere' or not could be suspended in the interests of practical politics), then some participation might be possible. We know that the change occurred following changes in Soviet analysis after the triumph of Nazism, when communist parties were urged to shore up the democracies. At this point the radicals and SFIO were ready for a deal, even if it did not (yet) mean PCF ministers. The new all-left formula had the radicals as its furthest-right component and succeeded in its immediate aim of providing stability. Continuing centrifugal pressure seemed to have produced a new dominant formula in the shape of the Popular Front.But the rôle of the radical party proved crucial again, as it shifted the centre of gravity back towards the centre by elbowing SFIO out of the majority and marginalising the PCF (with the latter's help, it must be said); if it could no longer set the general direction of politics, it was still able to counter the prevailing drift.

Republican party politics was characterised, then, by a continuous centrifugal, leftwards pressure, which, momentarily, seemed to have been stemmed by the time the republic ended. This feature of the party system is noteworthy for the way in which it affected alliance behaviour as shown above, but also for what it tells us about the underlying nature of that system. For sinistrisme is simply a reflection of how well the party system adapted itself to a changing environment. Generally, as new political demands emerge they are slowly aggregated by political entrepreneurs; these can work from existing parties or they can form new ones. Historically, it would seem that existing republican parties had difficulty in widening their initial scope to take in new demands, whether these be for more political change (radicalism) or more social intervention (socialism). The experience of other countries suggests that established forces can widen their scope to cut out, at least partially, the emergence of new, rival entrepreneurs, but in France, new demands tended to find expression through new organisations. In terms of party systems, however, this is relatively unimportant, for what matters is how the new demands are processed by the system as a whole. Established parties do not have to do this alone; they can accept the existence of new forces and admit or co-opt these into the party system in ways which they can, it is hoped, control.

This was the strategy adopted by republican parties in France. First, the mainstream parties gradually admitted the radicals, or at any rate submitted to the radical agenda. Then, radicalism, from its central position, admitted the SFIO as alliance partners. By the late 1930s, even the PCF had been given a strong involvement in a governing majority. All of these forces were originally outsiders with new demands, and one might postulate that the demands were more and more difficult to process with each successive new party. Radicalism wanted quicker political and cultural change; SFIO stood for sweeping social and economic change; the PCF sought the same, but via a new kind of revolutionary organisation, heavily involved with a major foreign power. Yet, gradually, these forces became part of governing combinations. Clearly, much of this process turns on the decision of the 'gatekeepers' (established parties) as to whom to admit and when; this is the full sense of Mayeur's remark.

The Bases of Republican Partnership

One useful basis for understanding party cooperation is to study the logic of government formation. The interwar years reveal some clear patterns (Table 5.2). A typical BN government was dominated by centre parties, particularly the GRep and the RepG. To this central spine could be added, as appropriate, a minor radical presence, a ministry for the RS (recognised by them and everyone else to be their due share) and some FR representation. Before the second Poincaré government it seemed clear that such FR representation should not exceed one major ministry. If it were argued against this that the seventh Briand government had four such men, then one can only reply that it barely lasted a week.[22] Clearly, a tacit tariff was at work here; the FR was never going to be given ministries in anything like the proportion of its weight in deputies. This was a cultural rule of the game, where gut loyalties counted more than votes won.

The cartel cabinets made no concessions to the moderate right and packed their ranks with radicals, the faithful RS (now better rewarded, as SFIO was not interested) and a still sizeable proportion of GRep and even RepG; these were the beneficiaries of *désistement*. Bourgeois republicanism still occupied a pivotal position and showed it with its votes against Herriot's fiscal policies. Similar types of cabinet would be formed after the cartel's 1932 win, with a large radical core surrounded by GRep, RS and left-independent support.

The Poincaré cabinets of the late twenties come closest to the idea of a national unity coalition, allowing for the fact that the radicals were removed from it by their own congress. Their absence was compensated for by further

22. François Marsal's 1924 government again had four FR and was slapped down even quicker, but this was part of a vain attempt by the president of the republic Millerand to deny the verdict of the ballot box in favour of the cartel.

reliance on the RS. The axis of such teams was slightly further to the right, with increased weight for the RepG and ARS, and even some FR presence. Such a broad church clearly reflected the party consensus that emergency action to steer the economy was necessary. The Doumergue team of 1934 again projected a deliberately consensual cross-party image, but this was done to obviate an emergency situation (the anti-parliamentary riots). Once calm had returned, Doumergue was duly dismissed when he began to favour decree-laws as a means of government.

Following the clear rejection of the cartel in 1928, the Tardieu/Laval type of cabinet shows a clear shift to the right. Radicalism was marginalised (one ministry in six cabinets – even the RS were given more), and the centre groups were flanked by FR and more conservative types of republican such as the ARS. Even the PDP made its first appearance in government.

1936 ushered in a new formula, the all-left cabinet. Clearly, radicals and SFIO took the dominant share according to the label of the premier, but this time there were no GRep or similar centre republicans, none of whom had in fact had *désistement* arrangements with the PF candidates. It would take the failures of PF policy and the adroitness of Daladier to marginalise SFIO and bring some of the moderates back into a formula slightly more to the right of the pure cartel; Reynaud would continue this process.

Cabinet formation then went according to party strengths. These may have been imperfect parties, but party government was a reality. In principle, a premier tried for a preponderance of his own men. This is easier to see on the left because the left parties articulated a clearer identity, but it should also be clear from our summary of centre-right experience (especially when one considers that a number of non-party men were ideologically and personally close to those RepG and GRep who formed the backbone of their teams). What is interesting is how far a premier was prepared to broaden his net. Generally, it seems that only in times of agreed national crisis was some attempt at this made, otherwise the preferred formula was to stray as little as possible outside one's own family. However, as majorities had to be formed in a multiparty system, this gave a strong position to the moderate centre groups and, increasingly, to the radicals. Without such formations, putting together a cabinet became increasingly hard, and these formations were the thermostat of the party system.

If parties concluded cabinet deals on the basis of parliamentary strength, their calculations were partly determined by the ways in which this strength was gained, that is election results. *Désistement* goes back a long way, to the time of the struggle of republicans against reaction, but the practice brought its consequences. In particular, the expectation arose that any republican party should make way for another to keep out the right, and it was assumed quite early on that this included SFIO. Before 1914, party federations were the allowed freedom to conclude second-ballot pacts. Later, with the setting up of the cartel to beat the BN, 'republican discipline' came to mean solidarity not just against reaction, but against conservative republicans: FR, ARS or even (on occasion and depending on local circumstances) RepG or GRep. The causes of this solidarity are both material and ideological. It meant certain election for many deputies, but it could also be justified on grounds of republican principle.[23] One was a member of the same family after all. Whatever the roots, the practice took powerful hold, on the right as well as on the left.[24] Such practices could not be neutral when it came to coalitions. If one has urged supporters to vote for, or if one owes one's election, to a deputy who has, by that very fact, been proclaimed to be politically quite close, then it is difficult to refuse support for such a deputy and his party in government, especially if the alternative is someone further to the right (or left, after 1928, say). In other words, the electoral system and its implied practices created of themselves powerful conditions in favour of co-optation and alliance. Even the PCF would be drawn into this game, especially after its earlier principled refusal to stand down cost it huge numbers of seats.[25]

One of the reasons for the success of republican co-optation was undoubtedly the establishment of tacit groundrules, to which all incomers knew they had to conform. Some of these rules were cultural. Perhaps the most important was the republican virtue of modesty; politicians were expected to claim their share, but no more. Day-to-day experience in the chamber would enable a party to know what that share was. Our figures from above suggest that there were indeed semi-official tariffs. Office was not something to be clung to with despair, rotation of cabinets was seen as quite healthy, especially as able men would figure in them repeatedly. It is often claimed that the system discouraged outstanding personalities and rewarded mediocrity; invariably the cases of Ferry, Gambetta and the ageing Clemenceau are put forward in support of this thesis. However, Ferry and Clemenceau had long spells both as premiers and in other high office; they were only overthrown when the parties felt that they had completed a particular job. Identical fates can befall strong personalities in two-party systems, as supporters of Baroness Thatcher would attest; bipartism is no more or less a guarantor of fairness than multipartism. For all his talent, Gambetta owed his fate to a crucial error of judgement, namely his obsession with PR. Party leaders can make mistakes under any type of party system, and it is absurd to blame the system instead of the man for making the mistake. Certainly, republican parties liked a type of leader who knew the system and his place within it, but when more decisive action was needed, the system invariably produced such a man. Waldeck-Rousseau and Poincaré are two obvious examples, but each knew when to go once his task was done. Each understood the modesty of republican culture. What is remarkable about such

23. In 1924, the cartel gained 47 seats more than it would have done under PR thanks to alliance tactics. In 1928, 87 radicals or RS and 63 SFIO were elected by *désistement* (Lachapelle, 1924: 27; 1928: VI).

24. In 1914, for instance, the FR, ALP and older right had had numerous single agreed candidacies (Lachapelle, 1914: 12).

25. In 1924, the PCF took 876,000 votes for a mere 26 deputies, compared with SFIO's 750,000 votes for 104 deputies (Lachapelle, 1924: 26).

a culture is the way in which it incorporated the strong without marginalising them. In this respect, the party system was a faithful reflection of the values, widely shared within French society, that it had done so much to propagate – reward for hard work, public service, and mistrust of *les gros*.

The very invisibility of the party groundrules was also part of the reason for the success of the system. The public tended to leave the business of government to the elected professionals in their 'house without windows', as the Palais-Bourbon came to be known. The professionals, with their high degree of shared culture and similar lifestyle, produced the compromises and deals which kept government going, using formulae at best only half-acknowledged. Historians armed with hindsight have implied a progressive alienation of the electorate from these arcane 'party games': was not the overthrow of the republic in 1940 the ultimate come-uppance for the professional manoeuvrers? This is to forget the massive and growing endorsement given the system at every election. Lachapelle underlines the high turnout at all polls and makes the point that it would have been even higher had electoral rolls been updated (by removing the deceased) and had national servicemen been able to vote. In his view, the real turnout sometimes topped ninety percent. This suggests a (male) electorate in harmony with the culture of its politicians. Voters expected the parties to behave as they did in parliament and judged them on results. They were not concerned with how the parties obtained these results.

These analyses suggest that the party system was fundamentally very well attuned to the political expectations of French society. Loose and weakly-based the party system may have been, but it gave France a working government. This system survived major tests – the various crises prior to 1914, the war itself and the depression. Criticism was rife, but voters continued to endorse the system. Essentially, it gave most of French society the political outcomes which it sought for enough of the time. It may have struggled as the demands upon it grew, particularly after 1919, but so did bipartisan systems like those of the US or UK. It is important to avoid the error of condemning the Third Republic party-system with hindsight, simply because the French army was defeated so brutally in 1940, but this is what much literature does, often by mere implication.[26] The French (and British) armies were smashed by a novel combination of air and armoured power, which was able to break through because of erroneous decisions taken years previously about where to site crucial defences. That was the reality. To extend the blame for this military defeat to the general state of French society (demoralised, cynical, selfish, etc., according to the explanation) is to push explanation to the point where it becomes an article of faith. It is equally questionable to blame the defeat on the parties. Would a bipartisan system, where one left party alternated regularly with a right-wing rival, necessarily have made the right decisions about how

---

26. For a lucid refutation of the varied allegations of French weakness (poor civilian morale, excessive influence of pacifism, inadequate production of war materials, etc.) see Irvine 1998. It is hard to dissent from his conclusion that 'it was not decadence which led to 1940; it is 1940 that has led us to view the late Third Republic as decadent' (p. 99).

to equip the French forces, where to site their defences and whom to put in command of them? Would it necessarily have solved foreign policy and security dilemmas any better, and worked out whether to push flat out for a Soviet alliance, or bring in Mussolini, and so on? Or even intervene in Germany in 1936? Simply to raise the questions in this way is to show how impossible they are to answer. It is better to refrain from moralising about the rôle of the parties and to conclude simply that the party system translated fairly faithfully, and for a long period, the wishes of voters. That is surely an achievement in itself.

6

THE FOURTH REPUBLIC
Nadir of Party?

☙

It can hardly be disputed that the difficulties faced by democracy in France for forty years are due in large measure to the shortcomings of the political parties
Julliard , La Quatrième République.[1]

The Political Context of the Liberation

After four years of the Vichy régime and Nazi occupation, which suspended normal political life, hopes were high at the Liberation of 1944 for a renewal of the political system, blamed (mistakenly as we have argued) for the French collapse. Yet by 1958, a new republic had collapsed amid further recriminations about the destructive rôle of the party system.

Retrospectively, the hopes placed in the post-Liberation settlement can be seen to have been exaggerated; even a major shock, such as the defeat and occupation, followed by a short civil war (resistance against collaborators), cannot be expected to alter longstanding mentalities and practices in the space of four years. Thus, when political reconstruction began late in 1944, a very real and widespread desire for change was to run up against some fundamental realities.

The classic literature on the Fourth Republic addresses these problems amply (Fauvet, 1959; Williams, 1964; Elgey, 1965–92; Macrae, 1967; Julliard, 1967; Chapsal and Lancelot, 1979; Gacon, 1987), and we shall keep here to the strict minimum necessary for understanding developments in the party system. The main argument will be that, while France experienced huge qualitative change in her social and economic structures and in her foreign relations, her domestic political structures failed to keep apace.

Economically, a much more active style of policy based on indicative planning (Hall, 1986) and building on extensive *dirigisme* developed under Vichy took the French economy to new heights of sustained growth on the basis of

1. 'Il n'est guère contestable que les difficultés de la démocratie française depuis une quarantaine d'années sont dues pour une large part aux déficiences des partis politiques'.

major infrastructural rebuilding; the decision to become a founder member of the EEC in 1957 served to confirm the increasingly outwards-looking orientation of the economy. This growth, assuring near full employment, rising income and consumption for three decades, was buttressed by the creation of strong welfare institutions in what is sometimes called a 'fordist arrangement' (Hewlett, 1998). This economic transformation, a success by any standards, had extensive social consequences. Most visible of these was the rapid shrinkage of the peasantry. The working class increased proportionally as many rural dwellers moved to the cities in search of jobs in new factories; so too did the middle groups, now composed increasingly of the technically qualified and the supervisory grades (*cadres*).[2] To some extent, this modernisation displaced many of the old middle classes – craftspeople in obsolescent trades and shopkeepers increasingly squeezed by more modern forms of commerce; the Poujade revolt of the mid-1950s would be a political reaction to this process. All these processes of modernisation impacted sharply on France from the late 1940s onwards, meaning that by the end of the Fourth Republic her economic and social structures were beginning to look much more like they do today than they had done even in 1939. However, these processes failed to be matched by political change.

The Fourth Republic officially came into being in November 1946, following a very grudging acceptance by referendum. Thus ended a two-year phase of institution-building during which France had been governed by provisional governments, headed originally by General de Gaulle from 1944 until his withdrawal from politics in January 1946.[3] From the point of view of our study, however, this formal re-establishment of republican legality changed very little; the logic of party politics was plain to all long before the first Fourth Republic government (Blum) was sworn in.

2. Some 90,000 people left the countryside annually from 1944 onwards. One farmer in ten left the land from 1949 to 1954, and one in three in the following eight years. Thus, the primary sector, which had still represented 37% of the population before 1939, had shrunk to 27% by 1954 and to less than 21% by 1962, by which time the secondary sector accounted for 38.6% and the tertiary 40.8% (Rioux, 1982: 224–5). These brute figures give some idea of the massive social mutations which underpinned the Fourth Republic.

3. The somewhat complex sequence of institution-building after Liberation is as follows. De Gaulle's provisional governments, formed in Algiers from 1943 onwards, took over in France in 1944. Until 21 October 1945 their authority was purely charismatic and not endorsed by any election. On this day, the French elected a new chamber and gave it power to draft a new constitution via a simultaneous referendum, thus massively rejecting the Third Republic. They also voted to submit the new constitution to a further referendum within 7 months.

This second referendum, in May 1946, rejected the draft constitution by a short head (1 million votes out of 20 million cast), essentially through fear of a too powerful mono-cameral arrangement. This necessitated the election of another constituent chamber on 2 June, which duly produced another constitutional draft, to be submitted again to referendum in October. This time the constitution scraped through by 9 million votes to 8, with a further 8.5 million not bothering to vote. Fatigue was more in evidence than enthusiasm, and on such a slim foundation of legitimacy was the Fourth Republic born. It only remained to hold a general election in November to complete the institutional jigsaw. Complex as the process seems, the underlying logic of the party system remained the same beneath the changing chambers and ongoing constitutional argument.

Table 6.1 Party Strengths, 1945-58 : Votes and Seats
Top line figures are percentage of vote cast on single PR ballot, lower line is number of seats won

	PCF	SFIO	Rads	UDSR	MRP	Indep	Gaull	Other[a]	Total seats
Election year + turnout									
1945	26.1	23.8	11.1		24.9	13.3		0.9	
77.9%	161	150	28	29	150	64		4	(586)
June 1946	26.2	21.1	11.5		28.1	12.8		0.3	
80.5%	153	129	32	21	169	67		15	(586)
November 1946	28.6	17.9	14.0		26.3	12.8		0.3	
74.5%	183	103	43	27	167	71		22	(618)
1951	25.9	14.5	10.0		12.5	14.0	21.7	1.4	
77.3%	101	107	76	19	96	98	120	10	(627)
1956	25.9	15.0	13.5		11.1	14.6	4.3	15.8	
80.2%	150	91	75	19	84	97	22	50[b]	(596)

a: some deputies in this catgeory elected under party labels, hence discrepancy between votes and seats
b: excludes 11 Poujadists disqualified by the chamber, out of 52 elected with 12.3% of the vote

Source: adapted from Williams (1964: 502 - 3) ; Campbell (1966).

This logic was partly determined by the new institutional arrangements. Aware of the weakness of the executive before 1939, the political class of the Liberation sought remedies. Already it was hoped that the emergence of newer, more disciplined parties (see below) would have a stabilising effect. The electoral system was changed back to departmental PR to facilitate this. An attempt had even been made in one of the draft constitutions to get rid of the senate. Fears of socialist and communist dominance of a jacobin chamber put paid to this, but it showed the desire for a strong government. The hand of the premier was supposed to be strengthened by measures making it easier to dissolve the lower house, and now he would not have to face a full investiture debate on the composition of his government. Such measures showed the impatience with the old system felt by the many new activists entering politics from the various resistance organisations – catholic, gaullist or left-wing.[4] A final feature of the new arrangements was the extension of the suffrage to women over 21. This more than doubled the size of the elec-

4. Berstein summarises well the political climate at Liberation (Berstein and Rudelle, 1992: 357–81). The 1940 débâcle tended to be blamed on parliamentarism, and especially the parties. Institutional renewal was considered essential and would stem, it was thought, from resistance and Free French élites. Berstein could even write that (p. 359) 'republican culture, recently held up as an unsurpassable model, was buried for being obsolete and archaic'. Events would show that this was an optimistic verdict.

torate, where women constituted fifty-two percent of the voters (Reynolds, 1999). The first elections saw patterns of female voting that tended to favour gaullism and moderate republicans as well as MRP. The left generally, and radicalism in particular, missed out on this new source of votes.

The success of the new institutions clearly depended on the parties (Table 6.1). Here, renovation was visible, but it vied with strong attachments to continuity.[5] On the left, the PCF emerged from the resistance stronger than it had ever been, with a membership of 800,000, heavy penetration of the main union centre CGT, powerful media outlets and an impressive network of satellite organisations, from its women's movement through the peace movement to farmers groups, and it consistently topped a quarter of the poll. Although the party had dissolved its clandestine militias and committed itself explicitly to democratic politics, its sheer bulk and organisational cohesion made it a feared opponent – or ally. SFIO also showed postwar growth (Sadoun, 1982), but it would prove to have a shallower base and to be shorter-lived. The radical party had done little during the resistance and would struggle to rebuild, relying much on prewar cadres, but it could still aspire to a tenth of the vote. Still based on a provincial, less dynamic France, it would slowly become a useful majority member once more. In the mid-1950s, the party would go into turmoil under the energetic leadership of Mendès-France, who tried to drag it away from its increasing conservatism and enthralment to the colonial lobby by an energetic style of leadership, concentrating on economic growth and pragmatic reforms against vested interests. The result of this would be the victory of his conservative 'neo-radical' oppponents and his own marginalisation, even though he briefly increased the popularity of the radical current, especially among workers and urban dwellers (Williams, 1964 : 114–31).

Essentially, the main prewar forces of the right, FR and the various groups which had sat for ARD, were scattered, either discredited by overenthusiastic support for Vichy (Flandin) or losing influence to new forces (Vinen, 1993; 1995). However, from 1948, under Roger Duchet, the CNIP would gradually attempt to pull together the various fragments of the moderate right, acting first as an electoral umbrella, then gradually trying to impose a party line (Williams, 1964: 148–59; Sirinelli, 1992, II : 588–662). The independents, as they now came to be called, grew in numbers if not in overall cohesion; there was always tension between a more liberal pro-European wing and a nationalist one, as well as between economic modernisers and representatives of rural France, often identified by the tag *paysan*, but they would play a major rôle both in steadying the system after 1947, and later, in destabilising it.

These older parties all faced new competition. The most remarkable was the Mouvement Républicain Populaire (Letamendia 1995; Dreyfus, 1988; Callot, 1978; Irving, 1973). MRP provided at last a serious organisation for the

5. It is worth remembering (Berstein and Rudelle, 1992: 361) that De Gaulle himself made sure that the parties had places on both the national council of the resistance and his Comité Français de Libération Nationale. He took pains to exhume the parties of the moderate right, which had virtually disappeared under the occupation.

political expression of catholic interests. To be sure, the party's official line said no such thing. At face value, MRP was a democratic party inspired by christian values (even the name 'christian democrat' was avoided where possible) and open to all. However, reference to the cleavage system in France makes it quite apparent what MRP represented. At long last the catholic subculture had found organised expression, thanks to the efforts of young élites formed in the prewar catholic social movements and honed in the resistance. What ALP should have achieved before 1914 now finally happened. The new party made a strong start in terms of voters, members and infrastructure, with impressive parallel organisations, union links and media ties. In programmatic terms it stood for a leftish version of modern christian democracy (Hanley 1994; Letamendia, 1995: 49–117), stressing solidarity and welfare issues and criticising liberal capitalism from the *personnaliste* viewpoint developed by thinkers like Mounier.

Another new entrant was smaller and, in its way, more complex (Duhamel, 1995 & 1996; Williams, 1964: 174ff.). Founded by ex- resistance fighters, the UDSR sought to straddle the centre-left space with its small cohort of deputies, specifically by bringing both laïc and catholic progressives into a broadly reformist party. This ambition was dealt a rude blow by the SFIO's reassertion of its traditional republican identity, especially under its new leader Guy Mollet (Graham, 1965; Quilliot, 1972; Sadoun, 1982: 216ff.) and, from the opposite direction, by the launch of the progressive MRP; there was to be no creation of a sort of Labour party with the anti-clerical sting removed. UDSR would always show a tension between its more conservative wing (Pleven) and a notionally more leftward pole (Mitterrand). Despite this, the party would soon become an essential pivot party, vital for the making of majorities in which its men often held key government posts. For much of the period, UDSR, along with the radicals, would be part of the large RGR group in the chamber, in a marriage of administrative convenience. Comparisons with the prewar RS are inevitably (and fairly) made.

There were two further major innovations. From May 1947, gaullism would make an appearance in partisan form as the Rassemblement du Peuple Français (RPF) (Purtschet, 1965); before this, numerous gaullist sysmpathsers had sat in the chamber as members of several groups. Based on resistance networks and on the popular appeal of de Gaulle, RPF sought to combine values that were reassuring to the right (assertion of national interest and strong government) with a vaguely progressive social programme (worker participation and an economic discourse that was dirigiste in tone). While its hard-core electorate came from the right or from MRP, it could make short-lived forays into more popular categories. Its late start, and steep decline after 1951, have led it to be seen as a 'flash' or 'surge' party; but it caused serious perturbations within the party system.

The title of 'surge' party is undoubtedly deserved by the poujadist movement, whose parliamentary incarnation, UFF (Union et Fraternité Française), elected over fifty deputies in 1956 (Hoffmann, 1956). Poujadism began as a social movement, articulating the fears and protests of small traders, businessmen and craftsmen threatened by economic competition and, as they believed, crushed by unfair taxation. Poujadism would live but briefly as a party force, but its short-term effects were noticeable.

In addition to these larger novelties, the system saw smaller groups often useful at the fringes of majorities. Of particular note are the few progressives (fellow travellers of the PCF) and the deputies from the empire (rebaptised the Union Française in 1946), who tended to divide between the Indépendants d'Outre-Mer (IOM), often from catholic backgrounds, and the more Black African- and Moslem-oriented Rassemblement Démocratique Africain (RDA) (Williams, 1964: 180–82). RDA would form a close alliance with UDSR.

These players would have to work in a society undergoing rapid change, an uncertain new institutional environment and, most of all, an external world which changed brutally. The wartime alliance between the Western powers and the USSR turned sour in 1947, and the Cold War set in. The consequences of this for a party system boasting (along with Italy) the biggest communist party outside the Soviet bloc can be imagined. At the same time the strains of empire started to tell; decolonisation began as the world war was ending. More so than in either Britain or the Netherlands, the effects of the break-up of empire were transferred in numerous ways, directly and indirectly, into the domestic political system (Kahler, 1984). Shortly, we shall analyse the effects on the party system of these external shocks of the Cold War and decolonisation which hit France simultaneously, but it can be said here that their impact may well have been more than could have been withstood even by a domestic political system more robust than that which France possessed.

Majorities and Governments

The parliamentary arithmetic of the chambers elected from 1945 confirmed that France was still a multiparty system, and a polarised one at that (Pétry, 1992). What remained uncertain was the degree of polarisation. It was also clear that between them the three big forces – PCF, SFIO, MRP – commanded well over half the seats; at one stage, the two marxist parties alone almost made up a majority. The desire to hold office and carry out vitally needed reforms was strong in all three parties, and so too was mutual mistrust. The MRP naturally feared the anti-clericalism of SFIO, and doubted the PCF's total commitment to electoral democracy. SFIO shared this doubt, and disliked MRP's mix of catholic identity and social progess (Mollet said that here was a party which should not exist). The communists doubted the commitment of both their 'reformist' rivals to serious change. The safest way to proceed was for all to go into coalition, and so began a series of tripartite governments which must count among the more successful of postwar France. In its two and a half years, tripartism laid the foundations for economic takeoff and built a solid set of social institutions in a France which occupation and war had left in a state of near collapse. Radicalism and the remains of the right could only watch from opposition as this work proceded; tripartism carried through the desire for change evident across all postwar Europe and which a document like the charter of the Conseil National de la Résistance summarises admirably. George Ross (1987) calls this 'left-Liberation discourse', and his phrase is a useful reminder that citizens expected purposive government action in the social and economic spheres as opposed to the immobilism of the 1930s.

If the big three could agree relatively easily on large areas of social and economic policy, such as the building of a welfare state and the need for government to spearhead economic recovery, major differences remained, and the study of these sheds much light on the dynamics of the system.

Even macroeconomic policy held pitfalls. Generally MRP and SFIO sought to keep inflation down by putting downward pressure on wages. The PCF, as a workers' party, could only accept so much of this. (When it eventually left government, the ostensible cause of its departure was prices-and-incomes policy (Rioux, 1980: 177)). The cultural clash also remained a potential menace. SFIO had never concealed its hostility to catholic schools, while MRP had by definition to protect them, and secure more benefits if possible. Colonial policy was another timebomb. All three parties colluded in repression of (Moslem-driven) Algerian nationalism in 1945 as unprogressive ; the outbreak of an anti-colonial rebellion in Vietnam was another matter (Shipway, 1996). This time, the nationalists demanding home rule as a prelude to independence were under the aegis of the Vietminh, led by the communist Ho Chi Minh. As overseas politicians and administrators (with complicity from some parts of the system in Paris) maneouvred France into a full-scale war against the insurgents, the position of the PCF became acute. A member of a government committed to modernising France and, notionally, anti-imperialist, it found itself having to support repression of an anti-imperialist movement led by a sister party. The contradiction between a stake in the domestic system and international (class-based) loyalties can hardly have been illustrated more cruelly. The PCF writhed uncomfortably for several months before a much bigger shock unhinged tripartism. This was the coming of the Cold War. In May, 1947 SFIO premier Ramadier sacked the communist ministers after they voted in the chamber against government wage policies, following a strike at Renault. The real reason for the break was that it had become apparent that Europe was split into two, and that the communists of Western Europe were henceforth to be put into quarantine as untrustworthy partners in government. Ultimately, their first loyalty was believed to lie with the USSR, whose hegemonic ambitions they were assumed to share. This policy of 'containment' would last till 1981. Thus, the irruption of changes within the international system forced modifications of party relationships in France, turning what had been a difficult situation into an impossible one.

The end of tripartism was marked by a wave of heavy strikes and protests through 1947–48 as the PCF and its CGT allies strove to put pressure on their erstwhile partners. At this stage, the prime aim was probably to be accepted again as an indispensable government partner, but the extraparliamentary

pressure was beaten off by governments not afraid to use the repressive apparatus of the state, and in which SFIO took a key rôle. It was clear that any
dreams of reuniting socialists and communists into one workers' party were
over and that the degree of polarisation in the party system was high. SFIO was
committed to the defence of electoral democracy, buttressed by membership of
the new Atlantic Alliance and NATO. The PCF was regarded by all other players as seeking the type of takeover which its fellow parties were busy carrying
out in Central and Eastern Europe, and its congenital inability to criticise Soviet
behaviour and heavy top-down style of internal organisation did nothing to
correct such impressions. Thus, the PCF was quarantined, but the systemic
implications were clear. A quarter of the deputies were henceforth unavailable
for supporting majorities, but the PCF was quite happy to help destroy these
majorities when it suited. The base for potential governments thus shrunk
sharply, the more so as a further squeeze was now applied from the right of the
spectrum. De Gaulle's angry withdrawal from politics early in 1946 did not last
long; he was soon arguing for a more powerful, essentially presidentialist executive which could curb the parties.[6] His RPF was founded in April 1947, and
soon made major gains in municipal elections. The chamber was still relatively
safe until the 1951 elections, although members of various groups who had
gaullist loyalties soon began to threaten governments.[7]

The system's answer was, in Williams' phrase, to call in the old political world
to redress the balance of the new, or, if one prefers, to invoke static France in
order to check dynamic France (1964: 449). If the two most dynamic parties
were opposed to the régime (the PCF had massive working-class support and
gaullism drew numerous votes from urban categories in the rapidly developing
parts of France), the other parties would have to form what soon became termed
'third force' governments. The two surviving components of the pivot of tripartism, MRP and SFIO, now moved to the centre of the system and increasingly became identified as the core of the régime. They needed support,
however, and this meant a revival of opportunity, in particular for radicalism,
which soon began to figure regularly in cabinets, but also for UDSR, whose
twenty or so votes became as indispensable as those of its RS godfathers in the
Third Republic. It also opened the door to the independents of the moderate
right. After the 1951 elections, when SFIO went into opposition (mainly over the
financing of catholic schools), these men would be essential enough to man several governments, and head two. (The two premiers Laniel and Pinay were both
prewar veterans, one from the FR the other from an ARD group. Their return
symbolised the weakening hold of the new ex-resistance men in politics).

This external pressure on the party system accelerated some of its internal
dynamics, pushing it back towards a prewar logic. A majority of three large,

6. As Berstein remarks, De Gaulle's resignation showed that his moral authority and historic
legitimacy only weighed so much, compared to the real weight of the forces sent to parliament
by universal suffrage (Berstein and Rudelle, 1992: 368).

7. According to Pinol (in Sirinelli, 1992, II: 601) the gaullist intergroup in the chamber contained 18 MRP, 6 UDSR, 12 independents and 4 radicals by early 1948.

relatively structured and disciplined parties, whose leaders were relatively new men with resistance backgrounds, was no longer available, hence the return of older, more loosely structured forces, often still led by men formed in the mores of the previous republic. Such men instinctively returned to the familiar habit of subordination to the chamber. Thus, from Ramadier (SFIO, but an ex-RS) onwards, prospective premiers accepted challenges from the deputies on the composition of their governments, and some would be rejected as a result. Gouin had already accepted the primacy of party by simply allotting various posts to the parties in his coalition and leaving them to fill in the ministers' names (Berstein and Rudelle, 1992: 369). These were huge sacrifices to the spirit of Grévy. They were, however, as much a symptom as a cause. The older, looser parties had to be allowed back in because of parliamentary arithmetic, itself dictated by external shocks. Coalitions were always going to be more fragile as a result. The instinctive behaviour of the old parties could only worsen the situation; it had not created it.

By 1950, party logic was working much as it had in 1939; short-lived coalitions, often giving way to broadly similar combinations of men, all based on compromise between mainstream régime parties, were the accepted norm. If anything, conditions were harsher than prewar, given the squeeze from the PCF on the left and the soon to be applied rightwards pressure from the RPF, which took one hundred and twenty deputies in 1951. This was in the context of a global Cold War (by now a shooting war in Korea), a colonial war in Indo-China and a massive task of socio-economic reconstruction, which stretched all governments. It is instructive to see how the party system digested these pressures.

We may usefully distinguish two dimensions of the system's response to pressure – actions against the enemies of the pro-system parties, and internal relations between the pro-system parties. The key action against the enemies was undoubtedly the change in the electoral law for the 1951 elections, which owed something to Queuille, a radical veteran (De Tarr, 1996). The system of apparentements allowed lists to make alliances in their departments, and any joint lists which topped fifty percent of the poll took all the seats. This was an invitation to core parties to line up against the PCF and RPR, and they did so, often in different combinations according to local strengths, in deals not unlike those of the Bloc National.[8] The arangement worked to the extent that for 47.6 percent of the poll, the two challengers only took 35.2 percent of the deputies, but this still left a powerful blocking group.

A second-phase offensive then made inroads into the RPF. Many of its deputies had used De Gaulle's aura to secure election, but not all of them shared his hostility to party government, and saw no reason not to support, or

---

8. For the highly variegated alliances according to local circumstances, see Williams (1964: 313–6). In 103 constituencies, there were 53 alliances of SFIO + MRP + radicals; in 36 of these, inependents were also on the ticket. In 31 of these constituencies, the régime parties won a majority and took all the seats. 25 of them were located along, or South of, the Loire, in classic republican heartlands. See also Goguel, 1951.

even join, a cabinet that might apply some of their policies. After careful over-
tures, the first gaullist appeared in René Mayer's radical-led cabinet in 1953,
and others would be key members of cabinets for the rest of that legislature
(and even of 'republican front' governments after 1956). Long before then, De
Gaulle had disowned the RPF and again retired from politics; this episode
simply confirmed that party logic had a power beyond even his charisma. The
core parties knew their men in the RPF, and provided an opening that enough
of them accepted to break the dynamic of the dangerous new challenger. Once
again, the system had absorbed a dose of venom only to emerge stronger.

Similar remarks could be made about poujadism, whose fifty members of
the 1956 legislature were easy meat for the parties. Elected to protest on
behalf of the obsolescent commercial classes of provincial France, these
deputies made much sound and fury, especially with their strident nationalism over colonial matters. Kahler believes that their presence helped pull
élite opinion towards colonialist positions (1984: 118–9). When it came to
obstructing the legislature or gaining advantages for their supporters, their
inarticulacy and sheer lack of technical competence meant that they could
largely be ignored by the core parties (who disqualified a fifth of them immediately upon their election anyway), apart from the small number who were
interesting enough to be wooed by the independents (Collovald, 1989).

The major threat, the PCF, was simply quarantined. For its part, it made
efforts to return to the fold, notably in its vote for the investiture of Mendès-
France in 1954, when the radical leader was put in to secure a respectable peace
in Indo-China following the French defeat by the Vietminh. In his investiture
speech, Mendès told the deputies that he would simply ignore PCF votes in
counting up any majority. Similarly, in 1956, when the PCF put out feelers
about supporting Mollet's 'republican front' government, it was made plain to
the party that there would be no places for it. In due course it helped vote down
both Mendès and Mollet, in alliance with the right. Any temptation for other
parties to soften the line towards the PCF was regularly weakened by international events such as the 1956 repression in Hungary, endorsed by a PCF whose
own internal structures replicated those régimes it supported.

Thus, by a mixture of refusal and partial incorporation, the system parties
held off their enemies. This did not mean that their own internal relations
were easy, however.

A glance at Table 6.2 reveals the profound logic of post-tripartite governments. The spine of these, with the brief exception of the republican front governments of 1956–57, was MRP. Basically, it could govern with SFIO, the other
main protagonist, or not. If it did, then the radicals and UDSR were invariably
included. As one or two independents also began to appear in cabinet from
Ramadier onwards, these combinations resembled the union nationale of the
Third Republic or, to put it differently, a 1940s version of 'from Blum to Marin'.
MRP could also face rightwards. The right's strong showing in the 1951 election (especially if we take the RPF vote into account), coupled with a drastic
MRP slippage, changed the rules. Henceforth, the natural combination was

Table 6.2 Party Composition of Governments, 1944-58
(Full ministers only)

	PCF	SFIO	Rads	UDSR	MRP	Indep	Gaull	Non-Party
De Gaulle I								
10.9.44; 21	2	4	3		3	1	1*	8ᵃ
De Gaulle II								
21.11.45; 22	5	5	1	2	4	1	2*	1
Gouin								
26.1.46; 20	6	7*			6			
Bidault								
23.6.46; 23	7	6		1	8*			1
Blum								
16.12.46; 17		17*						
Ramadier I								
22.1.47; 26	5	9*	3	2	5	2		
Ramadier II								
9.5.47; 24		11*	3	2	6	2		
Ramadier III								
22.10.47; 12		6*	1	1	3	1		
Schuman I								
24.11.47; 15		5	2	1	6*	1		
Marie								
26.7.48; 19		6	5		6	2		
Schuman II								
5.9.48; 15		4	4		6*	1		
Queuille I								
11.9.48; 15		5	4*	1	4	1		
Bidault II								
29.10.49; 18		5	3	2	6*	2		
Queuille II								
2.7.50; 22		5	5*	2	7	3		
Pleven I								
12.7.50; 22		5	5	3*	6	3		
Queuille III								
10.3.51; 22		5	4*	3	7	3		
Pleven II								
10.8.51; 24			7	2*	7	6+2		
Faure I								
20.1.52; 26			8*	3	8	5+2		
Pinay								
8.3.52; 17			5	2	4	4*+2		
R. Mayer								
8.1.53; 23			6*	3	6	5+2	1	

Table 6.2 (Continued) Party Composition of Governments, 1944-58 (Full ministers only)

	PCF	SFIO	Rads	UDSR	MRP	Indep	Gaull	Non-Party
Mendès-France 19.6.54; 16			5*	2	1	3	4	(+1 IOM)
Faure II 23.2.55; 19			5*	2	4	2+2	4	
Mollet 1.2.56; 14		7*	4	2				1
Bourgès-Maunoury 12.6.57; 14		5	7*	2				
Gaillard 5.11.57; 17		4	3*	3	3	3	1	
Pflimlin 14.5.58; 22		4	5	4	5*	4		
De Gaulle 1.6.58; 24		3	2	1	3	3	3*	9a

The premier's party affiliation is shown thus*, including General de Gaulle despite his objections.
In the Independent column, ministers indicated by + belonged to the Parti paysan.

a: many of these were clearly gaullists, in the absence of a proper gaullist party.

Source: adapted from Williams (1964 : 494 - 5).

skewed rightwards, even to the point of independents heading governments. SFIO dropped into opposition to these new versions of *concentration républicaine* or, to personalise it, 'from Herriot to Reynaud' (both still active). The left's revival in 1956, due largely to Mendès-France's drive to renovate the radical party (De Tarr, 1961), ushered in a phase of centre-left governments (they could not be called Popular Front because of PCF absence), from which MRP withdrew, but, from Gaillard onwards, the *union nationale* formula prevailed again as the christian democrats returned. Much of prewar coalition practice was resumed, then, though the old vocabulary tended no longer to be used to describe it.

In two important ways, however, the systemic logic differed from before the war. The two parties which made up the pivot were both forces which had previously been marginal. Until 1936, SFIO had been regarded (and certainly saw itself) as a genuinely revolutionary party. Its admission to the core of government in 1936 had been in the context of emergency, and it was levered out subtly, as we saw, by the older parties. Its famous 1946 congress, where Mollet assumed control, reinforced its marxist character by its deliberate refusal to become a broad-based social-democratic party including resistance groups and, significantly, eschewing anti-catholic sectarianism. It is widely agreed that in taking this direction the SFIO élites were above all concerned to strengthen the identity of their party so as to hang on to its space, hence their plunge back into tradition (Graham, 1994b: 267–365; Portelli, 1980 & 1992; Quilliot, 1972; Sadoun, 1982: 216–28). Revolutionary discourse apart, this party now found itself to be the main force defending the republic against internal threat, be it gaullist or communist, and the external threat of the USSR.

The main partner of the SFIO was another escapee from marginality. Although the direct successor of the PDP, MRP was a much larger organisation, with a vote more widely spread and some pretension to being a mass, structured national party.[9] It would soon become apparent that half of the MRP vote was fragile. This is usually attributed to the fact that the élites stood for a modernising type of christian democracy, which seemed too statist to voters more used to conservative values. Thus, the old right, as it recovered from its associations with Vichy, was able to win back some MRP voters. So too was gaullism, which not only appealed to more nationalist values but was also regarded as vaguely socially progressive and had clear associations with catholicism. Despite its weaknesses, MRP was probably the key party in the system. It is no small paradox that this rôle should fall to the representatives of that eighth of the voters whose attitude to politics was primarily determined by spiritual considerations, and who had been shut out of mainstream republican politics for generations for precisely that reason.

The system turned, then, on a partnership of christian democrats and anticlerical republicans with socialist aspirations. Compromise was never likely to be easy, given the strong attachments which characterise these political families.[10] What is all the more remarkable, then, is the amount that this axis and its party allies achieved in the decade before 1958.

During that time, the régime was successfully defended against internal challenges. The major work of postwar reconstruction was pursued, resulting in high growth rates and vast occupational and social change (the very emergence of a phenomenon like poujadism is proof of the extent of this change). Within the international political economy, France was steered firmly towards European integration with the signing of the ECSC and EEC treaties. In the security field, third force governments put France decisively into NATO, despite objections from the régime's enemies. Much is made of the failure to secure a diplomatic solution to the need for German rearmament via the EDC, and critics dwell on the strife within parties as well as between them which the project produced. The truth of the matter is that the political class was

9. In truth the only areas where MRP had a really solid mass base were Alsace and Flanders. The first of these goes back to the German occupation and the implantation of the Deutsches Zentrum, and the second reflects the work of catholic social organisations and the *abbés démocrates*, those politician/priests who captured a popular catholic following. (Letamendia, 1995: 151ff.). Elsewhere, the new party's roots were shallower, and it soon began losing out to gaullism or the old right.

10. Lefort (1996: 73ff.) gives clear examples of the sort of compromise necessary to put a new cabinet together; his perspective is sharply hostile to the parties and their system.

saved from its agony on this issue by outside intervention. A solution was imposed upon it by US and UK insistence on rearming West Germany as a full member of NATO. None of the political class, even gaullist, was capable of altering this outcome, and everyone knew it, even though they might not have admitted it (a majority of deputies was certainly ready to overthrow Mendès-France precisely for having persuaded the chamber to vote for the inevitable). Even on the difficult chapter of decolonisation, third force governments had enjoyed some success. By 1956, they had disengaged France from Indo-China (admittedly with some help from the Vietminh), Morocco and Tunisia were set for independence – despite obstruction from local colonialist interests and their Parisian allies – and the loi-cadre of Defferre was about to grant autonomy to French holdings in Black Africa. The problem of education was never entirely solved, as the grants to catholic schools made by centre-right combinations after 1951 were still resented by the left. This was a minor running sore, however, not the bitter strife of prewar years, and would be negotiated anew in 1959.

All this policy output was accomplished by the classic type of allegedly weak coalition. In terms of parties representing interests, which is our underlying theme, this must be seen as a highly successful exercise. Apart from some losers (poujadist victims of economic modernisation, the colonial lobbies), one could argue that Hoffmann's idea of a republican synthesis was still intact. The party system was providing governments which adequately identified and addressed the needs of most social groups for most of the time. Voters seemed to endorse this view with a consistently high turnout, though doubtless cynicism about politicians remained as high as ever. Dislike of those who run a system is not necessarily the same as dislike of the system, however.

The Limits of Party Control: Decolonisation

In view of the above, it will be asked how the Fourth Republic collapsed so ignominiously in May 1958 (its legal death came with the September referendum on the new constitution). The events have a pristine simplicity. The colonial war in Algeria, begun in November 1954, was going badly and increasingly dominated domestic politics. Despite huge budgetary and military commitment, the 'military solution', which official policy was designed to achieve, was not remotely in sight. At the same time, no major political leader dared advocate talks with FLN nationalists about autonomy or independence. The furthest anyone dared go was Mollet's famous 'tryptych' – cease-fire, elections and then negotiations. However, as FLN was never going to lay down its arms on the strength of a promise, this whole schema was unworkable. Following the investiture of Pflimlin's MRP-led cabinet, rumoured to be soft on Algerian independence, an alliance of settlers, colonial officials and military chiefs in Algeria staged a mini-insurrection. Party leaders in Paris panicked, fearing that they no longer had sufficient control of the military to restore order. Amid rumours of an imminent invasion of Paris by paratroops, they had recourse to the option that the insurrectionists would also endorse, namely, an invitation to De Gaulle to head a government. The insurrectionists saw De Gaulle as an *Algérie française* man, but to the political class he was its last hope of preserving some form of democracy; even presidentialism was better than army rule. The general, whose silence had been matched only by the hard campagning of his followers against the régime, especially in Algiers, stepped into the breach left by this ambiguity. His price was the writing of a new, presidentially-slanted constitution. Such are the bare bones of the situation. What needs to be explained is how the sophisticated party system we have described was caught out in such a humiliating way.

The party system had managed to offload many of France's overseas possessions prior to the Algerian conflict. This was not always an easy process, as alliances of settlers, colonial bureaucrats and their friends in the Paris parties often created obstructions. There were frequent illegal acts (proclamation of the independence of Cochin-China in 1947, deposition of the Sultan of Morocco, etc.) which invariably went unpunished, but the momentum of decolonisation carried the deputies with it, until Algeria. More numerous than elsewhere (one million out of a nine-million population), the settlers were better organised from the start in their determination to keep Algeria French. They had considerable penetration of metropolitan parties, especially radicalism and parts of the independent nebula.[11] Early attempts at reform such as the 1947 statute were effortlessly stymied by administrative cheating, endorsed by the resident-general Naegelen of SFIO. Once war broke out in Algeria, the administration, military and settler militias tended increasingly to dictate the conduct of operations on the ground, including massive repression of civilians and widespread torture, as well as violations of international law (physical attacks on neighbouring states, seizure of air traffic). All of this was 'covered' by Paris governments, and indeed, repressive modes spread increasingly into France, with interference in the output of critical newspapers and harrassment of pro-Algerian activists. The peak of such activity came after 1956, when office was held mainly by centre-left combinations in which SFIO and its longstanding minister-resident in Algiers, Robert Lacoste, were prominent.

11. The much shrunken postwar radical party had its strongest base in the old South-West heartlands, but little apart from this except islets of support around commanding local personalities (Mendès-France in Normandy, Faure in Franche-Comté), hence the relative importance of a new cluster, the North Africans. These included René Mayer, deputy for Constantine and friend of Senator Boutemy, known to be the distributor of political funds for the employers' organisation CNPF, as well as senators with strong economic interests in North Africa, like Bourgeaud and Colonna (Baal, 1994: 100–101). Mayer was premier once and an important king-maker in many coalitions. These men were able to work on a party mostly sympathetic to the idea that the colonies were a part of French identity, unsurprisingly perhaps, given that radical voters were over-represented among traditional categories – pensioners, farmers, shopkeepers and lower public employees. Even Mendès-France's first reactions to Algerian nationalism were jacobin (the problem was one to be solved by social and economic improvement, not independence). Only under the impact of Mollet's catastrophic policy did he take a more critical line.

If governments had increasingly colluded in policies that their more fore-sighted members knew to be futile, and if this had increasingly meant abandoning real authority to local forces on the ground, then they can hardly have been too surprised by the events of May 1958. This makes it all the more urgent to discover why the parties who formed these governments took such a disastrous path. We should beware of arguments that point to the sheer size and sophistication of the Algerian lobby, compared with that of either Morocco or Indo-China. It was well-organised and its target-parties were crucial to majorities; but after 1958, De Gaulle showed that it could be beaten. We also know that the professional soldiers were angry at their defeat in Vietnam, which they naturally sought to blame on politicians (survivors do so even today) and were determined not to see repeated, but again, De Gaulle would show, after 1959, that disgruntled soldiery can be brought to heel. The question here is how the soldiers ever got so far out of control in the first place. It is also a myth to believe that public opinion was overwhelmingly attached to keeping Algeria French, maybe as some kind of compensation for loss of status elsewhere, and that party leaders thus ran scared of it. Kahler has shown, following Ageron's work on public opinion (1976), that there was never a majority in France for *Algérie française* and that even the surge of what Werth called 'national molletism' after the absurd Suez expedition of 1956 was to some extent manufactured. Algeria was made into a burning issue by the lobby; it never was one spontaneously (Kahler, 1984: 370). In short, there were no massive, irresistible pressures pushing the parties unavoidably into such a position of weakness that the plotters of May 13 could easily roll them over. The parties made huge errors of judgement and paid for it.

What is crucial in this process are the decisions made by parties to adopt colonialist positions deliberately. To anticipate our argument briefly, some mainstream parties had good short-term reasons for doing so at the time, but they failed to see that the mid-term consequence of their actions would be to undermine the very party system in which they flourished. It was a gross piece of miscalculation by the élite. Leaving aside the case of radicalism, the most interesting cases are those of the SFIO, gaullists and independents. SFIO should have been expected to promote decolonisation fairly naturally, as the British Labour party tended to do. However, Kahler's illuminating comparison of the two cases reveals that anti-colonial ideology was never to the fore in the party's thinking (1984 : 161–230). Developmentalist theses of 'white man's burden' type had always existed in SFIO ideology and so had republican jacobinism, with its universal rights discourse and dislike of the traditional religions, archaic social structures and local particularisms which often fuelled anti-colonial revolt. This had always provided an ideological matrix in which defence of empire might flourish. All that was needed was a helpful context, and this came with the Cold War. Roped into the Western camp, SFIO tended to see international problems of any sort firstly in relation to the communists. Thus, if the USSR and PCF were in favour of Algerian independence (quite a generous assumption so far as the PCF goes),[12] then this should be resisted. This is merely context, however, for a quite instrumental decision to play the national card, taken by Mollet. There has been much speculation as to his reasons, with the visit to Algiers on 6 February 1956 often being cited. He and Catroux, his appointee in Algiers and a reputed liberal on colonial questions, were showered with eggs and tomatoes by a crowd of poor whites, many of them SFIO supporters. Whatever the source of his views, Mollet saw defence of Algeria as crucial to reinforcing the party's identity and he was ready to go a long way in seeking a costly military solution (this is the main reason why the other parties left him in office so long). By focussing on the need to keep Algeria French and thus, as he thought, preserve the republic, Mollet also sought to carve out a special SFIO identity. He was able to impose his view on the party by appealing to a residue of loyalty, by rewarding supporters (SFIO was in office) and using the disciplinary apparatus against the rising voices of dissent (Kahler, 1984: 225ff.). This was very much a top-down process, which makes it hard to agree with Macrae's claim that party militants exerted excessive pressure on their leaders (1967: 327).

The independents evolved in a similar way. They had generally gone along with North African decolonisation before 1956, and some leaders like Pinay remained openly liberal on Algerian decolonisation. The party's move to *Algérie française* positions after 1956, however, seemed to owe much to the desire to give the party a firm identity, in competiton with a gaullist rival on their right and with the new ultra-nationalist virus of poujadism. The need to anchor an identity became more crucial because this was also a period of serious party-building, as Roger Duchet attempted to give the moderate groups some kind of overall structure via his CNIP. A clear ideological profile was seen as part of this building process, and nationalism seemed an element that might pay off electorally (Kahler, 1984: 121). Kahler reminds us that the moderate right had never been particularly atttached to colonial nationalism, insofar as the empire was very much the product of a minority of republican politicians and interest groups (the so-called parti colonial) who operated stealthily as a sort of cross-party alliance along a large part of the republican spectrum. At any rate, the independents colluded in the wrecking of the *loi-cadre* on Algeria in 1957, which might have held out hope of some reform within that territory, and voted down all the last cabinets of the republic.

Gaullism played the same game more ruthlessly, especially after 1951. Its hope was to polarise the system betweeen itself and communism, squeezing the third force into its embrace. Thus, it proved to be the major source of cabinet instability until 1956, opposing all concessions in Indo-China and elsewhere (Kahler, 1984: 79ff.). The French presence in South-East Asia was linked to the struggle against communism; De Gaulle subscribed to what US politicians would later call the 'domino theory'. Although the general himself

---

12. Joly (1990) stresses the weight of the PCF's jacobin, nationalist and Jauresian legacies in explaining its general reluctance to commit itself to support of FLN and its repression of dissenters favouring this policy.

moved to more liberal positions on decolonisation (which he mostly kept to himself) after 1954, his withdrawal from leadership of the gaullist party meant that, in the absence of his charisma, it felt the need to move even further towards the adoption of nationalism as an identity-peg, as well as a means of weakening the hated régime. This need was felt all the more acutely as gaullism was now in sharp competition with the independents and the anti-Mendès wing of the radical party to win the support of nationalist opinion. Thus, although gaullists sat in the Mendès-France and Faure cabinets, which had a liberal agenda on North African decolonisation, Kahler sees them as having used their position to slow down change and points out that when these cabinets fell, some gaullist votes helped seal their fate. After 1956, despite disagreements on strategy among gaullists such as Debré and Soustelle, all were agreed in making defence of French Algeria a condition of support for any majority and they voted down the last governments of the régime for their shortcomings in this field. Inseparable from the colonial issue was the question of the régime itself; as the situation overseas degenerated, gaullism was not averse to using extraparliamentary means to provoke a crisis in favour of the general's return.

Overall, then, a wide spectrum of the party élites deliberately chose to play the nationalist card, principally in furtherance of partisan aims, that is to say consolidation of existing support and, for gaullism, the hope of destabilisating the régime. The consequences of such tactics, namely the growing insubordination by overseas officials and settlers, which would ultimately be highly dangerous for the delicately balanced party system, seem to have been completely underestimated by the opportunistic politicians (with the obvious exception of the gaullists) who applied them. Elite calculations failed to extract France from the war over her last big colony. For the parties were still élite-driven rather than mass-based. Only the PCF had a mass coverage of civil society. With high membership, numerous satellite organisations and mass media presence, all related to an extensive local government base, it was the only party that could claim to embody a true counter-culture. For this reason, and many others, it was systematically excluded from the party game. The other parties remained, with partial territorial exceptions for MRP and SFIO (the famous 'Bouches-du-Nord' grouping of Mediterranean and Northern strongholds), much nearer the organisational model of the Third Republic : notables' parties with few members and skeletal organisation. Even MRP and SFIO were heavily dominated by ensconced leaders,[13] and these leaders failed.

---

13. Letamendia confirms the oligarchical nature of MRP leadership, where power effectively rested with an 'inner circle' of senior parliamentarians. His figures also paint a cautious picture of the alleged mass-membership of the party. Numbers settled at some 30,000 annually from 1948, after an initial surge of enthusiasm which saw membership peaking at around 125,000 (1995: 296). Grassroots criticism tended to be muted, thus, ministers taking up very colonialist stances (Letourneau in Indo-China, Bidault in North Africa) were simply trusted to do a good job (1995: 248–9). SFIO's democratic traditions made it ostensibly harder to control, but Mollet and his team were usually able to get their way thanks to the backing of the big federations.

The Fourth Republic: Failure of the Party System?

This analysis suggests that the collapse of 1958 implied an irremediable failure of the party system and what we have tried to present as its finely-balanced workings. However, consideration of the parties' performance across the whole period suggests a more nuanced view. The system clearly struggled – and failed – with the overwhelming problem of decolonisation, but there are reasons for this, and to concentrate excessively on this one aspect is to miss out the many ways in which the system adapted to the huge changes within French society and continued to process the demands of its constituent groups.

The 1946 constitution was negotiated by the three big parties. As a result its workings depended on these. The possibility of firm government alliances backed by a large disciplined majority seemed much more plausible in a context where, from 1945 to 1951, the three majors held between seventy-four percent and seventy-nine percent of the seats, indeed the work of the tripartite governments showed what could be achieved beneath the normal party friction and jostling for advantage. France seemed to be heading for a much more structured type of party government than she enjoyed before 1939, in accord with what was needed to rebuild civil society and the economy. The irruption of the Cold War destroyed this new equilibrium at a stroke. In party-system terms, it turned a mild multiparty system into a highly polarised one, depriving the system of any influence that it may have been exerting on the PCF in terms of bringing it in as a regular member of the pool of potential governing parties. Whatever internal evolutions may have been taking place within the PCF, they were rudely interrupted. The new international situation forced the party to line up with the USSR, and it did so. Its withdrawal from the majority totally changed the dynamics of the system.

This opened a space for the older parties, and with this came a reinforcement of traditional republican behaviour (in the sense of deference to the chamber and a general mistrust of firm government). Yet this did not automatically mean the end of the régime. The basis of majorities obviously had to change; but it would probably have done so gradually in any case, once the immediate postwar reforms were out of the way. One could easily have envisaged other combinations of parties, for instance any two of the tripartite group, plus others. This is only speculation, however, and what matters is the eviction of the communists.

Once new majorities were created without the PCF, Third Force governments were very skilled at preserving democracy while progressing on the social and economic fronts. We have also suggested that in purely party-system terms, these combinations resisted two major challenges, in the shape of political gaullism and poujadism, with relative ease. All this was achieved without the support of a quarter of the deputies.

Panebianco (1988: 95–102) illustrates how Mollet continued the traditional alliance of central party bureaucracy, senior deputies and big federation leaders, bolstered by the rewards that office enabled him to offer.

Hence, the régime's base remained quite narrow. It is sometimes suggested by critics such as Julliard (1967) and Grosser (1967) that part of the reason for this is that the régime parties did little to educate the electorate or involve it more in politics. The mass media are also usually attacked for their failures on this point. The consequence of such a shortcoming, according to this type of critique, is that when crisis loomed in 1958, most electors simply did not care. The PCF sat on its hands, and few others felt it worthwhile demonstrating in favour of a system from which they were largely alienated; it was not a fundamental matter if a new set of politicians (De Gaulle and his team) replaced some of the old party professionals, even if the circumstances of the new men's arrival in office were slightly irregular. (And in any case many of the old professionals were taken into the general's transitional government).

These arguments owe much to hindsight, but they do address one key dimension of party, as it was understood by republicans, namely the nature of political mobilisation. Historically, voters were mobilised on polling day in very high numbers and they were mobilised above all by appeals to their underlying culture or 'family' to vote for their own kind (and, more importantly, against the enemy). After this, all mobilisation ceased and the elected deputies formed the coalitions and governed according to their judgement and the various rules of the game which became elaborated over decades. This was all that was required to keep the 'republican synthesis' going. Voters understood this and sought little more involvement in politics. It is true that, since 1900, parties had appeared which we conventionally treat as mass parties. Ostensibly, these parties sought to recruit a mass base and had internal structures which gave power to elected officials. Theoretically, such forces should have been immune to the parliamentary logic of the party system, and their gradual growth should have modified the behaviour of this system away from the sophisticated collaboration of the élites towards some other kind of relationship between big parties whose existence was not totally parliamentary.

The parties in question are those of the left. Unfortunately, political practice does not match up to the theory. Radicalism never got beyond a federation of locally based potentates, who could never be disciplined in parliament. The SFIO had all the structures of a mass party, even if it was always light on members, but in reality it was dominated by a small élite of professionals, who slipped easily into parliamentary logic. The democratic nature of the party meant that these leaders often had to work quite hard to square some of their actions with the membership, but they usually managed to do so by skilful use of rewards, sanctions and appeals to loyalty based on traditional maximalist rhetoric. Certainly, Mollet's leadership lasted far beyond the Fourth Republic. Mollet and his team were ready to put their party firmly at the centre of the parliamentary system. In the name of anti-communism and defence of democracy they reversed the traditional anti-system image of SFIO and made it a key régime party. One of the prices of this was full immersion in traditional party games, and these were played between professionals, without the involvement of the public beyond voting day. Once a party is fully involved in this kind of system, the mass party aspects (education of voters, participation) become much less important than the ability to deal quickly and flexibly with other parties in the system. The SFIO leadership had made this choice, and the party went with it.

The great exception to the above is the PCF. Here was a mass party, desperate to educate and socialise its following. Party schools, propaganda and media and local government apparatus were all used to mobilise voters along distinct lines. The problem with this is that it was too successful. To use Kriegel's phrase, the PCF created in the end a 'counter-community' of French people attached to a hypothetical vision of socialism which was not necessarily compatible with republican ideology. The existence of such a force made the party less, not more, attractive to potential collaborators, who were attached to the weak form of mobilisation described above. For all the political interests and commitment of the 'communist people', the party remained an efficient top-down operation, where policy was decided by a small coherent group whose directives would meet a high degree of compliance from members and voters, precisely because of the sense of belonging and loyalty which had been built up. The one successful example of a mass party based on widespread education and involvement was a very powerful incentive to continue the opposite tradition, namely, deals between largely autonomous groups of deputies. Big structured parties could be dangerous.

Thus, while in theory a better educated public should have seemed attractive to progressive parties, in practice, there were reasons for fearing such developments or, at least, for not striving for them ; participation got in the way of élite bargaining, and the system turned on the results of such bargaining.

Even within the more structured parties, tolerance of élite behaviour was high. SFIO militants could be critical, and the party's very structure had always tended towards factionalism (although the postwar statutes changed the system of electing the national executive in a way which favoured the big three federations), but after the debate the faithful could rally, via the famous motions de synthèse, to the 'comrade-ministers'. MRP was notorious for its easygoing attitude to ministers, especially on colonial affairs, where Bidault and Letourneau seemed to enjoy a very free hand.

Inseperable from the attitude of militants towards leaders is the frequently aired question of intra-party divisions. Generally speaking, divisions within parties were a less significant factor than might appear. The radicals are a clear exception to this, for, by 1956, the party had broken up over Mendès-France and the Algerian problem. Thus, the post-1956 governments would find part of the radical deputies voting down cabinets in which their own colleagues were prominent. Against this, it must be recalled that radicals in the Third Republic could be just as indisciplined. The independents could also fragment on some issues, and the moderate right had always done so. It was a part of the liberal credo that such behaviour was justifiable. Mostly, MRP and SFIO held together, even if SFIO did wobble over issues such as the European army, but this was in some ways an issue that did not linger. Threats to leaders from internal divisions were at most a secondary problem.

The conditions of successful operation of the system depended, then, on the quality of leadership élites and their decisions. It is clear that these élites made major mistakes on the Algerian issue that compounded similar errors made on previous colonial questions. These errors can be divided into two kinds: fundamental and conjunctural.

The fundamental error was never to establish a workable policy on Algeria; only De Gaulle was able to produce one after 1959. This does not mean that there was no agreement on a policy, however. On the contrary, the official line from the start was that of the military solution, reinforced by commitment to various degrees of internal reform according to the party in question. History and the FLN would show that this was a chimera, and, indeed, before 1958, some party figures said as much. Are the parties to be blamed for being wrong on this? De Gaulle is credited with solving the Algerian question by manoeuvring France towards disengagement with full independence by 1962, but nothing he did before 1958 suggests that he held such a course of action to be necessary; on the ground his followers certainly did everything possible to use the Algerian war to help bring down the régime. It is easy to say with hindsight that governments should have recognised the inevitability of independence and started negotiations with the FLN, but given the deliberate choice of mobilising nationalist opinion, which a number of key parties made, no durable coalition could ever have been put together on this basis. What is important is why such a choice was made. We have seen this to be a mixture of electoral calculation, anti-communism and the reluctance, built upon experiences undergone during the occupation, to see France lose further international status.

The major mistake of choosing a nationalist solution was compounded by other, apparently less serious errors. We refer here to the steady abdication of authority to colonial officials and soldiers which had been going on since Indo-China, and which had mainly gone unpunished. The reasons for this impunity are varied and would include in some cases the fact that key offenders had powerful political protection in parties deemed vital for coalitions. More important, perhaps, is republican culture. If the system continued to function despite certain abuses, there was a part of the republican mindset which always thought it better to forget about these and carry on (*passer l'éponge*). All the more so if investigation might reveal that some of one's own people were involved. In the circumstances, it was better to let sleeping dogs lie. Such attitudes might have entailed few consequences at the time, but their cumulative effect was to allow a culture of insubordnation to grow. As it became more difficult to form cabinets, mainly because few wanted the responsiblity for Algerian policy, the feeling of impunity at the periphery grew. Even so, many of the insurgents must have been surprised at the ease with which the parties in Paris capitulated.

Grosser and Julliard tend to blame this sequence of events on the quality of party élites, citing their lack of political courage. Julliard claims (1967: 254) that political leaders were short of political courage, not clearsightedness or ability.[14] While it is true that the politicians' capitulation was abject, such moral judgements do imply that it would have been enough for a few conviction politicians to stand up and argue a cogent case for independence, in order to carry parties and public with them. This is to underestimate the complex mechanics of the party system. As Grosser remarked (1972: 398), the PCF could have provided strength to a resolutely decolonising majority, but it was quarantined for other reasons. By then, the other parties had mainly chosen not to take this road. Once independents, SFIO and most radicals had opted for *Algérie française*, parliamentary arithmetic ruled out an alternative possibility. The core parties were roped into a situation where they steadily lost control to the point where they were finally forced out.

The manner in which the core parties were ousted is also highly revealing about the party system. Despite the mini-insurrection in Algiers, the army never made a coup d'état in Paris, and President Coty was constitutionally entitled to summon De Gaulle to form a cabinet. Apart from the PCF, Mendesists and some small groups, the parties endorsed this move, even to the point of accepting posts in what everyone knew to be a transitional government. Their concern was to preserve democracy, even in what they knew was likely to be an uncharted, presidential version; but that was better than military rule. By preserving democracy, the parties also preserved themselves.They would have been the first casualties of military rule. Furthermore, De Gaulle accepted their representatives on the drafting committee for the new constitution. Thus looking at it purely from the viewpoint of the parties, De Gaulle's advent defused the situation, stood a good chance of correcting the parties' mistakes in relinquishing authority and gave the parties a breathing space. They would now have to wrestle with gaullism in a new institutional environment not of their own choosing (though they would have a chance to influence that), but they would still be able to function. Compared with the outlook on the afternoon of 13 May, that might have appeared to be no bad prospect.

At the end of the Fourth Republic, the republican party system stood discredited; it was about to have to adapt to a new style of politics. It remained unclear how far the system had simply been caught out by an exceptional type of pressure, some other version, as it were, of the Nazi Blitzkrieg of 1940. Williams wonders whether any type of régime could have resisted the tornado from Algiers (1964: 449). Alternatively, it might have been the case that the party system was simply no longer able to process the new demands placed upon it by the mutations within French society and changes within the international system. For the moment, the parties could hide behind De Gaulle. Soon, the experience of the Fifth Republic would provide some answers to the question.

---

14. 'Ce qui a le plus manqué aux dirigeants de la Quatrième, ce n'est ni la lucidité ni le talent, c'est le courage politique'. For similar views cf. Grosser (1972: 397–406).

7

HUMILIATION AND RECOVERY
Parties in the Fifth Republic

༄

The parties are now even better placed to adapt and to control ... Their general capacity to constrain choice and change has been enhanced, and it is in this way that the 'old' parties manage to survive. They simply keep themselves going.
Mair, Party System Change

The Context of Politics: From Grevy to de Gaulle

The background to political developments in the Fifth Republic has been as dynamic as that of its predecessor. Economic growth was rapid and steady, until the oil crisis of the early 1970s heralded a new cycle in the world economy. Until that time, high employment and gains in real income were the norm; the working class expanded to its historic peak, and the numbers of the middle groups increased apace. The peasantry shrunk still further, as productivity increased, though the Common Agricultural Policy slowed down what would otherwise have been a brutal, market-driven exodus from the countryside. With the new developments in the world economy since 1974, the picture has been different. Increasing globalisation of the economy has put ever greater pressures upon firms to compete and upon governments to help them do so. One result of this has been the massive reduction in the industrial workforces of European states, as traditional industries like mining, shipbuilding and heavy engineering have slimmed down. As well as decreasing in numbers, the working class became more diversified. Large numbers of immigrants entered France, mainly from Africa. At the same time, many of the new, lighter industries employed an increasingly feminised workforce. In latter years, a substantial number of people have fallen into what can only be described as an underclass – permanently unemployed, poorly housed and much more heavily exposed to risk than those incorporated into jobs and the social structures that go with them, these *exclus* increasingly occupy the attention of politicians.

Culturally France has changed hugely since 1958. Religion continues to decline steadily, with the exception of Islam, which shows vigorous growth. The women's movement has grown in strength and confidence, addressing its demands to all political forces. Gay movements, environmentalism, anti-racism and many other social movements have grown considerably in influence. In short, the socio-economic and cultural base of politics has been in flux, constantly setting new demands for parties to address.

The international scene has also evolved rapidly. De Gaulle's early years saw the final liquidation of the French empire, bar a few fragments. French policy countered this loss by a twin strategy. On the one hand, French political investment in the EEC/EC was stepped up sharply, despite initial gaullist coldness. A key part of this strategy was a special relationship with Germany, aimed at making the 'Paris-Bonn axis' the driving force behind the EC's development. On the other hand, gaullian diplomacy promoted the idea that France could still be a significant player on the world stage, even in a bipolar world, with its concept of national independence. This did not involve neutralism between the Cold War blocs but consisted of carving out of a special rôle for France within the Western bloc. Deriving full publicity from French possession of nuclear weapons, French strategic postures would stretch membership of the Atlantic Alliance to considerable lengths, in an attempt to show that medium-sized powers could still enjoy a relative autonomy. The end of the Cold War after 1989 reduced the need for this kind of politics, but by then the whole problematic of 'national independence' had cast a large shadow over party politics.

Although domestic and international changes had a major effect on party politics, this was as nothing compared with the short-term political changes wrought by the new régime. Gaullian politics saw little use for parties, and the new institutional dispositions were designed to cut them back. The most that the party representatives on the drafting committee of the new constitution could do was to have some key passages drafted as ambiguously as possible (notably the famous *arbitrage* in Article 5 which describes the president's rôle as a decision-maker). However, constitutions can only ever mark out a framework in which *rapports de force* then operate, and these favoured gaullism hugely. The political class accepted that only the general could solve the Algerian dilemma, and that this meant that he had to be given the political means which he sought. The parties and De Gaulle thus concluded a sort of Faustian pact, in which the gaullian constitution was accepted in return for deliverance from Algeria and the army threat. De Gaulle duly delivered his part of the bargain, using his own ex-resistance networks to purge disloyal elements from the high command and accepting very early on (furtively at first and then with increasing openness) that Algeria would have to be given independence. After two failed coups in Algeria, the desired result was obtained in July 1962 and massively ratified by referendum, but during these four years, gaullism had extracted the full price from the parties, a price paid both in the wording of the constitution and, much more importantly, in the evolution of actual government practice.

By the time France emerged from Algeria, the pattern of presidential rule that would predominate in the Fifth Republic was already well set. The principal source of policy initiative was the president, and the prime minister was clearly his subordinate. The referendum of 1962, when De Gaulle persuaded the French to agree to the election of the president by universal suffrage (as opposed to the previous electoral college) legitimated this changed style of government while making it more visible. This 'bicephalous' executive (where one of the brains was obviously becoming ever stronger) still had to pass its legislation through the lower house, renamed the Assemblée Nationale as in 1871, but it now had many more constitutional tools to do this. The very sphere of law was narrowed down, preventing deputies from legislating on any topic, however small, as they had been used to do. Government now controlled the parliamentary timetable, could impose guillotines and force deputies to vote on its texts, ignoring amendments. It was no longer subject to interpellations; censure motions were made harder to put down, and abstentions on these were counted as pro-government votes. Article 49-iii allowed government to end delay by making a text an issue of confidence; it was deemed passed unless the very difficult censure procedure could succeed against it.[1] Laws could, if necessary, be referred to the new Constitutional Council for vetting (though this body would prove a two-edged sword as deputies learned how to use it against presidents, especially after Giscard d'Estaing made it easier to access). If, after all the above, a president still felt handicapped by the national assembly, then he was entitled to dissolve it , though not more than once in twelve months. All these devices were put in specifically to block the workings of old-style chambers; they were direct blows at the Grévy constitution, and so at the party system itself.

One further blow to the party system was the change in the electoral system for the lower house, which, from 1958 onwards, reverted to the two-ballot *scrutin d'arrondissement* of the mature Third Republic.[2] One clear aim of this was to cut down the big mass parties (which by then meant mainly the PCF), and in this it succeeded spectacularly. However, the second ballot is all about alliances, and it was at first unclear how these might be contracted between the established parties and the newly emergent gaullist party. A more drastic gamble suggested by Michel Debré, namely, adopting the UK system of one ballot plus first-past-the-post, was felt to be too far out of line with republican traditions, however effective it might have seemed in the short term.

1. This has only happened once in the entire Fifth Republic (against Pompidou's government on 4 October 1962).
2. This system has remained in use ever since, with the exception of 1986, when departmental PR was used. This was a ploy by Mitterrand to save as many socialist seats as possible and to divide the moderate right. It succeeded to the extent that the latter only achieved a bare majority, but at the price of seeing over 30 Front National deputies elected. None would have been elected under the old system, to which the new Chirac government promptly reverted. Frears (1991) is useful on this topic.

Table 7.1 Party Strengths in Assemblée Nationale since 1958

	Comm	Soc	Rad	ChrDem	Gaull	Indep	Other	NP
Election Year								
1958	(10)	43+4	37+2	49+15	199+7	107+10	66[a]	36[b]
1962	41	64+2	35+4	51+4	216+17	32+3		13
1967	71+2	116+5[c]		38+3[d]	180+20	39+3		9
1968	33	57[c]		30+3	270+23	57+4		9
1973	73	100+2[e]		30+4[f] 30[f]	162+21	51+4		13
1978	86	103+12	see UDF		143+11	108+14[g]		13
1981	43+1	265+20			79+9	51+11		11
1986	32+3	196+16			147+8	114+17	35[h]	9
1988	24+1	258+17	34+7[i]		127+3	81+9		12
1993	23+1	60+15	See UDF		258	206		13
1997	34+2	242+8	33[j]		134+6	103+6		5[k]

a: deputies elected for Algeria
b: includes the 10 PCF (not enough to form own group)
c: combined total for FGDS (socialists + radicals)
d: PDM group led by Duhamel and Pleven; includes ex-MRP and UDSR
e: socialists plus left radicals (MRG)
f: these two groups are the remains of radicalism and the MRP. Lecanuet's 'opposition centrists' waited till 1974 to join the majority. Duhamel's group had already done so in 1969
g: from 1978 this column refers to UDF
h: Front National
i: CDS formed its own group for this legislature
j: RCV group includes left-radicals, MDC and Verts, all allied to socialists
k: includes one FN

Source: Cole (1998); *Le Monde*

Fifth Republic governments thus acquired powerful leverage over parliament, the locus of party activity. They also sought, via the electoral system, to influence the type of party which actually achieved parliamentary representation. We may now see how the party system has coped with these unprecedented challenges.

Party and the New Institutions: The Major Phases

One visible symptom of change is the rapid re-emergence of a gaullist party. The rump which survived the 1956 election was never going to be an adequate vehicle for rallying support for the general. Although he had achieved power by extraparliamentary presssure, he could only govern with parliamentary support.[3] Despite his proclaimed contempt for parties and the refusal of his party to describe itself as such (the usual tags of 'rally' or 'movement' were used), De Gaulle allowed his collaborators, particularly Frey and Soustelle, to put together a UNR for the November 1958 elections (Charlot, 1967: 29–45). Aiming to recruit support for the general on a broad basis, it achieved a significant take-off (200 seats) and would remain, beneath its regular changes of nomenclature, one of the key parties of the new system. Clearly, the arrival of the gaullist party affected most the parties nearest to it (moderates and MRP essentially), from whom it took many votes,[4] but its implantation sent shock waves across the whole party system.

We can distinguish several general phases in the evolution of the party system since 1958. The first, essentially one of transition, runs to approximately 1962 and is characterised by the rise of a relatively dominant (but not majoritarian) gaullist party, which needed help from the moderates. During this time De Gaulle regained control over the armed forces and moved Algeria towards independence, while deepening presidential involvement in decision making across all policy areas (not just the so-called 'reserved area' of high policy, said by Chaban-Delmas and other gaullists to be the traditional sphere of presidents). During this time, party competition was muted, simply because the parties knew that the Algerian question had to be solved and the future of electoral politics secured before any change could take place.

These conditions were fulfilled by mid-1962, at which point the parties attempted to become competitive again and seize a rôle nearer to that which they had enjoyed previously. Quarrels over Europe, which led to the resignation of MRP ministers, and over De Gaulle's referendum on the new mode of presidential election, led to a censure vote being passed against Pompidou's government by all the non-gaullist parties (the *cartel des non*). Whatever their differences, they knew that the evolving gaullian practice of government was a serious threat to their traditional rôle. In the subsequent elections, De Gaulle, fortified by his referendum win, was able to pose as a successful champion of change against a divided group wishing to return to the past. His party, and the moderates who backed him (the Républicains Indépendants – RI – beginning to emerge under rising star Giscard d'Estaing), triumphed. The stakes of this contest were clear; it was about the classic conception of party and its rôle against the new presidentialist vision, where party was clearly subordinate to the president. With a strong president, vot-

3. Presidential need of a lower house majority has remained one of the fundamentals of the system, whatever its founder's feelings about the parties which have to provide such majorities. The absence of such a majority leads to the situation of cohabitation, where, effectively, the president hands over much decision-making power to the prime minister. In all *cohabitations* thus far, the latter has been leader of the biggest party in the winning electoral coalition. It would be hard to find a more eloquent proof of the persistence of party at the heart of the system.

4. The key election was 1962 when many CNIP and MRP supporters went over to gaullism (Brechon, 1995: 67–8 ; Ysmal, 1989: 249–53 ; Ponceyri, 1988: 141–3).

ers knew who was making policy and were minded to vote in deputies willing to back him; thus talk began of a 'coat-tail' effect. It was as if Anglo-Saxon practices were beginning to cast a shadow on French voters' behaviour.

The second phase of the system, which lasted until the mid-1970s, can thus be seen as a dominant-party sytem. Gaullism and its rump ally, the RI, controlled the assembly, winning a working majority in four elections (1962–73). For most of this period, they were opposed by the parties of the centre and left, operating at first in isolation and then trying to fashion alliances, with little success. This period of hegemony came easily, inspiring some to see gaullism as the natural party of government, much as the Tories claimed to have been in the UK. Only when the SFIO was revamped as the PS after 1969 and began an electoral alliance based on a joint manifesto with the still strong PCF did the system's shape begin to change. These years of gaullian hegemony saw a huge strengthening of the state, with active industrial and commercial policies, high growth, rapid social mobility and rising wealth, though failure to redistribute these social goods adequately was partly responsible for the civic unrest of May 1968. Voluntaristic foreign and security policy also helped popularise a concept of national independence, from which later politicians would depart at their peril. The opposition parties were quite ineffectual during all this period.

As the left alliance gradually grew, however, and as gaullism weakened after a long spell of office under the effects of the 1970s downturn, it became possible to see the system evolving towards a kind of bipartism; the favourite expression of the time was the *quadrille bipolaire*. What was meant was a two-bloc system of left and right, with two roughly equal forces in either camp. This was clearly the case by 1978 when the elections saw the clash of PS and PCF against gaullism and the new UDF of Giscard d'Estaing, who was narrowly elected to the presidency in 1974 in the absence of a plausible gaullist successor to Pompidou. The party system had now entered its third phase since 1958.

This equilibrium was relatively short lived. The landslide victory of the left in 1981 was hugely to the advantage of the PS, with a corresponding decline of the PCF. The right alliance also lost seats, in the short term at least. The system now seemed more like it had in the 1960s, with one major party in control of government for most of the two presidencies of F. Mitterrand (1981–95) except for *cohabitation* interludes from 1986–8 and 1993–5. Much as gaullism had expanded the French economy and pursued national independence twenty years before, so the socialists presided over a new phase of the internationalisation of the French economy and a deepening of political commitment to Europe. That this might not have been exactly what they intended upon election is irrelevant. Thanks to their control of government, the socialists performed a key function in imposing new policy directions on a France not well prepared, taking over in a sense from gaulllism.In the PCF, they had a semi-detached ally (except at the second ballot of elections), and were confronted by a more or less united right.

Since the savage beating taken by the PS in the 1993 elections, the rise of new parties, the diffculties of the right and the alternation of both camps in government, it could be argued that the system has now moved away from that of a dominant party towards a much looser kind of pluralism. We will address this fourth phase in our last chapter. Clearly the party system has undergone many mutations from 1958. We seek now to analyse these.

Explorations of Change

Numerous explanations are adduced for the extraordinary dynamism shown by the party system of the Fifth Republic (Wilson, 1982; Bartolini, 1984; Machin, 1989; Cole, 1990; Bell and Criddle, 1994b; Ignazi and Ysmal, 1998; Hanley, 1999a). Institutional factors normally occupy pride of place, particularly the effects of presidentialism.

As the presidency became the real political powerhouse, parties became dedicated to winning this office. This meant first having an electable figurehead, which is not always as easy as it might seem. Furthermore, party structures tended increasingly towards the 'rally' model – that is, the party increasingly became perceived as the vehicle for a particular candidate. This was less of a problem for gaullism, whose raison d'être was to help elect and then serve a leader, but the older mass parties of the left, with their ideology of member participation and their carefully constructed democratic hierarchies and rituals, found the transition to such a style difficult. The PS in particular found it hard to accommodate Mitterrand's leadership, which rode roughshod over party sensitivities, but militants knew that he was probably their only leading figure with the stature to win a national contest.

Bipolarisation is another important institutional effect. It was noticeable early on that the system tended to be squeezed towards a confrontation between left and right blocks, narrowing the space for other formations, especially the so-called centre (which meant the remains of radicalism and the christian democrats). The nature of the presidential contest was a major factor here, with its second ballot a shoot-out between the top two candidates from the first. This inevitably meant that the champion of the right faced his opposite number from the left. This would be bound to affect legislative contests, especially if they came soon after presidential polls, as frequently happened. The two-ballot system of election for deputies is already familiar, and we saw how important alliances were before 1939. This pressure to ally for the second ballot was given a further boost by the new rules, which forbade anyone to enter the second unless he or she had scored ten percent of the registered voters on the first (a threshold later raised to twelve and a half percent). Given an average turnout of around seventy percent, this makes the real threshold well above fifteen percent of the votes actually cast. Parties have responded to this pressure to ally with great sophistication. On the right, by the 1980s the situation was such that most first ballot contests had only one agreed candidate; unity was achieved well before there was any question of *désistement*, and usually according to some sophisticated tarrifs (Hanley, 1999b). The result of such processes is that the remains of christian democracy and radicalism have long since been forced to ally with either camp, mostly in fact with the right, though the left radicals still receive a small number of safe candidacies when the left parties agree their pre-election deals. The radicals and christian democrats now coexist uncomfortably under the umbrella of the UDF, imprisoned as much by electoral constraint as political desire.

A further source of party dynamism has been the rapid change within French society, giving rise to new political demands. During the Fifth Republic, the working class has waxed and waned, as well as changing in composition. It has become more feminised and far more culturally diverse. A vast new middle class has arisen, composed of skilled and qualified white-collar workers, many of them in the public sector with its educational and caring bureaucracies. All such groups had their political demands, and the traditional parties were not necessarily best placed to address them. More recently, extensive changes in value systems, themselves consequent upon raised educational and living standards, have brought forth different politcal demands,often summarised under the heading of postmaterialism (Inglehart, 1977); existing parties had little to prepare them for this type of demand.

Institutional changes, allied with socio-economic and cultural mutations, have, therefore, represented a major challenge for the party system. What is fascinating are the different ways in which it has sought to confront such challenges. These may be understood partly in terms of change, and partly in terms of continuity.

Right and Left within a New System

The major factor on the right is undoubtedly the swift and durable emergence of a viable gaullist party. Clearly, this vehicle was able to capture widespread support for the general as guarantor of democratic order and solver of the Algerian problem, and translate such support into continuing votes for the UNR and its avatars. This was done primarily at the expense of the moderate right and MRP; there is no doubt that the core vote of early gaullism was sociologically skewed to the right, with higher than average representation among the better-off, self-employed, aged, religious and rural. From 1973 onwards, these traits have, if anything, been accentuated, but at the peak of its influence in the mid-1960s, the party's electorate was very close to the social structure of the electorate in general (Ysmal, 1989: 278–87). To achieve such a coverage, it had won over a sizeable proportion of urban working-class and lower white-collar voters, who can only have come from the left parties, the natural vehicles for such categories. Gaullism could not hang on to such support in the long term, but it had done enough to be seen as a cross-class, catch-all party of a type not hitherto seen, stretching the right's influence beyond its historic boundaries.[5]

5. For geographical confirmation of these sociological features of the gaullist vote, see Bon and Cheylan (1988: 220ff.).

Tactical adroitness helped the gaullist success, but the party was aided by gross errors committed by the independents (Anderson, 1975: 249–68 ; Sirinelli, 1992: II, 668–713). In 1958, their vote was up with the gaullists, a performance reminiscent of prewar strengths. However, Duchet's insistence on hitching his party to the *Algérie française* wagon, even to the point of condoning terrorism, and then lining up against De Gaulle in the *cartel des non*, soon dissipated this capital of conservative votes. Voters wanted peace and stability and perceived any anti-gaullist as a threat to these objectives. The CNIP was, thus, severely sanctioned and began a decline into oblivion; it would never recover the votes lost to gaullism. Only the shrewd RI faction, which realised that the traditional moderates had to hide within the gaullist camp while awaiting better days, survived as a rump, dependent on a benign alliance with gaullism. Their regular, but residual presence in government, and their modest tally of deputies, show the limits of such an alliance; if not quite prisoners of gaullism, the RI were under house arrest, albeit comfortably.

Gaullism's corrosive capacities also ate into the political centre. MRP had already lost heavily to it in the Fourth Republic. A new christian-democrat party with a fragile base was always vulnerable to competition from a party owing obedience to a charismatic figure of catholic aura, standing for policies with welfarist tinges and picking up on traditional nationalist themes (Letamendia, 1995: 281–3). Some MRP personnel, and many voters, moved over after 1958, leaving a hard core of around a dozen percent which might still be said to represent the core catholic vote today.[6] There was still the problem for this remainder of how to position itself. Although MRP was wound up in 1967, its various successors from CD to CDS to today's FD have always faced the same problem. As the old multi-party system shifted towards a two-bloc format, the space for centre forces simply shrank. Christian-democrats could still attempt to fill a modest space so long as the left-right polarisation was taking shape (up to the late 1960s); the whole operation of Lecanuet's 1965 presidential campaign and the subsequent foundation of the CD are part of this logic (Hanley, 1991). Even at this early stage, however, the CD sought to downplay its specifically christian image and attract other remnants of the centre groups into a broad reformist alliance. In practice, this meant the radical party, briefly invigorated by Servan Schreiber. From 1971 to 1974, these two opposed traditions would cohabit as *les réformateurs* in a painful demonstration of how electoral and institutional constraints can force unlikely partners together; the Fifth Republic was far more efficient than the Cold War at making radical cohabit with centrist, freemason with catholic. After some short-lived explorations of a deal with the 'non-communist left', as it was depressingly called by then, which centred on the abortive campaign of Defferre to be a centre-left runner in the 1965 presidential duel, parts of the 'opposition centrists' gradually gave up and allied with gaullism.

6. This 'moderate, traditional, churchgoing France' (Ponceyri, 1988: 71) formed the core electorate of Lecanuet in 1965 and Barre in 1988, though Weil's 1989 list did not attract it fully. Geographically, it is centred on the departments of Maine-et-Loire, Mayenne, Vendée; Ille-et-Vilaine and Manche; Haute-Loire, Rhône and Haute-Savoie.

Table 7.2a Party Composition of Fifth Republic Governments (First Period)
Full ministers only

	Non-party	Gaull.	Indep/ RI/PR	MRP	Rad	SFIO
Debré 21.7.59–14.4.62; 27	5	12*	4[a]	4	1	1
Pompidou I 14.4–28.11.62; 24	1	15*	2	5	1	
Pompidou II 28.11.62–8.1.66; 22		18*	3		1	
Pompidou III 8.1.66–1.4.67; 17	1	13*	1		2	
Pompidou IV 6.4.67–10.7.68; 23		21*	2			
Couve de Murville 10.7.68–20.6.69; 19		16*	3			
Chaban-Delmas 20.6.69–5.7.72; 23		15*	5	3[b]		
Messmer I 5.7.72–28.3.73; 19		14*	2	3[b]		
Messmer II 2.4.73–27.2.74; 23	2	13*	6	2[b]		
Messmer III 27.2–27.5.74; 16	1	10*	4	1[b]		
Chirac I 27.5.74–27.8.76; 17	3	5*	5	4		
Barre I 25.8.76–29.3.77; 18	5*	5	4	4[c]		
Barre II 29.3.77–3.4.78; 15	5*[d]	4	3	3[c]		
Barre III 3.4.78–21.5.81; 24	5[d]	7	12*			

a: includes one IOM
b: PDM centrists (mainly christian democrats who joined majority with Duhamel and some radicals)
c: centrists including CDS and radicals ; joined up as UDF as of 1978
d: many of these were Giscardian fellow-travellers of the UDF

Source: Avril et al. (1989).

Duhamel took his followers (twelve deputies of the forty-one in the group) into Pompidou's majority after the 1969 presidential election. Lecanuet took the rest to Giscard in 1974, thus completing the process of bipolarisation. The old centrist parties continued to exist, but in truncated and modified form.

Gaullism was responsible for this process both by the institutional changes it imposed and by the way it then competed within these new structures. Such competitive pressure also caused the next stage of decline of the centre, viz: the creation of the UDF in February 1978 (Hanley, 1999b). Having become president by default (Pompidou died suddenly and gaullism had no obvious successor groomed), Giscard had difficulty in passing legislation through the lower house, where a big part of his majority was the obstructive gaullist party, now revamped aggressively as the RPR by Chirac after falling out with Giscard in 1976 (Offerlé, 1984). For the 1978 legislative contest, Giscard clearly needed to cut down the RPR, and the best way to do this was to have his own party. However, the weak RI, even revamped as the PR, was still a pathetic tool, a visible scion of the old independents; hence Giscard's co-optation of the christian democrats of the CDS, radicals and some dissident anti-communist ex-socialists into the UDF. The UDF has arguably never been a party worthy of the name 'party', rather a federation of mini-parties of quite different traditions, stitched together minimally as an electoral alliance and then as a parliamentary group; it owes everything to the force of institutional gravity. To put it more bluntly, it fights the left but fears the RPR at least as much. We have shown (Hanley, 1999b) how the UDF has never punched its weight, always accepting second place in terms of winnable seats, places in government and presidential candidacies. The second place has often been comfortable, but UDF is still visibly second to the RPR. This inferiority is due essentially to the fact that UDF has never developed any organic unity. Its component parts think of themselves in terms of their original identities. The fact that Madelin was easily able to pull the PR (now renamed DL) out of the UDF to conclude a (very ill-advised) electoral deal with the RPR for the 1999 euroelections is eloquent proof of this. In that sense, Giscard's original gamble of changing the *rapports de force* on the right has failed, but in systemic terms, this move (dictated solely by the pressure of gaullism) has further diminished the autonomy of the old centrist parties, forcing them to live in a common tent with the remains of the moderate right, and thus ruling out any of the old Third-Force type openings to the left.

Overall then, the rise of gaullism, making full use of the electoral systems it had put in place, has squeezed down the old moderates and forced the remains of the centre into an untidy cohabitation; on the right side of the political spectrum RPR remains hegemonic. The presence of such a large, well-structured force in a position of dominance on the right and exercising huge influence on the centre is one of the clearest breaks with pre-1958 systems.[7]

7. A succinct analysis of gaullism which deserves wider attention than it has had is CERES, 1976. It links the political streamlining carried out by gaullism to the need to modernise the French economy and open it outwards. Thus (p. 12), 'this coming together of a man, a policy and underlying trends within the French economy explain the strengths but also the weaknesses of gaullism'.

Table 7.2b Party Composition of Fifth Republic Governments since 1981
Full ministers only

	Non-party	RPR	UDF	PS	Left Rad.	PCF	Green
Mauroy I 21.5–22.6.81; 31	1			28*	2		
Mauroy II 22.6.81–22.3.83; 35	1			29*	1	4	
Mauroy III 22.3.83–17.7.84; 23				19*	1	3	
Fabius 17.7.84–19.3.86; 23	2			19*	1(+1 PSU)		
Chirac II 20.3.86–12.5.88; 29	2	14*	13				
Rocard 12.5.88–14.5.91; 20	6[a]			14*			
Cresson 15.5.91–1.4.92; 20	3			16*			1[b]
Bérégovoy 2.4.92–28.3.93; 27	7			18*	2		
Balladur 29.3.93–17.5.95; 30	1	14*	15[c]				
Juppé I 18.5-6.11.95; 29	1	16*	12[d]				
Juppé II 7.11.95–3.6.97; 28	1	16*	11[e]				
Jospin I 4.6.97–27.3.2000; 17				12*	1	2	1[f](+1 MDC)
Jospin II 27.3.2000; 21				16*	1	2	1[f](+1 MDC)

a: includes centrists like Durafour and Pelletier, signed up on an individual basis
b: Brice Lalonde of Génération Ecologie
c: of which 7 PR, 5 CDS, 1 rad and 2 UDF direct
d: of which 5 PR, 5CDS, 1 rad and 1 UDF direct
e: of which 3 PR, 4 CDS, 1 rad and 3 UDF direct
f: Dominique Voynet of Les Verts

Source: Avril et al. (1989); *European Journal of Political Research*, vols. 22, 24, 26, 30, 34.

The left-hand side of the political spectrum has seen similar turbulence, and again, the major cause of such turbulence was one party in particular, this time the PS. Its rise to a dominant position on the left was, however, a long and hesitant process. Mollet's SFIO soon went into oppposition against gaullism, stressing such policy areas as Europe, nuclear disarmament and the general drift of socio-economic policy, particularly education, where gaulllist willingness to finance catholic schools on a pragmatic basis (the Debré laws of 1959) fed the old republican reflexes of the socialist faithful. Socialist opposition to gaullism coexisted, however, with an equal mistrust of the PCF, which extended to the refusal of any collaboration for elections. As a result, gaullism had an easier time than it should have, being confronted not by a united opposition, but by a scattered group of parties, several of whom might run a candidate in the second ballot and simply divide the anti-gaullist vote. This situation could not last, if only for reasons of self-preservation, hence, even in the 1962 contest, there were a number of ad hoc désistements between the two main left parties. This raised the question of whether such arrangements should not be made more permanent, irrespective of the ideological differences between the left parties. The underlying logic of bipolarisation was becoming clearer. Either the two left parties combined systematically for electoral purposes (but electoral success surely involved the possibility of governing together, in which case a broad programmatic understanding would be necessary sooner rather than later); or else gaullism and its allies would continue to win by default in the absence of any credible alternative.

Socialist fear of the PCF still proved strong enough to delay acceptance of this logic for some time, however. The mid-1960s were spent searching for a non-gaullist alternative, which would somehow shut out the PCF – a concept spoilt only by the fact that it was numerically impossible to realise, given that the PCF still pulled a good twenty percent of the vote. Thus, the SFIO, radicals and some of the republican clubs, which were essentially refuges for ex-socialists and left sympathisers (Mossuz-Lavau, 1970; Loschak, 1971) invested in the electoral alliance known as the FGDS until 1968 (Simmons, 1970). It proved moderately successful in the 1967 poll, and there was even a sort of shadow cabinet to support the leader Mitterrand, but it was a shallow structure, which fell apart under recriminations after the events of May 1968 and the failure of the parliamentary left to extract anything other than electoral humiliation and the revelation of its general irrelevance to the France of the 1960s. Even FGDS had represented a reduced ambition. The original hope had been to federate the MRP and possibly even some of the moderates around the left pole which eventually emerged as the FGDS. This type of alliance-building centred around the failed campaign of 'Mr X' (Gaston Defferre) to spearhead a centre-left presidential bid in 1965. The moderates and MRP still felt that his campaign was too socialist, and he eventually withdrew and left the field to Mitterrand, whose campaign targeted more traditional left-leaning loyalties. MRP and some of the moderates then attempted to play the card of 'opposition centrism', but despite the false dawn of Lecanuet's

15.6 percent in the 1965 presidential poll (a figure artificially swollen by many far right voters angry with De Gaulle for abandoning Algeria, but unwilling to vote for a *laïc*), the centre was never able to expand beyond narrow limits. Eventually its leaders accepted their fate as members of the right block.

Shorn of the centre's support and unable to build any credible alliance via FGDS, which had been shown to be utterly irrelevant during 1968 (L. Bell, 1989), SFIO had one more humiliation to endure. This was the mere five per-cent scored by Defferre in the 1969 presidential election. The shock proved terminal in that the party was forced to begin a rebuilding process culminat-ing at the Epinay congress of 1971, during which time it became the PS. Given the depth of the hole into which the socialist party had fallen, the process of its rebuilding was swift. The ageing anti-communist generation of Mollet was effectively sidelined; new blood was recruited into the party, particularly from the quite numerous clubs and groups now functioning in the space of the 'non-communist left'. Mitterrand, a national figure who had taken De Gaulle to a second ballot in the 1965 contest, became leader. The team which ran the new party included most of the incomers, the Marseille federation of Defferre and crucially the CERES, a neo-marxist grouping staffed by young *énarques* and dedicated to party renewal (Hanley, 1986). These allies won con-trol of the 'new' party on the understanding that there was to be a clear elec-toral and programmatic deal with the PCF. This duly ensued with the signing of the Common Programme of Government in 1972 (Poperen, 1975; Johnson, 1981; Nugent and Lowe, 1982). By the 1973, elections the new allies clearly offered a viable challenge, each taking over twenty percent of the vote.In a brief time, the dynamics of the party system had been transformed from com-fortable dominance by gaullism to a situation of genuine competition.

This balance between right and left would only be temporary, as 1981 saw a major displacement of forces within the left. Mitterrand's presidential win was followed by a PS victory in the legislative elections that was gained as much at the expense of the PCF as of the right. The communist vote shrank to 16.1 percent (a loss of 4.6 percent) and would only decline further, slipping below the ten percent threshold in the mid-1980s to stabilise at roughly seven percent at the onset of the millennium. We have argued that from 1981 it makes more sense to see the PS as the new dominant party within the system, certainly until 1993, when a more plural system set in.

Such a change tells us much about the capacity of party to adjust to new sit-uations. The rise of the PS certainly owes much to the failings of the PCF (see below), but it is also a remarkable example of how political entrepreneurs can identify a new market – and win it – by doing a 'makeover' of a product which was near terminal exhaustion. The SFIO of 1969 had been out of office for a good decade; it had an obsolete doctrine of crude class antagonism couched in the vulgar marxist language of 1900, even down to its anti-cleri-

---

8. For an evocative impression of the decrepitude of SFIO in the sixties the CERES polemic of Chevènement and Motchane (Mandrin, 1969) still repays reading.

calism; its members were increasingly ageing public sector officials, often teachers; its vote was slipping away rapidly and its major asset was probably its grip on a number of town halls like Lille or Marseille.[8] Yet, within a dozen years this, party could plausibly be seen as dominating the party system.

What happened was that a part of the leadership (those who sponsored the winning coalition of motions at Epinay) recognised that the electorate had changed as well as the institutions. Their revamped party would address both. The programmes of the new PS would target the new middle classes born of economic modernisation (skilled white-collar workers, middle management, public sector professionals) rather than the manual workers at whom SFIO discourse had mainly been aimed.[9] A key part of this was the development of the discourse of *autogestion* (Brown, 1982) which stressed political participation in decision making at every level; the decentralisation put through after 1982 is very much in line with this thinking. While offering numerous chances for increased participation to educated and articulate groups, the PS also distinguished its offering from the socialism of the PCF which, for all brave talk of a 'French socialism' still seemed uncritically close to the soviet model in the eyes of many potential left voters. PS discourse was nourished by lively internal debate within the party, where its long tradition of organised factionalism came into its own. In particular, the exchanges between the Rocardian current, bringing many new left ideas of grassroots participation and an emphasis on the importance of civil society (Evin, 1979; Rocard, 1972) as opposed to state-led types of social transformation, and those of the CERES, which vulgarised a succinct and bold neo-marxist analysis of contemporary capitalism (Hanley, 1986: 60–121), which produced a creative tension and feeling of excitement among the activists of the 1970s. One crucial factor was the effective downplaying of anti-clerical themes. In this way, catholic activists from the CFDT trade union and the remains of christian democrat movements were encouraged to enter the party. By the 1980s, the PS was able to win seats in previous 'mission lands' like Brittany or Alsace. Such a reversal of the classic ideD logy was not always to the taste of older militants, any more than was the other major policy reversal of abandoning unilateral nuclear disarmament in 1977. Pushed through by Mitterrrand (Buffotot, 1998: 342–74), who was aware of the popularity of gaullian deterrence, perceived as highly cost-effective by a majority of voters, the lifting of this taboo removed a further obstacle to the left's winning office.

Sweeping changes to doctrine were made to accommodate new social demands. Institutional reality was recognised by the ready acceptance of an electoral deal with the PCF and a joint manifesto which nowadays would be considered extreme for its advocacy of economic planning and extensive nationalisations as macro-economic tools. To be sure, the PS watered down the PCF's demands in repeated negotiations, even to the point of provoking a rupture in 1977 that cost the left the 1978 legislative elections (beneficially

9. Portelli (1980: 119–41) sees the PS unambiguously as the party of the new salaried middle classes. For a less convincing attempt to see it as still a workers' party (based mainly on the social origins of its élites), see Kergoat (1983: 269–87).

as it turned out in hindsight; by 1981 the cracks in the giscardian edifice were much more visible to voters in an increasingly sour international economic climate). At the same time, the PS left enough of classical socialist ideology in its manifestos to appeal to the still considerable part of left voters, many of them PCF, who believed in statism. 1981 was not 2000, and voters were only at the beginning of a steep learning curve.

The biggest recognition of institutional realities was, however, the hiring of Mitterrand as leader of the new party. In a gambit more familiar to systems such as those of Israel or Canada, a new figure with a national reputation, won entirely outside SFIO, was enthroned as a presidential standard bearer. He would run the party very much on his own lines, while paying notional attention to its traditional democratic mechanisms. He usually got his own way, because it was realised that he alone was a potential national winner.

It is hard to argue with the success of such boldness. By the mid-1970s, the PS was forging ahead of its communist partner, justifying Mitterrand's gamble that a reformed PS would always have the preference of voters over a stalinist PCF. On the second ballot it was winning a hundred percent of the transfers from PCF first-round voters, but when it was a communist who made it to the second ballot, only two-thirds of socialist voters reciprocated. Clearly there was a glass ceiling to PCF support, and the PS pulled this ceiling ever lower. It was the main beneficiary of the heavy municipal wins of 1977 by joint left lists, and by 1981, although the PCF had tried to escape from the alliance, its voters would not allow it to. Thus, at least a quarter of PCF votes disappeared overnight to Mitterrand on the first ballot, never to return. By now, voters knew that to put the right out they had to *voter utile* (vote tactically); but utility meant credibilty, which meant the PS.

The argument is, then, that ruthless and swift adaptation by party élites to changed circumstances paid off handsomely (and quickly) in electoral terms. Experience in office confirms this view further. The saga of the Mitterrand experience is far too well known to be repeated here (Favier and Martin-Roland, 1995–7; Machin and Wright, 1985). Suffice it to say that a serious attempt to carry out the keynesian and dirigiste policies of the joint manifesto was made, but as balance of payments, currency and debt problems loomed, course was changed with succinct brutality from 1983 onwards. Since then, the PS has stood for an increasingly market-driven, neo-liberal agenda, not always admitted in its official texts (Ladrech and Marlière, 1999), in which deregulation and privatisation have begun to figure more prominently (which is not to say that it has totally abandoned any socialist references). Central to this agenda is a will to anchor France firmly in Europe with acceptance of the single currency and commensurate economic discipline. This is a long way from the joint manifesto or any PS texts of the 1970s, which were far more ambitious in terms of social transformation; the 1972 programme was blithely entitled Changer la Vie. However, it has been successful in that the PS almost escaped defeat in 1986 and has, with the brief aberration of 1993–97, been the dominant party. Clearly, it has read the evolution of opinion better than its rivals and adjusted strongly when necessary. Some explanation is needed for this ability to remain one step ahead of the game, as it were.

Opportunities Sized and Chances Missed

One obvious starting point is the quality of leadership. Mitterrand's adroitness is usually cited in this context (Cole, 1994). He was sharp enough to see that a deal with the PCF would not necessarily redound to its advantage. On the contary, as he told a meeeting of the Socialist International soon after signing the deal, three million communist voters out of five million could be persuaded to vote socialist. The key to such a development was first to set a up a credible left alternative to gaullism. In the short term this could only be a PCF/PS deal based on equality (or even real PCF predominance), but in the medium to long term, the *rapports de force* would switch in favour of the PS, both because of the intrinsic limitations of the PCF (there really was a glass ceiling) and because the PS was better able to identify changing electoral markets and appeal to them. In this sense then, Perrineau's view of Mitterrand as the gravedigger of the PCF is apt.

Mitterrand was, however, only one factor of socialist leadership. His own majority faction in the party was increasingly staffed with high quality politicians, many of them *énarques*; so were the rival Rocard and CERES groups. These talented young politicians might have had an easier entry into politics if they had gone with the gaullist movement, like Rocard's contemporary at ENA, Jacques Chirac, but through a mixture of social origins and political conviction they had soldiered on in the wilderness of the old SFIO or in the uncharted spaces of the 'second left' – the CFDT and other social movements, often christian in character, which sought to find a space between the socialist party and the PCF before rallying to the new party after 1971 (Hamon and Rotman, 1982).[10] As the new formation proved viable, there was a rush of young talent to join it, with the appearance of promising leaders such as Fabius or Jospin. By the late 1970s, the PS was seen as the party of the future and the place to make a career; the gaullist party now seemed less attractive to those seeking positions within the political élite. Leadership was extremely important. Under Mitterrand's aegis, the new party was fleshed out with highly competent leadership teams, able to appear as a plausible alternative government, present different and attractive programmes and argue articulately with gaullism.

Leadership renewal also took place at sub-national levels of the party. If national bodies, both official and factional, were dominated by *énarques*, the leadership at federal and city level changed too. Increasingly, the old primary school teacher would be replaced by a graduate professional, often from the public sector, who would be the party's public face and eternal can-

10. The Rocard current actually joined in 1974, after Mitterrand's near miss in the presidential election.

didate at local level. More women appeared, though still at a disappointingly low level. The party was like a series of concentric circles. The national élite were high-ranking énarques or professionals; federal leaders were probably graduates, but of middling rank, and local leaderships might be slightly less well qualified; working class members would tend to occupy fairly low functions and be less and less numerous in any case (Portelli, 1980: 119 -30).[11] One would doubtless have to count the PS as a mass party, though at its peak it probably never had more than 200,000 real members.[12] However, it certainly became a catch-all party in terms of voters. By 1981, its electorate could show the broad coverage of the social map that gaullism had achieved in the 1960s (Ysmal, 1989: 243–8). Such a performance is the best evidence that its leaders had, indeed, diagnosed social demand better than their rivals.

The recruitment of a national leader and powerful support enabled the new party to carry out the ideoogical and strategic renewal necessary for it to make a comeback. Once this process was underway, further talent, members and voters were attracted in a kind of virtuous spiral, but to concentrate exclusively on the internal dynamics of PS success would be to forget a key extrinsic factor, the performance of its rivals, especially the PCF.

The decline of the PCF has been obvious in recent years (Ranger, 1986). The loss of a good two-thirds of its regular vote, the shrinking of its parliamentary group to the bare minimum, falling membership rolls, the weakening of the link with the CGT labour movement and an increasing difficulty in hanging on to the last major asset, the local government heartlands, all bear testimony to the probably terminal decline of a once-great party. Our account has stressed the active rôle of PS strategy in the PCF's decline. It would also be tempting to adduce the collapse of the USSR and the Soviet model generally after 1989, except that the party's decline was well under way before then; the collapse of the Berlin Wall was more a symptom than a cause. The ultimate causes of the PCF's decay are to be found within the party itself.

When the PCF embarked on the joint programme in 1972, it could reasonably have expected to be the main beneficiary of an admittedly conflictual partnership; it was far ahead of the socialists in terms of votes, members and general infrastructure and resources. The PS was probably envisaged as the figleaf which would enable the PCF to become once more a government contender, but to the PCF mindset, no further adaptations beyond the alliance tactic were necessary. In other words, a majority of voters could be won over to an analysis of French society which postulated the dominance of a few financial groups and their political representatives, in accordance with the theory of State Monopoly Capitalism (stamocap) that adorned the party textbooks of this period. All other sectors of society were deemed to be oppressed

11. From about 1978, the party has been coy about giving a sociological breakdown of membership, precisely to avoid being seen as a party of the educated middle classes (Hardouin, 1978).

12. French parties, generally, have never compared well with those of other European states, particulary in Northern Europe. It is surely no accident that the country missing from Katz and Mair's survey (1992) is France.

by this dominance, and could only rally behind the sole pole of resistance to capital, namely the working class and 'the party which it has given itself', the PCF. Peasants, the old petty- bourgeoisie and the 'intermediate layers' (this old Gambetta-like term did not even grant them the status of a middle class) should have no difficulty in falling in behind working-class leadership. Electoral victory by the representatives of the exploited would then usher in a phase of 'advanced democracy' based on public ownership and economic planning . Little else was known of the contours of such a society, save that the party was always careful to deny that it would be like the soviet model. Such were the assumptions on which the PCF based its activity until quite recently. A brief flirtation with the ill-defined concept of eurocommunism in the mid 1970s, which, whatever else it may have meant, clearly involved greater readiness to criticise the Soviet model, was brought to a crashing halt in 1979, when Marchais proclaimed support for the soviet move into Afghanistan and awarded the USSR 'postive marks on the whole'.[13]

Such a take-it-or-leave-it offering was likely to be of limited appeal to an electorate growing in sociological diversity as well as in general political competence thanks to better education. Indeed, it makes more sense to ask why this type of offer had been electorally successful for so long. Following Lavau (1981), theorists have stressed the tribune or protest function of the party; voting PCF was a way of venting political anger, even if there were few direct results to be had from it. Thus, the party arguably played a stabilising rôle in the political system. Kriegel (1968) saw the problem in more anthropological terms: the PCF was a counter-community with its shared values and hopes (all hanging on rejection of the present capitalism) into which the disadvantaged came in from the cold. Whatever the explanation, by the 1970s the PCF's recipes were proving of limited attraction to newer social groups. They retained their appeal in areas of heavy industry with a real proletariat and several generations of militant anti-capitalist culture, and in the party's rural bastions with their old republican cultures, but such areas were more of the past than the future. The economic future belonged to the skilled white collars and other intermediary groups; unlike the PS, the PCF had nothing to say to these. Its discourse remained predicated on the skilled, male manual worker, unionised and quite likely to be in the public sector; the miner and the railwayman were typical communist icons.

It could not be otherwise, given the structure of the PCF. Ever since it was 'bolshevised' in the 1920s, it had retained tight control over its leadership selection. The mechanics of 'democratic centralism' meant that the leading élite controlled access to every position of responsibility below it in the hierarchy, down, ultimately, to branch level. This élite made sure that only people like itself rose within the hierarchy. Sociologically, such cadres tended to be ex-skilled workers (they usually became full time bureaucrats on reaching the federal or departmental level). Ideologically, they were fiercely loyal to the party line and generally very pro-soviet (many would have gone to party

13. 'bilan globalement positif'.

schools in the USSR). Their loyalty to the party could only be reinforced by the awareness that, after years as a *permanent*, they were probably unemployable elsewhere. Thus, the party hierarchy tended to be self-reproducing and well entrenched against criticism, and it was easy to lever out dissenters at lower levels before their dissidence got up a head of steam, thanks in particularl to devices such as the banning of factions and the insistence on vertical, as opposed to sideways, communication.

Such an apparatus could be very effective at embracing incomers within a counter-community or even at mobilising them in protest. Where it had difficulty was in reading signs of change within society and within the electorate. Thus, reformers in the party who wanted it to address the new middle classes, or who worried that its reluctance to analyse the soviet model properly would limit its appeal, were ousted as disloyal; the PCF apparatus was very good at shooting the messenger. Thus, as voters' demands evolved beyond mere protest and a semi-plausible left alternative at last began to appear in the shape of the PS, there was a relatively sudden exodus from the PCF.

In truth, the party has been trying to digest this ever since 1981. Its attitude to the PS typifies its dilemma. It accepted posts in the 1981 government, only to walk out in 1984, far too late; by this time it was bound to share the blame with the PS for the disappointments felt by voters. From then until 1997, it remained in half oppposition when the PS was in office, always allying with it at election time, sometimes criticising it, but never daring to bring it down (as it might have done in Rocard's premiership). At the same time, it has slowly begun to question its own iron structures; democratic cenralism has now gone, factions are tolerated, even deputies do not always toe the line in votes. However, the party remains uncertain as to what it is. It was a leninist party, built for a scenario which never happened, viz. a 1917-type coup in France. Latterly it has lost much of its leninist character but cannot simply become a social-democratic party (not least because there is a perfectly viable one already). It lives on its remaining electoral and municipal capital, eyeing the future anxiously.

We will return to the PCF in our conclusion, but in systemic terms it seems clear that there has been a permanent shift in the balance of the left block. This clearly owes something to international circumstances and also to the adroitness of the PS entrepreneurs, but the major factor is surely the inertia and mistakes of the PCF. The Italian example shows that old communist parties do not have to become slowly decaying rumps, but to avoid such a fate they need a capacity for social analysis, political invention and an ability to communicate their new ideas ; a capacity which clearly was not present in the PCF.

The Death of the Centre?

Bipolarisation firmed up the left and right blocs, while also allowing for powerful distortions within both. Its cruellest effect was, however, on the centre.

We saw that, before 1958, radicalism and christian democracy were pivotal parties in the Third Force and its successors. Both groups have undergone severe decline, especially the former. In some ways it might be argued that radicalism did well to hang on to around a tenth of the popular vote after 1945. The active elements of its programme had long since been prosecuted, and it remained only as a conservative force catering for parts of provincial France where republican roots ran deep. The party shared the gradual move of the mainstream parties of the Fourth Republic into outright opposition to De Gaulle, but its situation was aggravated by the weight of the Algerian interest within its ranks. Leaders like Morice and Marie engineered a debilitating split in 1956, ruining the attempts of Mendès-France to recast radicalism as a force of economic and social modernisation. Part of the defeated *cartel des non* in 1962, radicalism has been searching for a bolt-hole ever since. It invested in the FGDS after 1965; but when this replay of the old *cartel des gauches* failed in 1968, the party moved into a loose partnership with Lecanuet's christian democrats known as *les réformateurs*. With the entry into the party of J. – J. Servan Schreiber, the millionaire publisher, hopes were raised that the revamped party could still find a space between the fast-reviving socialists and the right. The radicals' anti-communism stopped them from joining the 1972 left union, but if left unity could be refused, the logic of bipolarisation could not. Increasingly, the few radical deputies found themselves wondering where their second-ballot votes would come from. In most seats it was from the left, but in others it was the right, as had been the case even before 1939. The presidential election of 1974 gave organisational substance to this existential dilemma, when the party split. The MRG of Robert Fabre joined the left unity pact, while the remaining radicals sided with Giscard, later entering the UDF.

So it has remained to this day, despite periodic talks of unifying the radical family. With few seats (all of them owed to election deals with either right or left) and a minute percentage of the vote, radicalism survives in the form of two rumps as an artificial vestige, kept alive solely by bigger parties for reasons of local tactical advantage that are not always clear.[14] The fact that a radical party (or even two of them) continue to exist, may be seen as proof of the freezing thesis of Lipset and Rokkan ; but if so, the freezing owes as much to the tactics of neighbouring parties as to any ineradicable behaviour patterns of voters.

The small size of radicalism and its visible obsolescence may be felt to make it an irrelevance in terms of the party system. This would be harder to argue of christian democracy, however, if only because it remains a vibrant and electorally succesful party across the EU and outside. The MRP of 1958 had a distinct electorate, geographically and sociologically, as well as standing for a recognisable set of policies. Yet, it has also struggled to avoid mar-

---

14. The influence of the Baylet family and its Dépêche de Toulouse newspaper in the South-West would be one good example, however. J.- M. Baylet is president of the PRG, as the old MRG is now called.

ginalisation. Its falling out with De Gaulle left it vulnerable to the loss of voters to gaullism. Later on, its avatars would face a similar squeeze on their more reform-minded supporters from the new-look PS. The christian-democrats tried longer than anyone to fill a centre space in an increasingly bipolar world, but have used ambiguous tactics to do so. Lecanuet's 1965 campaign, followed by the setting up of the CD, attempted to offer a refomist type of policy, sounding not dissimilar to 1960s Labour (Hanley, 1991), but the CD deliberately downplayed any references to christian values, in an attempt to spread its audience beyond its hard-core catholic vote and bring in radical or SFIO sympathisers. Although the 'opposition centrists' (mainly CD) did quite well in 1967, they, too, were decimated by the gaullist landslide of 1968, confirming the difficulties of working the centrist space. Some of the former radicals or UDSR, like Pleven and Duhamel, joined Pompidou's majority as early as 1969. Lecanuet's followers made one more attempt to build a centre with the *réformateurs* experiment, but eventually gave way to the force of political gravity in 1974 and backed Giscard in return for cabinet posts.

This painless drift into the embrace of the right was not (nor is it today) to the taste of many christian-democrat activists. Thus, the 1970s saw an attempt to stiffen the christian-democrat identity within the 'centre'. In 1976 the movement was rebaptised the CDS. When it became part of UDF in 1978, it still strove to keep a separate identity, and commentators spoke of the possibility of its leaving UDF and moving back to a deal with the socialists as in old Third Force days (such practices had continued at municipal level till 1977 in venues as important as Marseille, Nantes and Nancy). The guarantee of a number of seats thanks to second ballot deals with the right proved a powerful deterrent to any such impulses, however. Nor did the rising PS, confident of its pact with the PCF, feel much need for other alliances.

Only with the waning of PS dominance after 1986, and the emergence of a Rocard government in 1988 without a real majority, did the scenario of leaving UDF come to the fore again. Despite Mitterrand's talk of *ouverture*, no formal pact was made between the left and the CDS, which did, however, form its own parliamentary group for the 1988–93 legislature.[15] A number of known christian democrats, like Rausch or Théo Braun, joined cabinets as individuals, but there was no partisan basis to this, and CDS as a party stuck with the right. The 1993 elections provided a generous if short-term reward for this tactic, as prime minister Balladur gave the CDS a share of ministries some way above the normal tarrif in return for its support for his 1995 tilt at the presidency.

Since then, under the leadership of Bayrou, CDS implantation within the right has increased. Bayrou incorporated the last remains of the anti-left-unity SFIO (such as André Santini), who had joined UDF in 1978, into his

15. There was also an independent CDS list for the euroelections of 1989, put up under pressure from the grassroots and without great enthusiasm from leaders. Significantly it was led by Simone Weil, not a christian, presumably as a signal that it was intended to reach beyond the classic former MRP electorate. It still took over 8%, confirming the existence of a bedrock of christian democrat support in the traditional heartlands of East and West, and south of the Massif Central.

party which now became FD. This recruitment from the opposite pole of politics (republican and masonic) is reminiscent of Lecanuet's attempts, in 1965, to broaden his appeal, as are FD references to laïcité and the party's increasing reverence for liberal economics (long mistrusted by mainstream christian democracy and the personalist thinkers who inspired CDS). So far, it is hard to see whether these addenda amount to much. Bayrou is obviously anxious to create a presidential vehicle for 2002, when UDF might at last produce a runner from within its own ranks, which it has not managed to do since Giscard. On the face of it, such a party has to be broadly based, but by running down the christian identity at the core of this particular party and trying to make an amorphous catch-all party, he is more likely to throw the baby out with the bathwater. Whatever the outcome, the vicisstudes of the grandchildren of MRP demonstrate the difficulty of keeping alive a distinct species of party within a highly constraining, bipolarised institutional environment.

Both of the main centrist parties have had to evolve in subordination to electoral logic. A PR system would have allowed them to stand their candidates everywhere, with a distinct programme and take whatever percentage of the seats voters chose to give them. After that, open-ended negotiations about coalitions might begin on the basis of acquired strength, not hypothetical claim and counter-claim about how much party x or y is 'really worth on the ground'. The Fifth Republic system forces the centre groups to conclude their deals in advance, which means bargaining a certain number of seats and in return accepting parts of a broad programme that might not normallly be endorsed wholeheartedly. If the (right-wing) alliance wins, cabinet seats may well be shared out proportionally, but those proportions will have been determined by bargaining in the first place.[16] It is an altogether more constraining world than that which existed before 1958.

Conclusion: The Fifth Republic and the Parties – Half a Success?

This chapter has tried to identify the fundamental shifts in the party system that have taken place under the mature Fifth Republic. The founders aimed to cut back party influence, and to some extent they succeeded, although not perhaps in the way they hoped. Certainly, party as a form of political linkage has remained essential; charisma had its place early on, but once it became routinised, party inevitably came back to centre stage.

The electoral and institutional changes have put great pressure on party, but parties have simply found ways of adjusting to these. If, on the one hand,

16. Members of an alliance can, in fact, receive more than their fair share, as is shown by Balladur's generosity to UDF in general and CDS in particular (Hanley, 1999b), but this has more to do with roping the christian-democrats into Balladur's 1995 presidential bid than with any desire to practice fairness.

the normal style of government is presidential, then parties have to find themselves a potential winner of a national contest and work behind him. If, on the other hand, *cohabitation* sets in, party becomes more important than ever: only a disciplined coalition led by a dominant party will be strong enough to govern in the teeth of presidential obstruction and the Sword of Damocles represented by the possibility of dissolving the chamber. *Cohabitation* can be seen as a rehearsal for 'normal' presidential rule, and during such periods, the premier/leader of the biggest majority party is, in effect, preparing a presidential bid for the next election. Whether France is under straight presidential government or *cohabitation*, however, party remains crucial.

Even the constraints placed on deputies can be turned to the advantage of party. Once a party leader is in power with a programme to carry out, he can use all the devices put in place to overrule obstruction. The beauty of such devices is that they can be used as much against one's own side as against the opposition. Provided party discipline holds, the head of government is as powerful as his Westminster equivalent.

The mature Fifth Republic presents great opportunities for parties, but only if they know how to adapt. This means being fairly well disciplined and cohesive, having a clear leader and programme and being able to reach across a wide sector of the electorate in order to gain critical mass. For it is obvious that only parties of a certain size can really make use of the opportunities sketched out above. Perhaps the biggest contribution of the Fifth Republic to the party system has been to bring out the importance of size. The gaullian legacy in fact offers huge opportunities to parties, but only if they know how to become big enough to seize them.

Our analysis suggests that two such parties, the gaullists and the PS, have fully mastered these requirements. Each in turn reached a critical mass, spread its influence widely and was clearly the leader and motor of any coalitions in which it took part, and each seemed to be a natural party of government for its epoch, carrying out a number of historically necessary changes.[17] These two success stories show that party remains essential. The failures of the communists, and to a lesser extent the UDF and its components, support this theory. Here were parties who did not know how to adapt to the new circumstances and as a result lost out. The loss was arguably less serious for the UDF, but it was no less real for that. What might this party have achieved had it managed to attain a real organic unity comparable to that of the gaullists?

Party remains as crucial as it has ever been at the onset of the milennium. It remains to examine the state of the party system today, with a view to future developments, and then to synthesise the long-term evolution of the system as we have followed it across more than a century.

17. Pierce (1992) links the growth of clear partisan identities (as opposed to vaguely left or right feelings) to the success of the gaullist and socialist parties in standing above others in their camp. They gave partisan expression to institutional tinkering which was aimed, above all, at clarifying and simplifying electoral choice.

8

PARTY AND SOCIETY
A Politics of Partial Accomodation?

⁊ᴥ

> Parties continue to provide essential organisation, expertise, financial resources and signifying labels. They still «structure the vote», and we are not yet ready to abandon them.
>
> Lawson and Ysmal, Do The Parties Matter ?

In this chapter we examine the system as it stands presently and assess its immediate prospects. We then essay a wider conclusion which summates the historical findings presented above.

The Party System Today

Of late, commentators have found cause for gloom when loooking at the party system. It is said to be subjected to a number of growing pressures, not all pushing in the same direction. The net result of these is felt to be increasing stress, with the possibility that the system might be becoming less able to discharge its functions. The general tenor of this book has been such that readers will be unsurprised to learn that we find such analyses unreasonably pessimistic, nevertheless, they must be considered.

Various pressures of different kinds can be distinguished, beginning with the obvious fact that, since 1981, the party system has shown sharp oscillations in terms of providing government. A socialist-communist government gave way in 1984 to a socialist team; 1986 saw an RPR/UDF governing tandem. However, 1988 saw the second presidential win by Mitterrand, which ushered in a series of socialist governments until the left was trounced in the 1993 legislative elections. The RPR/UDF ruled till 1997, fortified by Chirac's presidential win in 1995, until an early dissolution let in the left again, but

---

1. The plural left also includes the remains of left radicalism, nowadays called the PRS under J. – M. Baylet and the MDC of Chevènement, operating as an independent mini-party outside the PS. Both small groups received a handful of safe seats in return for their support of the PS, and the viability of either, outside such a cosy symbiotic relationship, is questionable.

this time a 'plural left' of PS, greens and PCF, as opposed to previous combinations of the PS plus one or two 'fig-leaves'.[1] Some of these majorities were threadbare (1986, 1988). All of this suggests some dissatisfaction with party performance in government and a willingness by voters to ring the changes fairly quickly. To Anglo-Saxon analysts more used to longer spells in office for parties and less readiness by voters to change sides, such behaviour can be seen as potentially destabilising the party system.

We also know that turnout has been going down latterly, albeit slowly in most kinds of national elections. Earlier Fifth Republic turnouts could top eighty percent, and even these fell short of the incredibly high participation of prewar years; today percentages in the high sixties are more the norm. At the same time, the number of spoiled ballots is rising. Additionally, a significant number of people never register in the first place, perhaps as many as one in twelve of the notional electorate (Appleton, 2000); these tend to come disproportionately from among town-dwellers, the young, unemployed or poorly skilled. All these trends can also be seen as evidence that party is failing. One could ignore the consistently poor opinion ratings for politicians as a group (Mossuz-Lavau, 1994: 349), if only because this is a profession which has probably never commanded high respect in France in any case, but recent dips in even a modest level of popularity for career politicians cannot be seen as a sign of faith in parties.[2]

One symptom of party weakness is often adduced as a cause, the involvement in *affaires* and scandals of various sorts. Politico-financial scandals have long been part and parcel of republican politics, but often concerned individuals or cliques (e .g., Stavisky, the Panama *chequards*) rather than party machines. During the 1990s, however, a regular series of disclosures came to the fore concerning party finance. Noone was exempt. If the PCF had long attracted attention from journalists about its various business enterprises and / or its alleged clandestine handouts from the soviet communist party, all the main parties – PS, RPR, even the christian-democrats who prided themselves on ethical politics – were subject to legal pursuit at local and national level. The picture was usually depressingly similar. In order to raise funds, national (or more usually local) officials would award tenders for consultancy work to certain agencies. These would often have a shadowy existence and receive large fees for carrying out very small (and often completely irrelevant) amounts of work. Creative accounting techniques were then used to recycle this money into party funds.[3] Thus was completed a process whereby public monies paid in by taxpayers were redistributed to private organisations (parties). In some cases, individuals also appear to have done particularly well out of these operations (e.g., the wife of the RPR mayor of Paris and the PS finance minister who resigned late in 1999 on suspicion of such practices). The party finance scandals were also accom-

2. Leyrit (1997: 227) speaks of a 'general atmosphere of mistrust, if not to say suspicion, of the whole political class' revealed by polling.

3. According to some estimates, up to 1% of the annual turnover of the entire construction industry might have been finding its way into party coffers by such routes (Camby, 1995: 47).

panied by more traditional abuses, such as that of the PS development minister who appeared to have availed himself overgenerously of expenses from special funds, or the mayors of Nice and Angoulême who appear to have enjoyed themselves at taxpayers' expense before departing for exile in South America. It was undoubtedly true that the financing of parties by dummy consultancies was a long established practice, which left and right had both used happily. It was also true that the real costs of running a party (headquarters to rent, staff to pay, constant campaigns to fight) were far superior to anything that a party could generate from membership fees or even from the (little-known) area of private donations. Nevertheless, revelation of the systematic syphoning-off of public funds to fuel partisan activity was a shock, which hit party prestige hard. The passing of several laws on party finance since 1988 has gone some way towards alleviating this situation.[4]

The final blow to the party system was seen in the florescence of new parties. During the 1990s the FN has become a considerable electoral force. The greens have long suffered from internal divisions which undoubtedly stoppped them from exerting their full weight within the system, but even they had deputies elected to the European Parliament (EP) in 1989 and at one point chaired a regional council. By the late 1990s they were strong enough to conclude an alliance with the PS that brought them their first National Assembly deputies and a place in government, followed by a major performance in the 1999 EP elections, when they beat the PCF by some way. French trotskyism has also been active for a long time and was as subject to internecine fighting as its cousins in other countries.Traditionally, it could be written off as largely irelevant to wider party politics, whatever the intensity and commitment of its activists, but by 1999 an alliance of the two main families, LCR and LO, was electing regional councillors and also achieving EP representation. In short, a number of new parties seemed to be emerging as viable contenders within the national system. Political scientists might be expected to see this as proof of the vitality of the French partisan system and of its capacity for self-renewal, but often the first reaction was to fear that this rich new form of expression could only bring instability.

4. A series of laws, from 1988 to 1995, has attempted to clean up an area where total opacity was the rule (Camby, 1995: 45–67). The 1988 law recognised parties as legal personalities, entitled to receive public and private monies, subject to strict accounting. State funding is disbursed annually and comes in two tranches; the first relates to the number of votes won in National Assembly elections (parties have to field a minimum of 50 candidates), while the second is based on the number of parlementarians (in both houses) formally affiliated to the party. While the 1990 law allowed gifts from firms, this was quashed by the 1995 law, which allows only individual gifts (to a maximum of 50,000 francs per year and only by cheque). Parties can only receive monies through a designated trustee who must publish annual accounts. Generally, public money has become the predominant source of income for parties (Camby, 1995: 64), putting them well within the catgory of Katz and Mair's 'cartel parties'. There are some variations, however, with the PCF and FN, for instance, seemingly receiving greater support from members and individual donors. The use of public monies to finance parties seems to have split opinion: a 1994 poll showed 50% against, but also 41% for. Generally one can agree with Camby's view (p. 64) that these measures have brought much greater transparency into the life of parties.

There is a tendency to see the partisan system today as deeply unpopular because of the policy failures of parties, their financial misdemeanours and the apparent ease with which newcomers force their way in. In particular, commentators became highly exercised a few years ago that an ever-decreasing percentage of the vote kept going to the serious or core parties (defined as the only ones with realistic hopes of forming a government, which in practice meant the PS and the RPR/UDF tandem). By the mid-1990s, this trinity was 'only' winning less than two-thirds of the vote, with the rest going to 'protest' parties. This was felt by some analysts to bode ill for the future of party within the political system.

As with many critiques of party, such approaches underestimate the plasticity of parties as organisations and their ability to cope with pressure (Appleton, 1995).

Some of the longer-term trends are probably not good for party (if they continue), particularly the evidence on turnout, but their effects so far seem containable. Cole notes (1998: 266) a combined total of some thirty-five percent for non-voters and spoiled ballots in the 1997 poll. This puts the actual expression of the vote below the UK figure for the same year (seventy-one percent, which itself was a drop of seven percent from 1992). Yet, already in 1962 the figure for abstainers and ballot-spoilers in France was thirty-three percent, and it has hovered around this level since 1988. This suggests some disaffection on the part of voters, but not yet of criticial proportions (US presidents tend to be elected with around fifty-five percent of the poll, for instance). Furthermore, these figures include five or six percent of voters who actually turned out to vote but deliberately spoiled their ballot (a much higher proportion than in the UK). This means that voters have faith in the political process, but are serving notice of their displeasure on the range of parties currently avaliable.[5] It could be said, then, that this is a positive opportunity for party to correct its image or policies; it would be more worrying if such voters simply stayed at home. A further reassuring factor is that turnout usually increases by three to five percent on the second ballot. Some voters actually believe that the first ballot does not really count, but they will mobilise for the *tour décisif*.[6]

We should also be prepared to distinguish between readiness to be politically active (or to vote at least) and readiness to support party. The difference is confirmed by the fact that turnouts in presidential contests have usually been several percent higher than for legislative elections (as high as eighty-three percent in 1965 or 1974, and still over seventy-five in the demobilised

5. Spoiled ballots or votes blancs et nuls (a convenient expression which conflates two different types of behaviour, error and protest) have received little attention, though Brechon (1995: 15–38) and Bon and Cheylan (1988: 305–17) are helpful. This type of voting held steady for a quarter of a century before 1981 at between 1.5% and 2% of votes cast. Since then it has been more volatile, with peaks such as the 5% of the second ballot in the 1981 presidentials and 6.3% on the second ballot in 1997 (compared with 4.9% on the first).

6. Schlesinger and Schlesinger (2000) underline the rôle of the second ballot in reinforcing the hold of established parties which are able to conclude alliances, as opposed to newcomers, particularly the FN, who find this more difficult.

Table 8.1 Abstention in Postwar France (%)

Legislative Elections			Presidential Elections		
	1st ballot	2nd ballot		1st ballot	2nd ballot
1945	20.1				
June 1946	18.1				
Nov 1946	21.9				
1951	19.8				
1956	17.2				
1958	22.8	25.2			
1962	31.3	27.9	1965	15.2	15.7
1967	18.8	20.3			
1968	20	22.2	1969	22.4	31.1
1973	18.7	18.2	1974	15.8	12.7
1978	16.8	15.1			
1981	29.1	24.9	1981	18.9	14.1
1986	21.5				
1988	32.3	30.1	1988	18.6	15.9
1993	30.8	32.4	1995	24.5	26.3
1997	32	28.9			

Source: Brechon (1995); Le Monde, *Dossiers et Documents.*

climate of 1995, when the right seemed guaranteed a walkover). The nature of presidential contests is, of course, to pit the broad camps of left against right rather than one party against another. To that extent, it might be slightly easier to mobilise the extra few voters who see politics as about issues or personalities, but disconnected from the political machinery which links them all, viz. party. The overall conclusion from this disparate set of evidence about voter behaviour might be that party certainly cannot afford to be complacent, but equally, it is far from terminally ill in the voters' eyes.

Evidence other than voter turnout is sometimes adduced to support fears about the long-term unpopularity of politics and parties and the threat posed by the 'crisis of representation'. Mossuz-Lavau's surveys (1994) showed an increase in the percentage of those viewing politics as a dishonourable profession (this was when the party financial scandals were beginning to bite), but that did not imply a lack of interest by citizens in politics. On the contrary, they were better informed than ever and just as ready to identify themelves in block terms, if not in precise party terms (over ninety percent agreed to classify themselves along the left/right spectrum). There was disappointment with party performance in government, especially among left-wing supporters, and a certain scepticism about the value of alternation, perhaps because many felt that politics was increasingly powerless to affect the economy anyway. Many felt that politics did not offer them enough as individuals, and others felt they did not understand the political process and were put off voting by this. There was a general concern that full-time professional politicians were increasingly likely to be out of touch with the concerns of ordinary people. Few felt able to identify fully with the programmes of their preferred party.

Some of these traits are hardly new and others less disturbing than they might seem. If voters see politics as a dishonourable activity, it does not mean that they consider it unnecesary or that they will not carry on voting for the unfortunates who have to carry it out. Nor has it ever been necessary for supporters to identify one hundred percent with their party. It would be interesting to know the (surely minute) proportions who have ever done so. What matters is that they show sufficient identification to go and vote, preferably on a repeated basis. The seriousness of both the above criticisms of politics can only be judged by the voting behaviour of citizens, and we have seen that this has, by no means, reached disquieting proportions as yet.

The concerns about failure by party in office, the meaninglessness of alternance and the general inablity of politics to influence the economy are more worrying. They are three different aspects of the same question, namely the extent to which politics can or cannot change voters' lives. It seems clear that the capacity to effect such change is much less than it ever was, but that is a threat to party only so long as electorates continue to hold unreasonable expectations about what governments can and cannot deliver. One of the main functions of party is to influence such expectations, and it is no accident that, for a decade or more, the main effort of most mainstream parties of left or right in the developed world has been directed towards lowering voter expectations. Coded language such as the 'third way' (beloved of certain social-democratic leaders) or the calls by right-wingers for moderate, centrist, sensible and consensus-based approaches can be boiled down to a common desire to convince voters that governments and parties can deliver relatively little outside a narrow status quo. In the global economy, there can be sensible management, but not radical innovation. To that extent, France is like the rest. The loss of power by governments forces parties to rejig their messages, but it does not necessarily put them out of business.

Our conclusion, then, would be to agree with Daalder (1992) or Reiter (1993) that anxieties about the 'crisis of representation' or 'party failure' (Lawson and Merkl, 1988) are overplayed. Voters continue to vote for parties, and governments continue to be formed from them. There is never perfect satisfaction and indeed much complaint, but there is no real alternative to party, and citizens know it. So do parties, but they also know that if they are perceived as falling short, there are other parties which can take their place. There is no room for complacency.

This much is apparent from the recent movements within the party system, namely, the rise to apparent viablity of a number of formations. Latterly, the FN, greens and trotskyites have all managed to elect their candidates to either the National Assembly or the European Parliament, as well as winning seats on regional and other sub-national councils. Some would see this surge as a threat to the stability of the party system, but in our view such reactions miss the central point, viz., that the challenge to established parties is not taking place from outside the system (some 'new social movement' or charismatic populism, for instance), but from within, via competing parties. The rise of new parties is never necessarily threatening to system stability, since so much depends on both the causes of the rise of a new force and the ways in which established forces respond to it. However, since the relatively sudden rise of three contenders, all of them fairly vocal against the established parties, might be seen as cause for concern, we shall investigate the phenomenon more closely.

To take the most important first, it seems clear that the FN has profited from the failures of mainstream parties, particularly, but not exclusively, the RPR/UDF, to deliver adequately when in office. The sharp governmental alternation between PS-led majorities and the right is both symptom and cause of the Front's rise. Research has established (Mayer and Perrineau, 1992; Mayer, 1999; Birenbaum, 1992) that the FN caters, above all, for a type of voter who has some social capital (job or small firm, savings, property), but is anxious about the future. Such voters, who include an above average proportion of males, are seduced by an authoritarian discourse that blames outsiders (immigrants, European bureaucrats) for socio-economic difficulties and promises brusque remedies. Emotionally, they feel included in a polity defined exclusively as French (the more so because some of their neighbours/competitors are deliberately excluded). Of course, the FN's discourse is brutal and its policy recommendations hardly stand up to close analysis, but that is irrelevant. It has mobilised a steady ten percent since the mid-1980s and has, on occasion, come close to the fifteen percent threshold. As such it poses a major challenge to the established parties. Our purpose here is not to analyse in depth why the FN exists, and even less to speculate as to whether it is a transitional phenomenon or a symptom of *anomie* (Todd, 1988: 270), or to conclude, comfortingly, that, like the erstwhile PCF, it has a glass ceiling, and hence it is only a matter of time before it declines. We are interested in how the party system actually copes with this challenge.

It is clear that some poles of the system find it a bigger problem than others. However many one-time communist or PS voters the FN has won over (figures are not conclusive on this), its natural clientèle consists of people who either voted for the mainstream right or who could be reasonably expected to do so.[7] Therefore, the moderate left can welcome its presence in the party system, provided it stays within certain limits, simply because it is always going to take

7. Mayer (1999: 203–46) sees the FN as having two electorates. One is composed of right-wingers from bourgeois backgrounds with traditional values often close to catholicism; the other is popular (though does not necessairily have a past record of voting for the left) and votes against the political class and the political system in general. To some extent, the Mégret/Le Pen opposition mirrors this cleavage. From the point of view of the moderate right parties however, both of these types of voter should normally be capable of being won over.

more votes off the right.[8] On occasions, the FN can actually be encouraged, furtively, by the left; the locus classicus is Mitterrand's introduction of PR for the 1986 election which gave the FN over 30 deputies and almost cost the moderate right a working majority. Even the left's triumph of 1997 would have been paper-thin without the maintenance of FN candidates in many second-ballot duels, which cost the right seats (Buffotot and Hanley, 1998). Left parties could even hint that such an arrangement was to be preferred, in that it allowed some popular anger to be vented at the first ballot, before voters sobered up and voted sensibly at the second. Such disingenuous arguments need not be taken seriously, as they are simply rationalisations of a *rapport de force* within the system that happened to favour the left.

The RPR/UDF had a very different perspective in that they had to win back lost voters. It might be argued that a successful spell in office, implementing the neo-liberal and increasingly European-integrationist policy which has characterised both the right and the PS for some fifteen years, would have sufficed. Voters would see that the moderate right could succeed without needing to veer towards authoritarian and xenophobic stances. Unfortunately, government output since the 1980s has left an increasing number who perceive themselves as losers, on whom FN discourse preys. The benefits of the strong franc, single currency and single market have not yet trickled down in sufficient quantity to impress a majority of voters. Because of this, the right has felt unable to adopt a wait-and-see policy, but has, from time to time, used themes and vocabulary designed to attract FN sympathisers. The various manipulations of nationality law are one obvious symbol, as are throwaway remarks by certain leaders about FN and moderate right voters sharing common values. Officially, the line has been that the moderate right should have no truck with racism and authoritarianism, but the odd nod and wink, especially at local level, showed that the right was ready to harden its line a little in the hope of winning back converts.

This mix may be said to have worked in that the right won in 1993 and 1995, despite a good FN showing. However, the 1997 result raised the question of whether a deal with the FN at some levels might be necessary. Hints and gestures have their uses, but if the FN was likely to prove strong enough to stop the right from winning clear majorities in the future, then perhaps strategy needed rethinking. The 1998 regional elections raised the dilemma cruelly when, in four hung councils, local rightwingers concluded deals with the FN to ensure a majority in support of their own chairmanship of the council. After a heavy quarrel in Lyon, Millon, the former UDF chief, was forced out, and a UDF chair installed with PS support, but the other arrangements continued quietly.

This ungainly débâcle illustrated perfectly the difficulties faced by party systems in admitting newcomers. The alliance of the right and the newcomer

8. In the 1997 elections, for instance, only one-quarter of the FN's working class voters expressed any attachment to the left, compared with a third who expressed attachment to the right and 42% who felt close to neither – what Mayer calls les 'ni-ni' (1999: 216).

was one logical response to the basic need of all democratic systems: finding a majority to support the executive. It fell because, eventually, the price of collaboration with the newcomer was judged (tardily, and in some quarters, reluctantly) to be too high. This price should not be seen in terms of places on the executive (which were not offered) or even programmatic commitments (language is usually flexible enough to find a way round these), nor should we be too fixated on the endless moralising about whether the FN was really 'republican' or not. The price demanded by the FN was, effectively, legitimation as part of the pool of potential governing parties ; entry to the establishment club. After reflection, the national leaderships of the RPR/UDF decided (not unanimously) that the price was, as yet, too high to pay – in Lyon at least. (The furore in that city drew attention away from the quiet experiments being pursued in Languedoc-Roussillon by UDF boss Jacques Blanc.) The implications for future partnerships with the FN were too threatening : acceptance of the FN as a possible coalition partner by the moderate right could conceivably strengthen it at the latter's expense, in the same way as the PS had profited from the Common Programme of the left in 1972, signed with a then much stronger PCF. For now it was better to cut an ad hoc deal with the PS and see off the FN locally. In this way, options could be preserved while awaiting an electoral upturn.

This PS/right deal was never extended to national level; there was to be no 1990s Popular Front against extremism. Such a deal could easily have been agreed had the will been there, yet obviously the left had no real interest in removing a sizeable thorn from its oppponents' feet, and the right dare not be seen to be too close to the PS. The net effect of such collaboration might be to persuade many angry voters that there really was no difference between the mainstream parties, hence a vote for the FN represented the only radical alternative. Perhaps, less dramatically, it was feared that some voters might simply see such a compromise as an attempt to cartellise the political space between a group of entrepreneurs who were offering products not altogether competitive and so stay at home. Above all, neither left nor right can have felt that the FN dynamic had achieved sufficient momentum for them to suspend their own competition and make the primary competition the (joint) struggle against the interloper. At any rate, the establishment parties as a whole were not ready to react together to that interloper beyond a certain minmum level.

Potentially, the pressure exerted by the FN on the system represented the gravest challenge it had faced for some time. In the event, the system was saved from having to make a response beyond the minimal one just described by factors peculiar to the FN. We refer, of course, to the split within the movement that occurred from late 1998 onwards, culminating in the emergence of two separate parties, with Mégret's FN-MN (Mouvement National) competing with Le Pen's maintained FN. The split involved generational issues as well as tactical (whether to seek alliances with the moderate right or try to supplant it by direct confrontation), but the causes are less important than the consequences. The European elections of 1999 revealed a clear break in the dynamic of the extreme right, as the two lists combined polled only 8.97 percent, and Mégret's failed to win any seats in the EP. For the moderate right, the pressure was thus palpably eased; a short-term reaction to the slackening-off of this pressure could be seen in the split within the RPR that occurred during the European campaign, when Charles Pasqua allied with the former UDF leader Philippe de Villiers to run a list that would later constitute itself as a party, the RPF (Rassemblement pour la France). Significantly, the basis of the split was the issue of sovereignty; the RPF refused any further European integration, thus laying claim to the defence of national identity which was the FN's major feature. The new movement also sounded hard enough on law and order issues to appeal to potential FN supporters. In systemic terms, the weakening of an external challenge served, paradoxically, to liberate further fissiparous forces within the established system parties. Naturally, it remained to be seen if this split would prove definite, but at the start of the millennium it seemed more than a temporary quarrel between party chiefs.

The challenge from the left side of the system has been handled differently. By the 1990s the PCF had ceased to be a serious threat. With a vote of around seven percent, a shrinking local government empire, declining membership and resources, much weakened ties with already very weak unions and increasing internal factionalism, it was a party mainly concerned with survival. Mitterrand's bet that the pact betweeen PCF and PS could only redound to the long-term benefit of the PS had paid off handsomely. The PCF could now only hope to work the rather narrow space on the left-wing of social democracy, which meant hoping for the election of a PS-led government and trying to extract from it as much as possible for its working-class and poor rural supporters. The only question was whether such objectives were best achieved within or outside government. Those who continued to see the PCF as a peripheral party outside the 'natural' group of government candidates were thus taking an extreme view, predicated on the ineradicably revolutionary or protest character of the party. Jospin's PS had no such illusions when it offered the PCF an electoral deal and places in a coalition government for the 1997 elections. Both PS and PCF recognised that the natural place of the PCF within the system was that of a partner, but a junior partner, in a broad left alliance. The PCF had been brought in from the cold in a way that is probably definitive. If it continues to exist it will do so in this capacity.

Part of the reason for its readiness to slot in in this way is that the more radical social demands of generally ignored groups are now being carried by newer vehicles. The trotskyites of LO and LCR have, after many years of feuding, made common cause to elect MEPs and also some regional councillors in 1998. To be sure, these organisations remain committed to working-class revolution led by a vanguard party and only use democratic elections for propaganda purposes, but in systemic terms they have gained a foothold by performing a function traditionally associated with the PCF (not that the PCF has relinquished this willingly, but it is hard to maintain a purist discourse as it seeks to diversify its appeal).[9] We are not suggesting that the trotskyistes have become safely integrated into the party system and do not challenge its functions (as the PCF clearly no longer does); they have, in fact, won representation on the periphery of the system, to institutions with little power and where generous PR régimes operate. For the time being they can be left alone by the other parties, as their challenge is not yet serious.

A more complex challenge came from the greens. Despite levels of support which have reached double figures (the 1993 legislative elections for example), the green movements had never secured representation other than for one term in the EP (leaving aside their success in some regional council elections). Internal divisions between the more fundamentalist greens led by Waechter, and a pragmatic current led by Lalonde willing to ally with anyone in power and the mainstream current, committed to electoral politics but with a distinct programme, were the main reason for the shortfall (Boy, 1998). But Jospin's inclusive offer for the 1997 election clarified the choice for green activists, and the majority current led by Voynet accepted a deal which gave them parliamentary seats for the first time ever, followed by representation in government. Few parties can have jumped the legislative and executive hurdles in one. This represents a bold move by the party currently at the heart of the system, the PS. By incorporating the greens into a left majority, the PS challenged them to move from a rôle of protest to one of political management: Voynet was given the environment ministry. This is by no means a hazard-free operation, as the core demands of green activists have severe implications for the normal type of macro-economic management carried out by social democracy. Clearly, the PS and greens envisaged a phase of creative tension, as the newcomers bargained for their policy demands, from within the system. It is too early to say if the greens can be incorporated seamlessly as a distinct part of the 'plural left', but the move is a bold one in systemic terms. A key core party has judged that a certain type of challenger has now assumed sufficient weight to be admitted to the system of governing parties and has acted accordingly.

The PS tactics in 1997 amounted to a recognisable wish to reshape the party system. The PS recognised that majority government of 1981 style was a chimera. The wide range of political demands emanating from increasingly diverse social groups cannot be carried adequately by one all-purpose party, ceratinly not in a country with as diverse a party history as France. Better, then, to admit diversity but to try and organise it. Hence, the formula of the plural left, with its alliance of 'old' communists and 'new' greens flanking a catch-all party (the PS) seen increasingly as the vehicle for the new salaried middle-classes. All this makes for a constant and delicate bargaining process

9. The main argument within the PCF is whether it should harden its line in an attempt to cling on to or win back support among the most disadvantaged traditional sectors of society, or whether it should try and look outside this limited group (in which case it clearly has to try and be more inclusive and consensual).

within and between the left parties, but the alternative may well have been permanent division on the left and an open door for the right (or the FN). In that sense, the deliberate moves by the PS to remodel the party system in line with perceived pressures are far-sighted and intelligent. To borrow again the language of marketing, here were entrepreneurs who knew how to diversify their product in response to visible shifts in demand ; intelligence and far-sightedness are characteristics which have always been present in the French party system and the élites who run it.

The System in Historical Perspective

It is clear that over a century and a quarter, the French party system has evolved a character of its own, which previous chapters have attempted to illustrate. We present now, in synthetic fashion, the ongoing and underlying features which give the system its shape.

First, pluralism is endemic to the party system. Political demand has always been fragmented and has often evolved rapidly. It has suited voters, and the political entrepreneurs seeking to satisfy their demands, to link these demands with the political process via numerous, diverse and generally weakly structured parties. Thus, all the main types and subtypes of party family have been and remain present in France, mostly operating at quite viable levels still. Voluntaristic attempts to simplify them or boil them down by institutional tinkering have, on balance, had a fairly limited effect. There has been little 'unfreezing'. This has meant that government has usually been carried out by a core group of parties: republicans in the early years of the Third Republic, to whom were added radicals, then gradually catholic conservatives, socialists, christian democrats and even communists. Today, greens are also being given their chance to work with the core parties. The reconfiguration of the right after 1958, under the aegis of gaullism, did not really change this underlying pattern, it simply meant that the conservative republican tradition enjoyed a golden era under a slightly changed guise. Within the pool of governing parties, combinations were usually available that permitted a clear left or clear right orientation, or a less clear compromise, according to circumstances as interpreted by the political élites. Today, the left/right polarity seems unavoidable insofar as it is based on the existence of two recognisable sub-cultures (though with the arguable reduction in policy space between left and right, especially on issues such as economic management or European integration, the opportunities for combinations running across the left/right frontier become more real). At any rate, the plural party system provided coalitions which functioned in all save the most abnormal circumstances.

At the heart of the system lay a crucial regulating mechanism. This was the process of admission to the pool of governing parties. From the start, a certain group of parties were natural candidates for office, because they translated most adequately the limited wishes of a still largely rural and small-town electorate. These were the different republican factions discussed in Chapters Three and Four. However, the future of the party system was to be determined by the way in which these early groups conducted their alliance strategies.[10] We saw that, by the 1880s, they were increasingly accepting collaboration with radicalism. For all the common cultural roots it shared with the mainstream republican current, radicalism represented different groups with more urgent demands, some of them potentially troubling for economic liberals like the orthodox republicans. Radicalism was also an extremely aggressive force, prepared to play brinkmanship games in a system where the anti-republican right was still strong. Partly as a result of its aggression and partly owing to the realism of mainstream republicanism, radicalism became co-opted as an acceptable governing partner and came to dominate the republican camp until 1914. In this way, one of the key systemic mechanisms was enacted: the co-opting of a new member of the governing bloc. After entering the system as a challenger (radicalism wanted one chamber and no president, for instance), the new force was admitted to the governing club. In making this transition, it toned down its demands. This does not mean that radicalism sold out on its goals for the sake of office. On the contrary, it pushed very hard and took risks with the stability of the system until it secured the key objective of separation of church and state and the winning of this objective left it freer to temporise on some of its other objectives, such as those just listed.

A process of give-and-take thus ensued which would often be repreated. The circle of governing parties and ruling élites was thus widened in a process that was undramatic, slow and largely invisible; this was the way in which the republican party system irrigated itself and maintained its own reproduction. It is a fine illustration of Parkin's claim that élites cannot survive indefinitely if they remain perfectly closed; they have to know when to expand and take in new elements. Exactly the same is true of party systems, precisely because parties are run by élites.

Shrewd republican élites began a process of 'civilising the barbarians', as it were.

Successive challengers would appear at the periphery of the party system, bearing new and seemingly unacceptable demands (such as the socialisation of the means of production or, more recently, a policy of 'national preference' with public resources allocated towards French citizens only). The initial reaction of the gatekeeper parties would be to ignore these challengers, or at best denounce them; only when they threatened to achieve critical mass would they be taken seriously. This could occur before they reached a significant level of blackmail potential, to use Sartori's term, for the core parties could show active anticipation when it suited them. Thus, the coming of war in 1914 was used to introduce the SFIO into a modest share of government; a precedent had been laid down for the future that would again be used in 1936. We

10. In the words of Laver and Schofield (1990: 201) these core parties decided which of their competitors was 'non-coalitionable'.

have shown how the PCF, sworn enemy of the system, was first taken into a majority and then into government before being ghettoised thanks to the Cold War, but even during this period, it was kept warm within the left majority and even readmitted to government, once the PS thought it safe to do so. What is striking about all these co-options is not that the incomer had a huge weight of support that made its acceptance inevitable; in a fragmentary system like France, noone was ever likely to achieve such scores. Clearly, a certain level of support had to be achieved to suggest that the challenger was not ephemeral (this is why noone thought the Poujadists worth co-opting). Equally, a well-supported force like the PCF could be cold-shouldered (admittedly with some difficulty) for quite long periods. What mattered was recognition by the core pool of parties that here was a rival who had some status and who could potentially be entrusted with a share in government.

The focus of our study has been the national level of politics, but this focus risks ignoring one key mechanism of co-opting : the use of sub-national levels. With the growth of decentralisation, such levels have come to assume a greater stabilising rôle within the system than previously. It was long true that challenger parties often built a base in local government at the same time as (or just before) they began to win serious national mandates. The SFIO and PCF are classic exemplars of this. It is also true that such heartlands served various purposes in maintaining the parties through difficult times; they were a source of resources and jobs and above all a proof that the party could actually run some public institutions convincingly. What is perhaps insufficiently understood about this from a systemic point of view is that the process of insertion/legitimation at sub-national level helped stabilise the national party system. This it did by absorbing the energies and aggression of the challengers and canalising them into real political output, which voters could then evaluate. Whatever their strictures against the socio-political order, challenger parties were implicated in managing parts of it, not least because the cumul des mandats turned local figures into national ones and vice versa; such responsibility could only, over the longer term, modify their behaviour.[11]

We have tended to see periods spent by parties in parliamentary opposition as a kind of ante-chamber to the club of governing parties. It might be useful to envisage the achievement and consolidation of local power by a party as one stage further back in the ascent to governability, or at any rate, a process to be undergone coterminous with serving one's time in opposition. Whichever way one considers it, local experience was a useful preparation for admission to the national core.

---

11. It will be interesting to see how attempts by the Jospin government to reduce cumul des mandats to insignificance will affect the party system. This policy is based on the argument that local and national mandates are now full-time jobs in themselves. This is a technical rationale for breaking what is an essentially political link. One of its consequences will certainly be the creation of subsystems within (and across) parties, meaning that the process of élite accomodation will be more complex, involving more actors.

This consideration has been of particular relevance in recent years. The obvious case is the PCF. From 1947, it was made very clear to all that it had been expelled from the core and had no real hope of readmission so long as the Cold War threatened to become hot. Its negative, spoiling reaction to this marginalisation is well-known, but the PCF represented millions of voters; it made no sense to alienate these totally from the system. The party's strong municipal presence and control of a few *conseils généraux* was one means of mitigating its isolation. We are not suggesting that the core parties were particularly enlightened or generous or that they wanted to be fair, but they were intelligent enough to read *rapports de force* within French society and not to believe that the PCF could be killed off simply by denying it the right to exist. In theory, it would have been possible for them to conduct a much fuller attack on the PCF's municipal strongholds than actually occurred (we know that, initially, the 1958 change in the system of electing deputies cut down PCF representation hugely). That the other parties refrained from doing so suggests that their élites knew when to let up in the interests of overall stability. They judged that stability would be better protected by allowing the PCF some influence within a *chasse gardée* than by carrying out an overall assault whose consequences might be unpredictable.

Similar considerations have undoubtedly obtained more recently with the refusal to change electoral systems for the European Parliament (admittedly the subject of a supranational agreement) or the regional councils, both of them run on PR. The net effect of this has been to award seats to the FN as well as trotskyistes and greens. Despite indignant rhetoric about the need to outlaw extremism, no changes have yet been made. This may not be due to the overcrowding of parliamentary timetables or similar technical excuses, but to the awareness that it may well be better to allow peripheral forces some meaningful expression than to outlaw them by sharp practice which may well rebound in the faces of its authors. This indulgence is made easier by the fact that the institutions in which the 'extremists' win a modest amount of seats are, by and large, fairly peripheral to the making of decisions that have major impact on daily life. The core parties have made very sure that the hardline challengers face a maximum of obstruction in the search for parliamentary seats, but parliament is a body that still matters. In short, the party system has used its sub-national levels with some sophistication to ensure that challenger-parties and the angry voters whom they represent are given some modest representation within the safer zones of the political system. This is a very low level of inclusion, but it holds out some hope for the newcomers – provided they can show that they have learned the logic of republican politics. Republican pedagogy thus continues.

Inclusion or co-option of new forces has always depended on the judgement of the core parties. Such judgements were heavily political in nature and were made – and continue to be made – by party leaderships, not by party machinery, whatever the democratic trappings of the PS or MRP. At the heart of the gatekeeping process, therefore, stands a republican political élite.

The Republican Elite – From Lawyers to Enarques

The party élite in France can be considered sociologically and historically. Sociologically, it was, until recently, dominated by what one might term the organic intellectuals of the republic: legal professions, educationalists and other public servants, as well as the more traditional middle-class categories of small business and professions. Until the Fifth Republic, such categories often had a strong provincial flavour. They held a high degree of common republican culture and values, as we have suggested, involving a tight matrix of beliefs about human nature and politics. Elites also tended to show high sociological continuity across the spectrum from left to right. Thus, the early republican groups and radicalism were dominated by such 'organic' categories (Priouret, 1959; Gaudemet, 1970). Even when socialism began to elect deputies, many of them – certainly the most effective leaders, who set the strategy for SFIO and determined its relationship to the party system – would still come from such categories. The likes of Briand, Millerand, Jaurès and Viviani were closer, in many ways, to Poincaré or Clemenceau than to some of their miner or metalworker colleagues who found themselves suddenly in the Palais-Bourbon. The communist party was an exception, with its deliberate purge of early leaders (drawn very much from traditional republican élites) and their replacement by workers-turned-bureaucrats, often from a trade-union background, whose loyalty to the CPSU was unflinching. Thereafter the PCF always carefully cloned its élites from among the same categories. This was undoubtedly a major inhibitor to the induction of the PCF into the core parties (and it was done for precisely that reason; the PCF did not want its élites contaminated by 'reformism'). Leaving aside the PCF, though, the élites of the other parties had a certain common culture, which would affect their perception of the party game. It would make it easier for challenger-parties to understand some of the assumptions and rules of the game which governed basic republican political practice. There would always be links between parties, stretching over the left/right divide.

Even the changing nature of contemporary élites has not gone against this trend. It is customary today to evoke the technocratic nature of much party leadership and, in particular, to cite the iron grip of *grandes écoles* graduates, especially *énarques*, on party machinery. The argument is that such professional administrators, with their wide formation in law, politics, administration and international relations, as well as their inside knowledge based on their placements in key parts of the state apparatus, possess skills which make it easy for them to control party machinery and sideline traditional élites. Clearly, empirical evidence suggests that there is much truth in such assertions, if we take only such basic facts as the number of *énarques* in government or in senior positions in parties. What needs to be remembered, however, is that this type of élite is to be found in virtually every party (even the PCF latterly promoted a small number of *grandes écoles* graduates to positions of influence). They are not just a property of the right; Hardouin (1978) and Portelli (1980) long since demonstrated their salience within the PS. To some extent, the rise of such categories is a mere symptom of the more complex environment in which politics occurs; it is a sharper universe where more diverse skills are needed. We are not concerned here with estimating the relative importance of such categories in relation to more traditional élites (for instance in calculating how far *énarques* have displaced schoolteachers within the PS or small businessmen within gaullism). We simply wish to underline the ubiquity of such élites with their professional approach to politics based on a strong sense of public service and attachment to classic republican values. Just as in 1890, a certain type of élite and its values are to be found across the political spectrum today; this is a factor that can only help mitigate conflict.

The French Party System and the Resolution of Conflict: An Original Approach?

France devised a way of managing conflict through a political system in which party played a key rôle. We aim in conclusion to set this practice into a theoretical context.

Classically, party sytems have either produced majoritarian government or coalitions. The latter type of system has been given some of its most sophisticated theorising in the work of Lijphart (1968; 1977; 1997), with the concept of consociational democracy. Lijphart identified a number of plural societies which managed their differences by an elaborate, constantly constructed compromise between all the major segments within them; no segment could aspire to majority control, but had to respect and work with the others. His theory defined plural societies as those with profound ideological differences which bore political implications. These differences should produce recognisable segments or subcultures within society, easy to distinguish from each other (for example the catholic, protestant, liberal and socialist 'pillars' in the Netherlands). Each segment was relatively isolated from each other (maybe geographically concentrated in some cases) and largely ran its own affairs (educational, health and welfare, cultural and even economic apparatuses; media, voluntary associations and, crucially for our purposes, party). Compromises were arranged nationally by the élites of each segment, working with a relatively free hand and the confidence of their members. Concrete manifestations of such compromise were coalition governments and perhaps share-outs of resources and positions on a fairly proportional basis. In this way, democratic stability prevailed. Central to this delicate mechanism was the process of élite accomodation; élites had to know what was politically possible and stick within such boundaries. If they did this, their segments could be expected to follow loyally.

It is not our intention to claim that such a model applies to France, where political reality was always much more blurred than the rather tidy divisions required by Lijphart's theory. Nevertheless, there are elements of the model which shed some light on the French process, particularly the rôle of élite accomodation, and it is worth considering the applicability of Lijphart's theory to the French party system and its history.

Prima facie, France would qualify easily for the title of a plural society, with its history of violent social conflict and its absence of overarching groups which could subsume different factions into a wider entity (such as the Labour movement or the Conservative party in the UK). The degree of conflict within French society was always much higher than that of the Netherlands before the 'pacification' of 1917, which is held to have inaugurated the era of consensus politics. The problem is, however, that the different sub-groups in France (catholics, secularists, liberals, socialists) never organised themselves into the closed type of community central to Lijphart's model. The exception to this might be the communist party, which sought, with some success, to create a counter-community, but it could be argued that the price of this was precisely to be excluded for a long time from the compromises elaborated by other élites, and that the PCF did, in the end, recognise the error of its ways and join the community of compromise.

The other social segments are, however, striking by their refusal to organise in a hermetically sealed way. Attachment to one's own education system was the main manifestation of closure by subcultures, and schools were for a long time the main object of poltical conflict. All of the non-catholic segments shared a strong attachment to the republican school, whatever their differences on other issues. In other areas of social life the picture was patchy. There were catholic hospitals and newspapers, but nothing ressembling a national network. A vigorous associative current would only arise after 1919 with the (late) appearance of catholic trade unions, youth organisations, etc. It is uncertain how far the catholic hierarchy wanted its people to consider itself as a separate entity within France (such active identity-building by élites is a central feature of Lijphart's model). If the catholic pole of French society was not sealed off, the same was even more the case for the other sub-cultures. Lijphart's model relied heavily on the distinct sense of identity of Dutch catholicism, which in a sense obliged others to follow. If catholics do not opt for closed structures, the other groups are less likely to do so.

Turning to the specific field of politics, we see no evidence of a willingness to create tight unitary structures on the part of groups in France. Catholics expressed their political demands through a variety of oulets (monarchism and anti-republicanism, conservatism, which might well include moderate republicanism and reformist christian democracy). The liberal and secularist camp had a range of structures, centring on the loosely organised, moderate republican parties or the separate force of radicalism, and its non-political organisations were weak and informal (masonic lodges, educational leagues, etc.). The socialist and working-class groups eventually formed their own party, but they never had much by way of ancillary organisations in civil society, and even the SFIO had very strong cultural and even personal links to mainstream bourgeois republicanism.[12]

In other words, for all the reality of historical conflict, and for all the angry memories of it – exploited rhetorically at election time – the contending groups in French society never formed cast-iron, closed institutions of their own. The structures were always looser, and there were always bridges, manned and built by an élite of political entrepreneurs, who did not want particularly strong partisan structures, because they were felt to be constraining; the loose, shifting formations characteristic of the Third and Fourth Republics allowed for much more flexibility and negotiation.[13] Given that these élites regularly secured re-election on high turnouts, it seems fair to conclude that they correctly interpreted the wishes of most of French society as to how it wished its politics to be negotiated. French voters were seldom ready to form mass organisations, seeking to control deputies and pressure them to fulfil elaborate ideological agendas. Their demands were general in scope (and at the same time could often be very local and particularistic). They would judge elected officials (*élus*) on polling day by how they performed, but it was up to the officials, not any intermediary force, to make sure that they performed well. This did not imply deference on the part of the voters, either; voters believed in giving their *élus* responsibility in return for accepting their judgement.

It is important to give full credit for the way in which republican élites transmitted preferences into political action. It would be quite fair to say that these early élites contributed actively to the definition of partisan politics in modern France, that they created a style of party politics which has survived, thanks to careful management and adaptation, down to this day. In other words, the republican élite were one of the most important causes of the way the party system turned out.

The way in which the republican élite negotiated its compromises depended heavily on party, but not the kind of well-supported mass-party typical of consociational democracies. Here the picture is of leaders negotiating on behalf of big battalions, often in a fairly visible and proportional way;

12. Typical of the weak links between left parties and organisations in civil society is the divorce which occurred between the nascent socialist party and the main labour union CGT in 1894, when, under the influence of revolutionary syndicalists, the CGT severed all ties with the party.

13. This point is highly relevant for the discussion of the relationship between internal party structures and coalition bargaining (Laver and Schofield, 1990: 15ff.). The tighter a party's formal structures (ideological and organisational), the harder it should be in theory for élites to bargain meaningfully with competitors, because they are likely to be challenged from within. In fact, virtually all French parties have always kept structures which are far more supple in reality than their written constitutions imply. This gives the leadership, especially when in office, that degree of control which is necessary if we are to speak of 'party government' (Blondel and Cotta, 1996: 2). The exception would be the PCF with its well-known vertical discipline, but, paradoxically, that meant that if the PCF leadership did decide to negotitate a deal then it could be even more sure of carrying it through than the leaders of looser formations. Whether rigid or supple, French parties were always able to bargain purposefully, as if they were that 'unitary actor' whose exis-

the bigger the party, the easier it is to determine the proportions. French élite accomodation was more of a low-key, long drawn-out and and frankly attritional process. Initially, adversaries of the bourgeois republic (whether self-proclaimed, like the revolutionary socialists or suspected, like *rallié* catholics) were held at arms length in the coalitional logic, then gradually inducted into the core of government-worthy parties by the mechanisms described above; they became 'coalitionable'. For this induction to occur, the core parties had to feel that the challengers' demands had been sufficiently blunted to warrant their incorporation. Such incorporation might, in any case, be only temporary (like the SFIO in 1936, or even the PCF admitted into the majority, but no further, at the same period), if the core parties felt threatened again by the newcomers. Gradually over time, newcomers came to know what was expected of them if they were to be in government; thus they were socialised into the logic of republican politics partly by the tutelage of the core parties, and forced to embark on a steep learning curve. Once a party had entered the club of potential rulers, it would join in the gatekeeping function, gradually socialising wilder elements which were closer to it ideologically.

It is not our intention, resting on the benefits of hindsight, to see this as a smooth, deliberate or preodained process, a kind of republican theodicy, but process it undoubtedly was. Republican party élites worked at bringing their challengers into the frame of democratic politics, by setting rules and targets for them. It was a kind of republican pedagogy, and the challengers eventually accepted democratic logic. Sometimes the process was conflictual, but generally it worked. France was spared civil war and performed as a democratic state, which discharged all of the complex functions increasingly demanded of such states. Given the depth and breadth of conflict within French civil society, this is no small achievement. The republican élites and their 'weak' parties deserve a much fuller recognition of their rôle in anchoring democracy in France. The defeat of 1940 and the putsch of 1958, supported by self-serving forces within the system that then took full advantage of it, are, from a long-term perspective, temporary blips in a secular process of democratic adjustment, of which party was the heart.

A Politics of Limited Accommodation?

Lijphart's scheme for classifying democracies depends on the relationship between the masses and the élites. According to whether the élites are cooperative or conflictual, or whether the masses are segmented or exposed to several cross-cutting cleavages rather than to one dominant one, a political system can be placed into one of four categories:

Figure 8.2 Types of Democracy According to Lijphart

		Masses	
		Cross-cutting Cleavages	*Segmented*
Elites	*Co-operation*	Depoliticised Democracy	Consociational Democracy
	Conflict	Centripetal Democracy	Centrifugal Democracy

Source: Lijphart (1968)

In such a schema, countries like the Netherlands, Belgium or Switzerland are clear examples of consociational democracy, whereas Italy, Weimar Germany or the Third and Fourth Republics are examples of the centrifugal variety.

Like all ideal types, this model is intended to be challenged. Few of the catgeories are ever likely to be found in pristine form, and assessment of cases is always likely to be a matter of degree. We are not arguing that France has ever resembled a consociational democracy, but we cannot consign her blithely (as too many studies do) to the untidier end of the centrifugal camp. This is because there has always been a huge degree of collusion between party élites, much larger than that which the centrifugal model implies with its strict notion of 'competition'. Competition in republican party politics has always been, as we have tried to show, a collusive affair, with its own rules of the game, its own exclusions, incorporations and invisible tariffs, its own version of serving one's time before being rewarded. To be sure, there were never the formal agreements typical of consociationalism, such as minority vetoes and proportional shareouts (though there were less-than-fair shareouts, which became part of the game), but there was accommodation behind election-day- and chamber-of-deputies rhetoric.

Perhaps it is best to speak of a politics of limited accommodation, mediated by the parties. It was certainly not conflict free, and the system was never able to get away with the delaying and depoliticising tactics that the consociational democracies use to muddle through major policy dilemmas ('putting the hot potatoes in the fridge', as it is sometimes called). At key moments in French history, the protagonists fought the issues out directly. The major moments were around 1900, with the final affirmation of the primacy of electoral democracy and the related issue of separation of church and state. Once these issues had been settled, it is possible to see the rise of a much more collusive and inclusive type of politics, with the enemies of yesteryear (catholics) and of tomorrow (socialist and communists) gradually, grudgingly, but cleverly inducted into the group of the 'coalitionable'.[14]

Republican party élites with their 'weak' organisations were the architects of this politics of limited accommodation. In terms of Lijphart's model (fig. 8.2), their work should put France nearer the centre of the diagram than towards the bottom right corner. She is not consociational enough to join the members of that band and not centripetal enough to join the UK or US, but she is nearer to those cases than we might at first think.

Lijphart used his model to ask how far consociationalism had helped democracy. We can do the same with our adapted version of it. For him, a stable democracy was one in which the capabilities of the system were sufficient to meet the demands placed upon it (1975: 70). This meant more than the maintenance of a stable order; problems, tensions and conflicts should be resolved and not allowed to pile up. A healthy democracy was characterised by gradual peaceful change or dynamic stability.

Democracy in France has always been party-driven, and to judge its record is to judge the record of party. The demands placed on the system by society were huge. In our view the parties have mostly met them – not always as smoothly as Lijphart suggests should happen, but effectively enough and by the means which we have outlined. It has not always been a glorious record, but it has been honourable. Democracy remains strong, and so do parties. The health of the one will continue to depend on the condition of the other.

tence is questioned by theorists.

14. Even the manner of the separation is indicative of a will to set limits to conflict. The way in which the question of church property was handled (Briand's *associations cultuelles*) offered the hierarchy a dignified way out (which it admittedly took a long time to accept). This indicates a desire, not to eliminate the competitor (whatever radical party congresses may have thought), but to keep him in the frame, once certain vital objectives had been secured. It may have been limited accommodation, but it was still accommodation.

BIBLIOGRAPHY

Adamthwaite, A. (1995) *Grandeur and Misery: France's Bid for Power in Europe, 1914-40*. London: Arnold.

Ageron, C–R. (1976) 'L'Opinion française devant la guerre d'Algérie', *Revue française d'histoire d'outre-mer* 63: 256–85.

Albertini R. von (1961) 'Parteiorganisation und Parteibegriff in Frankreich, 1789-1940', *Historische Zeitschrift* 193: 529–600.

Anderson, B. (1983) *Imagined Communities*, London: Verso.

Anderson, M. (1974) *Conservative Politics in France*, London: Allen and Unwin.

Appleton, A. (1995) 'Parties under Pressure: Challenge to "Established" French Parties', *West European Politics* 18 (1): 52–77.

———. (2000) 'The France That Doesn't Vote: Non- Consumption in the Electoral Market' in Lewis-Beck, M. ed.) *How France Votes*, New York/London: Chatham House, pp. 206–26.

Avril, P. (1990) *Essais sur les partis politiques*, Paris: Payot.

Avril, P. et al. (1989) *Personnel politique français*, Paris: PUF.

Baal, G. (1977) 'Combes et "la République des comités"', *Revue d'Histoire Moderne et Contemporaine* 24 (2): 260-85.

———. (1994) *Histoire du radicalisme*, Paris: La Découverte.

Barral, P. (1968) *Les Fondateurs de la Troisième République*, Paris: Colin.

Bartolini, S. (1984) 'Institutional Constraints and Party Competition in the French Party System', *West European Politics* 7 (4): 103–127.

Becker, J.- J. and Berstein, S. (1990) *Victoire et frustrations, 1914-1929*, Paris: Seuil.

Bell, D. and Criddle, B. (1987) *The French Socialist Party: Emergence of a Party of Government*, Oxford: Clarendon Press.

———. (1994a) *The French Party System: from Polarised Pluralism to Consensus Fatigue*, Aston Papers in European Politics and Society 2.

———. (1994b) *The French Communist Party in the Fifth Republic*, Oxford: Clarendon Press.

Bell, L. (1989) 'May 68: Parenthesis or Staging Post in the Development of the Socialist Left?' in Hanley, D. and Kerr, A.P. (eds.) *May 68: Coming of Age*, London: MacMillan, pp. 82–99.

Bergounioux, A. and Grunberg, G. (1992) *Le long Remords du pouvoir: le parti socialiste français, 1905-1992*, Paris: Fayard.

Bernard, P. (1975) *La Fin d'un monde, 1914-29*, Paris: Seuil.

Berstein, S. (1980 and 1982) *Histoire du Parti Radical*, 2 vols., Paris: FNSP.

Berstein, S. and Rudelle,O. (eds.)(1992), *Le Modèle républicain*, Paris: PUF.

Billard, Y. (1993) *Le Parti républicain-socialiste de 1911 à 1934*, Université de Paris IV thesis.

Birenbaum, G. (1992) *Le Front National en politique*, Paris: Balland.

Birnbaum, P. (1979) *Les petits contre les gros*, Paris: Grasset.

———. (1993) *La France aux Français: histoire des haines nationalistes*, Paris: Seuil.

Birnbaum, P. (ed.) (1994) *La France de l'affaire Dreyfus*, Paris: Gallimard.

Blondel, J. and Cotta, M. (eds.) (1996) *Party and Government*, London: MacMillan.

Bock, F. (1998) *Un Parlementarisme de guerre: recherches sur le fonctionnement de la Troisième République pendant la Grande Guerre*, 3 vols., Paris: IEP thesis.

Bomier-Landowski, A. (1951) 'Les Groupes parlementaires de l'Assemblée Nationale et de la Chambre des Députés de 1871 à 1940' in Goguel, F. and Dupeux, G. *Sociologie électorale: esquisse d'un bilan, guide de recherches*, Paris: Colin, pp. 75–89.

Bon, F. and Cheylan, P. 1988) *La France qui vote*, Paris: Hachette.

Bonnefous, G. (1956-67) *Histoire politique de la Troisième République*, 7 vols., Paris: PUF.

Borne, D. and Dubief, H. (1989) *La Crise des années trente, 1929-38*, Paris: Seuil.

Bourdieu, P. (1981) 'La représentation politique', *Actes de la Recherche en Sciences Sociales* 36–7: 1–25.

Boy, D. (1998) 'L'Ecologie au pouvoir' in Perrineau, P. and Ysmal, C. (eds.) *Le Vote surprise: les élections législatives des 25 mai et 1er juin 1997*, Paris: FNSP, pp. 207–24.

Braud, P. (1998) *Êtes-vous catholique?*, Paris: FNSP.

Brown, B. (1982) *Socialism of a Different Kind*, New York: Greenwood.

Bruguière, M. et al., (1982) *Administration et parlement depuis 1815*, Geneva: Droz.

Budge, I. and Newton, K. (eds.) (1997) *The Politics of the New Europe: Atlantic to Urals*, London: Longman.

Buffotot, P. (1998) *Le Socialisme français et la guerre*, Paris- Brussels: Bruylant-LGDJ.

Buffotot, P. and Hanley, D. (1998)'Chronique d'une défaite annoncée: les élections législatives des 25 mai et 1er juin 1997', *Modern and Contemporary France* 6 (1): 5–20.

Burdeau, F. (1996) *La Troisième République*, Paris: Monchrestien.

Bury, J. P. T. (1973) *Gambetta and the Making of the Third Republic*, London: Longman.

———. (1982) *Gambetta's Final Years: The Era of Difficulties, 1877-82*, London: Longman.

Callot, E. – F. (1978) *Le Mouvement républicain populaire*, Paris: Rivière.

Camby, J. – P. (1995) *Le Financement de la vie politique en France*, Paris: Monchrestien.

Campbell, P. (1966) *French Electoral Systems*, 2nd edn., London: Faber.

Le Canard Enchaîné (1993) *Les Fromages de la République*, special dossier.

Carrère, J. and Bourgin, H. (1924) *Manuel des partis politiques en France*, Paris: Rieder.

CERES (1976) La Décomposition du gaullisme. *Repères* 38.

Chagnollaud, D. (1996) 'La haute Administration au pouvoir? Les grands commis de la IVe. République', *Pouvoirs* 76: 107–16.

Chapsal, J. and Lancelot, A. (1979) *La Vie politique en France depuis 1940*, Paris: PUF.

Charlot, J. (1967) *L'UNR: étude du pouvoir au sein d'un parti politique*, Paris: Colin.

———. (1989) 'Les Mutations du système de partis français', *Pouvoirs* 49: 27–35.

Cholvy, G. and Hilaire, Y. – M. (1988) *Histoire religieuse de la France contemporaine, vol. III, 1930-1988*, Toulouse: Privat.

Claudin, F. (1975) *From Comintern to Cominform*, Harmondsworth: Penguin.

Cointet, J. – P. (1998) *Marcel Déat: du socialisme au national-socialisme*, Paris: Perrin.

Cole, A. (1990) 'The evolution of the party system' in Cole, A. (ed.) *French Political Parties in Transition*, London: Dartmouth, pp. 3-24.

———. (1994) *François Mitterrand: A Study in Political Leadership*, London: Routledge.

———. (1998) *French Politics and Society*, Hemel Hempstead: Prentice Hall.

Collovald, A. (1989) 'Les Poujadistes ou l'échec en politique', *Revue d'Histoire Moderne et Contemporaine* 36 (1): 111–33.

Daalder, H. (1992) 'A Crisis of Party', *Scandinavian Political Studies*, 15 (4): 269–87.

Daalder, H. and Mair, P. (eds.) (1983) *Western European Party Systems: Continuity and Change*, London: Sage.

Delbreil, J.-C. (1990) *Centrisme et démocratie chrétienne en France des origines au MRP, 1919–44*, Paris: Publications de la Sorbonne.

Delcros, X. (1970) *Les Majorités de reflux à la Chambre des Députés de 1918 à 1958*, Paris: PUF.

De Tarr, F. (1961) *The French Radical Party from Herriot to Mendès-France*, Oxford: OUP.

———. (1996) 'Henri Queuille, un homme de la Troisième République, sauveur – à titre provisoire – de la IVe', *Pouvoirs* 76: 97–106.

Dogan, M. (1953) 'La Stabilité du personnel politique sous la Troisième République', *Revue française de science politique* 3 (2): 319–48.

———. (1961) 'Political Ascent in a Class Society' in Marvick, D. (ed.) *Political Decision Makers*, Chicago: Free Press, pp. 59–90.

———. (1967) 'Les Filières de la carrière politique en France', *Revue française de sociologie* VIII: 468–92.

Donegani, J. – M. and Sadoun, M. (1994) *La Démocratie imparfaite: essai sur le parti politique*, Paris: Gallimard.

Dreyfus, F.-G. (1988) *Histoire de la démocratie chrétienne en France: de Chateaubriand à Raymond Barre*, Paris: Albin Michel.

Dubief, H. (1976) *Le Déclin de la Troisième République, 1929-38*, Paris: Seuil.

Duhamel, A. (1989) *Les Habits neufs de la politique*, Paris: Flammarion.

Duhamel, E. (1995)'Pleven et Mitterrand', *Vingtième Siècle* 45: 67–75.

———. (1996) 'L'UDSR, un parti charnière', *Pouvoirs* 76: 81–96.

Dunleavy, P. (1991) *Democracy, Bureaucracy and Public Choice*, London: Harvester.

Duverger, M. (1976) *Les Partis politiques*, revised edition, Paris: Seuil.

Elgey, G. (1965-92) *Histoire de la Quatrième République*, 3 vols., Paris: Fayard.

Elwitt, S. (1975) *The Making of the Third Republic*, Baton Rouge: Louisiana State UP.

———. (1986) *The Third Republic Defended: Bourgeois Reform in France, 1880-1914*. Baton Rouge: Louisiana State UP.

Estèbe, J. (1982) *Les Ministres de la République*, Paris: FNSP.

Evin, K. (1979) *Michel Rocard ou l'art du possible*, Paris: Simoen.

Fauvet, J. (1959) *La Quatrième République*, Paris: Fayard.

Favier, P. and Martin-Roland, M. (1990-96) *La Décennie Mitterrand*, 3 vols., Paris: Seuil.

Fiechter, J. – J. (1965) *Le Socialisme français de l'affaire Dreyfus à la Grande Guerre*, Geneva: Droz.

Frears, J. (1991) *Parties and Voters in France*, London: Hurst.

Furet, F., Julliard, J. and Rosanvallon, P. (1988) *La République du centre*, Paris: Calmann-Levy.

Gacon, J. (1987) *1944-58, Quatrième République*, Paris: Messidor- Editions Sociales.

Gallie, D. (1983) *Social Inequality and Class Radicalism in France and Britain*, Cambridge: CUP.

Garrigues, J. (1997) *La République des hommes d'affaires, 1870- 1900*, Paris: Aubier.

Gaudemet, Y. – H. (1970) *Les Juristes et la vie politique de la Troisième République*, Paris: PUF.

Gaxie, D. (1977) 'Economie des partis et rétribution du militantisme', *Revue française de science politique* 27 (1): 123–54.

———. (1996) *La Démocratie représentative*, 2nd edn., Paris: Monchrestien.

Gibson, R. (1989) *A Social History of French Catholicism, 1789- 1914*, London: Routledge.

Girardet, R. (1983) *Le Nationalisme français*, Paris: Seuil.

Goguel, F. (1946) *La Politique des Partis sous la Troisième République*, Paris: Fayard.
———. (1951) *Géographie des élections françaises*, Paris: Colin.
Gouault, J. (1954) *Comment la France est devenue républicaine*, Paris: Colin.
Graham, B. (1965) *The French Socialists and Tripartism, 1944-47*, London: Weidenfeld and Nicolson.
———. (1994a) *Representation and Party Politics*, Oxford: Blackwell.
———. (1994b) *Choice and Democratic Order: The French Socialist Party, 1937-50*, Cambridge: CUP.
Greene, N. (1969) *Crisis and Decline: the French Socialist Party in the Popular Front Era*, New York: Cornell UP.
Grévy, J. (1996) *Les opportunistes: milieu et culture politiques, 1871-89*, Paris: IEP thesis.
———. (1998) *La République des opportunistes, 1870-1885*, Paris: Perrin.
Grosser, A. (1967) *La Quatrième République et sa politique extérieure*, Paris: Colin.
Guérin, A. (1980) *La Vie quotidienne au Palais-Bourbon à la fin de la Troisième République*, Paris: Hachette.
Guiral, P. and Thuillier, G. (1980) *La Vie quotidienne des députés en France de 1871 a 1914*, Paris: Hachette.
Guyomarch, A. (1995) 'The European Dynamics of Evolving Party Competition in France', *Parliamentary Affairs* 48 (1): 100–23.
Hall, P. (1986) *Governing the Economy*, London: Polity Press.
Hamon, H. and Rotman, P. (1982) *La Deuxième Gauche*, Paris: Ramsay.
Hamon, L. (ed.) (1991) *Les Opportunistes: les débuts de la République aux républicains*, Paris: Maison des Sciences de l'Homme.
Hanley, D. (1986) *Keeping Left: CERES and the French Socialist Party*, Manchester: Manchester UP.
———. (1991) 'Christian Democracy in France, 1965-90: Death and Resurrection?' in Atkin, N. and Tallett, F. (eds.) *Religion, Society and Politics in France since 1789*, London: Hambledon.
———. (ed.) (1994) *Christian Democracy in Europe: A Comparative Perspective*, London: Pinter.
———. (1999a) 'France: Living with Instability' in Broughton, D. and Donovan, M. (eds.) *Changing Party Systems in Western Europe*, London: Pinter, pp. 48–70.
———. (1999b) 'Compromise, Party Management and Fair Shares: the Case of the French UDF', *Party Politics* 5 (2): 167–85.
Hardouin, P. (1978) 'Les caractéristiques sociologiques du PS', *Revue française de science politique* XXVIII (2): 220–56.
Harismendy, P. (1994) *Un Héritier de la République: Sadi Carnot, 1837–87*, Paris: Université de Paris IV thesis.
Hazareesingh, S. (1994) *Political Traditions in Modern France*, Oxford: Oxford UP.
Hewlett, N. (1998) *Modern French Politics: Analysing Conflict and Consensus since 1945*, London: Polity.
Hoffmann, S. (1956) *Le Mouvement Poujade*, Paris: Colin.
———. (1963). 'Paradoxes of the French political community' in Hoffmann, S. (ed.), *In Search of France*, New York: Harper and Row, pp. 1–117.
Huard, R. (1994) 'Aboutissements préparés et cristallisations imprévues: la formation des partis' in Birnbaum, P. (ed.), *La France de l'Affaire Dreyfus*, Paris: Gallimard, pp. 86–119.
———. (1996) *La Naissance du parti politique en France*, Paris: FNSP.
Hudemann, R. (1979) *Fraktionsbildung im französischen Parlament: zur Entwicklung des Parteiensystems in der frühen Dritten Republik, 1871-75*, Munich: Artemis.

Ignazi, P. and Ysmal, C. (eds.) (1998) *The Organization of Political Parties in Southern Europe*, Westport: Praeger.

Imbert, C. and Julliard, J. (1995) *La droite et la gauche: qu'est-ce qui les distingue encore?*, Paris: Laffont/Grasset.

Inglehart, R. (1977) *Silent Revolution: Changing Values and Political Styles among Western Publics*, Ann Arbor: University of Michigan Press.

Irvine, W. (1979) *French Conservatism in Crisis: the Republican Federation of France in the 1930s*, Baton Rouge: Louisiana UP.

———. (1989a) *The Boulanger Affair Reconsidered*, Oxford: OUP.

———. (1989b) 'Royalists, Mass Politics and the Boulanger Affair', *French History* 3 (1): 31–47.

———. (1998) 'Domestic Politics and the Fall of France in 1940', in Blatt, J. (ed.) *The French Defeat of 1940: Reassessments*, Oxford: Berghahn, pp. 85–99.

Irving, R. (1973) *Christian Democracy in France*, London: Allen and Unwin.

Jackson, J. (1985) *The Politics of Depression in France, 1932-36*, Cambridge: CUP.

———. (1988) *The Popular Front in France: Defending Democracy, 1934-38*, Cambridge: CUP.

Jacques, L. (1913) *Les Partis politiques sous la Troisième République*, Paris: Sirey.

Jeanneney, J. – N. (1976) *François de Wendel en République: l'argent et le pouvoir, 1914-40*, Paris: Seuil.

———. (1977) *Leçon d'histoire pour une gauche au pouvoir: la faillite du Cartel (1924-26)*, Paris: Seuil.

Jenkins, B. (1990) *Nationalism in France: Class and Nation since 1789*, London: Routledge.

Johnson, R. W. (1981) *The Long March of the French Left*, London: MacMillan.

Jolly, J. (1960-72) *Dictionnaire des parlementaires français*, 7 vols., Paris: PUF.

Joly, D. (1990) *The French Communist Party and the Algerian War*, Basingstoke: MacMillan.

Judt, T. (1976) *La Reconstruction du parti socialiste, 1921-26*, Paris: FNSP.

Julliard, J. (1967) *La Quatrième République*, Paris: Calmann- Lévy.

Kahler, M. (1984) *Decolonisation in Britain and France: The Domestic Consequences of International Relations*, Princeton: Princeton UP.

Kalyvas, S. (1996) *The Rise of Christian Democracy in Europe*, Ithaca: Cornell UP.

Katz, R. and Mair, P. (eds.) (1992) *Party Organisations: A Data Handbook on Party Organisations in Western Democracies*, London: Sage.

Kayser, J. (1962) *Les grandes Batailles du radicalisme: des origines aux portes du pouvoir, 1820-1901*, Paris: Rivière.

Kergoat, J. (1983) *Le Parti socialiste*, Paris: Le Sycomore.

Kirchheimer, O. (1966) 'The Transformation of West European Party Systems' in LaPalombara, J. and Weiner, M. (eds.) *Political Parties and Political Development*, Princeton NJ: Princeton UP, pp. 177–200.

Knapp, A. and Le Galès, P. (1993) 'Top Down to Bottom Up? Centre-Periphery Relations and Power Structures in France's Gaullist Party', *West European Politics* 16 (3): 271–93.

Kriegel, A.(1968) *Les Communistes français*. Paris: Seuil.

Lachapelle, G. (1914) *Les Elections législatives des 26 avril et 10 mai 1914*. Paris: G. Gressin.

———. (1920) *Les Elections législatives du 16 novembre 1919*. Paris: Roustan.

———. (1924) *Les Elections législatives du 11 mai 1924*. Paris: Roustan.

———. (1928) *Les Elections législatives du 22 et 29 avril 1928*. Paris: Roustan.
———. (1932) *Les Elections législatives du 1 et 8 mai 1932*. Paris: Roustan.
———. (1936) *Les Elections législatives du 28 avril et 3 mai 1936*. Paris: Roustan.
Ladrech, R. and Marlière, P. (1999) 'The French Socialist Party' in Ladrech and Marlière (eds.) *Social Democratic Parties in the European Union*, London: MacMillan, pp. 64–78.
Larkin, M. (1974) *Church and State in France after the Dreyfus Affair: The Separation Issue*, London: MacMillan.
———. (1995) *Religion, Politics and Preferment in France since 1890*, Cambridge: CUP.
Larmour, P. (1964) *The French Radical Party in the 1930s*, Stanford: Stanford UP.
Lavau, G. (1953) *Partis politiques et réalités sociales*, Paris: Colin.
———. (1981) *A quoi sert le Parti communiste français?* Paris: Seuil.
Lavau, G., Grunberg, G. and Mayer, N. (eds.) (1983) *L'Univers politique des classes moyennes*, Paris: FNSP.
Laver, M. (1989) 'Party Competition and Party System Change', *Journal of Theoretical Politics*, 1 (3): 301–24.
Laver, M. and Schofield, N. (1990) *Multiparty Government*, Oxford: OUP.
Lavergne, B. (1966) *Les deux Présidences de Jules Grevy, 1879- 1887: mémoires de Bernard Lavergne*, Paris: Fischbacher.
Lawson, K. (1980) *Political Parties and Linkage: A Comparative Perspective*, New Haven: Yale UP.
Lawson, K. and Merkl, P. (eds.)(1988) *When Parties Fail: Emerging Alternative Organisations*, Princeton NJ: Princeton UP.
Lawson, K. and Ysmal, C. (1999) 'Do The Parties Matter?' in Lewis-Beck, M. (ed.) *How France Votes*, New York-London: Chatham House, pp. 127–43.
Le Béguec, G. (1989) *L'Entrée au Palais-Bourbon: les filières privilégiées d'accès à la fonction parlementaire*, Paris: Université de Paris X thesis.
———. (1992) 'Le Parti' in Sirinelli, J. (ed.) *Histoire des droites en France*, Paris: Gallimard, Vol. II, pp. 13–59.
Lefort, B. (1996) 'Les Partis et les groupes sous la Quatrième République', *Pouvoirs* 76: 61–79.
Lefranc, G. (1963) *Le Mouvement socialiste sous la Troisième République, 1875–1940*, Paris: Payot.
———. (1967) *Le Mouvement syndical sous la Troisième République*, Paris: Payot.
Letamendia, P. (1995) *Le Mouvement républicain populaire: histoire d'un grand parti français*, Paris: Beauchesne.
Lévêque, P. (1994) *Histoire des forces politiques en France, vol. 2, 1880-1940*, Paris: Colin.
Leyrit, C. (1997) *Les Partis politiques: indispensables et contestés*, Paris: Le Monde Editions.
Lhomme, J. (1960) *La grande Bourgeoisie au pouvoir, 1830-80*, Paris: PUF.
Lidderdale, D. (1954) *Le Parlement français*, Paris: Colin.
Ligou, D. (1962) *Histoire du socialisme en France*, Paris: PUF.
Lijphart, A. (1968) *The Politics of Accommodation: Pluralism and Democracy in the Netherlands*, Berkeley: University of California Press.
———. (1977) *Democracy in Plural Societies: A Comparative Exploration*, New Haven: Yale UP.
———. (1997) 'Changement et continuité dans la théorie consociative', *Revue Internationale de Politique Comparée* 4 (3): 679–98.
Lipset, S. and Rokkan, S. (eds.) (1967) *Party Systems and Voter Alignments: Cross-national Perspectives*, New York: Free Press.

Loschak, D. (1971) *La Convention des institutions républicaines*, Paris: PUF.
Loubet del Bayle, J. (1969) *Les Nonconformistes des années trente*, Paris: Seuil.
Machefer, P. (1974) *Ligues et fascismes en France, 1918-39*, Paris: PUF.
Machin, H. (1989) 'Stages and dynamics in the evolution of the French party system', *West European Politics* 12 (4): 59–83.
Machin, H. and Wright, V. (eds.) (1985) *Economic Policy and Policymaking under the Mitterrand Presidency, 1981-84*, London: Pinter.
MacMillan, J. (1996) ' Catholicism and Nationalism in France: The Case of The Fédération Nationale Catholique' in Tallett, F. and Atkin, N. (eds.) *Catholicism in Britain and France since 1789*, London: Hambledon, pp. 151–64.
MacRae, D. (1967) *Parliament, Politics and Society in France, 1946-58*, New York: St. Martin's Press.
Magraw, R. (1992) *France 1815-1914: The Bourgeois Century*, revised edition, London: Fontana.
Mair, P. (1984) 'Party politics in Western Europe: A Challenge to Party,' *West European Politics* 7 (4): 170–84.
———. (1989) 'The problem of party system change', *Journal of Theoretical Politics* 1 (3): 251–76.
———. (1995) 'Political parties, popular legitimacy and public privilege', *West European Politics* 18 (3): 40–57.
———. (1997) *Party System Change: Approaches and Interpretations*. Oxford: Clarendon Press.
Mair, P. and Katz, R.(1995) 'Changing models of party organisation and party democracy: the emergence of the cartel party', *Party Politics* 1 (1): 5–28.
Mair, P. and Smith, G. (eds.) (1990) *Understanding Party System Change in Western Europe*, London: F. Cass.
Mandrin, J. (1969) *Socialisme ou socialmédiocratie*, Paris: Seuil.
Marcus, J. (1958) *French Socialism in the Crisis Years*, New York: Praeger.
Martin, B. (1976) 'The Formation of the Alliance Libérale Populaire: An Example of Party Formation in the French Third Republic', *French Historical Studies* 9: 660–99.
Mayer, N. (1999) *Ces Français qui votent FN*, Paris: Flammarion.
Mayer, N. and Perrineau, P. (eds.) (1989) *Le Front National à découvert*, Paris: FNSP.
Mayeur, J. – M. (1966) *La Séparation de l'Eglise et le l'Etat*, Paris: Julliard.
———. (1973) *Les Débuts de la Troisième République, 1871-1898*, Paris: Seuil.
———. (1980) *Des Partis catholiques a la démocratie chrétienne, XIXe et Xxe siècles*, Paris: Colin.
———. (1984) *La Vie politique sous la Troisième République*, Paris: Seuil.
Mény, Y. (1992) *La Corruption de la République*. Paris: Fayard.
———. (1993)'La Décennie de la corruption', *Le Débat* 77: 14–25.
———. (ed.) (1997a) 'La Corruption de la vie publique', *Problèmes politiques et sociaux* 779: 1-78.
———. (1997b) 'La Corruption: question morale ou problème d'organisation de l'état?' *Revue française d'administration publique* 84 (10-12): 585–91.
Mollier, J. – Y. and George, J. (1994) *La plus longue des Républiques, 1870-1940*, Paris: Fayard.
Mossuz, J. (1970) *Les Clubs et la politique en France*, Paris: Colin.
Mossuz-Lavau, J. (1994) *Les Français et la politique*, Paris: Odile Jacob.
Nicolet, C. (1982) *L'Idée républicaine en France: essai d'histoire critique*, Paris: Gallimard.

Nugent, N. and Lowe, D. (1982) *The Left in France*, London: MacMillan.

Offerlé, M. (1984) 'Transformation d'une entreprise politique: de l'UDR au RPR, 1973-77', *Pouvoirs* 28: 5–26.

———. (1987) *Les Partis politiques*, 3rd edn., Paris: PUF.

Panebianco, A. (1988) *Political Parties: Organisation and Power*, Cambridge: CUP.

Passmore, K. (1997) *From Liberalism to Fascism: the Right in a French Province, 1928–39*, Cambridge: CUP.

Pennings, P. and Lane, J.-E. (eds.) (1998) *Comparing Party System Change*, London: Routledge.

Perrineau, P. (1994) *L'Engagement politique: déclin ou mutation?*, Paris: FNSP.

Pétry, F. (1992) 'Coalition Bargaining in the Fourth French Republic, 1946-58' in Laver, M. and Budge, I. (eds.) *Party Policy and Coalition Government*, London: MacMillan, pp. 380–407.

Pierce, R. (1992) 'Toward the formation of a partisan alignment in France', *Political Behaviour* 14 (4): 443–69.

Plessis, A. (1973) *De la Fête impériale au mur des fédérés*, Paris: Seuil.

Plumyène, J. and Lasierra, R. (1963) *Les Fascismes français, 1923–63*, Paris: Seuil.

Pomper, G. (1992) 'Concepts of Political Parties', *Journal of Theoretical Politics* 4 (2): 143–59.

Ponceyri, R. (1988) *Les Elections sous la Ve. République*, Toulouse: Privat.

Poperen, J. (1975) *L'Unité de la gauche, 1965-72*, Paris: Fayard.

Portelli, H. (1980) *Le socialisme français tel qu'il est*, Paris: Presses Universitaires de France.

———. 1992) *Le Parti socialiste*, Paris: Monchrestien.

Portier, P. (1993) *Eglise et politique en France au Xxe. siècle*, Paris: Monchrestien.

Pouvoirs (1996) special number on 'La Quatrième République', no. 76.

Prelot, M. and Gallouedec-Genuys, F. (1969) *Le Libéralisme catholique*, Paris: Colin.

Priouret, R. (1959) *La République des députés*, Paris: Grasset.

Purtschet, C. (1965) *Le Rassemblement du peuple français*, Paris: Cujas.

Quilliot, R. (1972) *La SFIO et l'exercice du pouvoir (1944-58)*, Paris: Fayard.

Rabaut, J. (1974) *Tout est possible: les gauchistes français, 1929-44*, Paris: Denoel.

Racine, N. and Bodin, L. (1982) *Le Parti communiste pendant l'entre-deux-guerres*, 2nd edn.,Paris: Colin.

Ranger, J. (1986) 'Le Déclin du parti communiste français', *Revue française de science politique* XXVI (1): 46–62.

Rebérioux, M. (1975) *La République radicale?, 1889-1914*. Paris: Seuil.

Reiter, H. (1993) 'The Rise of the "New Agenda" and the Decline of Partisanship', *West European Politics* 16 (2): 89–104.

Rémond, R.(1968) *La Droite en France*, Paris: Aubier-Montaigne.

———. (1969) *La Vie politique en France depuis 1789*, 2 vols., Paris: Colin.

Rémond, R. and Bourdin, J. (eds.) (1977) *Edouard Daladier, chef de gouvernement, avril 1938 -septembre 1939*, Paris: FNSP.

———. (1978) *La France et les Français en 1938-39*, Paris: FNSP.

Renouvin, P. and Rémond, R. (eds.) (1967) *Léon Blum, chef de gouvernement*, Paris: FNSP.

Reynolds, S. (1999) 'Outsiders by birth? Women, the Republic and political history' in Alexander, M. (ed.)*French History Since Napoleon*, London: Arnold, pp. 127–46.

Riot-Sarcey, M. (ed.) (1995) *Démocratie et représentativité*. Paris: Klimé.

Rioux, J. – P. (1973) *Révolutionnaires du Front Populaire*, Paris: Union Générale d'Editions.

————. (1980; 1983) *La France de la Quatrième République, 1944-58*, 2 vols., vol. 1, *L'Ardeur et la nécessité, 1944-52*; vol. 2, *L'Expansion et l'impuissance, 1952-58*, Paris: Seuil.

Rocard, M. (1972) *Questions à l'état socialiste*, Paris: Marabout.

Rosanvallon, P. (1998) *Le Peuple introuvable: histoire de la représentation démocratique en France*, Paris: Gallimard.

Ross, G. (1987)'Adieu vieilles idées: the middle strata and the decline of Resistance-Liberation left discourse in France' in Ross, G. and Howorth J. (eds.), *Contemporary France* I: 57–83.

Roussellier, N. (1992) *Phénomène de majorité et relation de majorité en régime parlementaire: le cas du Bloc National en France dans le premier après-guerre européen (1919-24)*. Paris: IEP thesis.

————. (1997) *Le Parlement de l'éloquence*, Paris: FNSP.

Rudelle, O. (1982) *La République absolue: aux origines de l'instabilité constitutionnelle de la France républicaine, 1870-79*, Paris: Publications de la Sorbonne.

Sadoun, M. (1982) *Les Socialistes sous l'Occupation*, Paris: FNSP.

Sanson, R. (1992) 'Centre et Gauche, 1901-14: L'Alliance Républicaine Démocratique et le Parti Radical-Socialiste', *Revue d'Histoire Moderne et Contemporaine* 39: 493–512.

Sartori, G. (1976) *Parties and Party Systems*, Cambridge: CUP.

Schattschneider, E. (1975) *The Semisovereign People*, Hinsdale, Ill.: Dryden Press.

Schlesinger, J. and Schlesinger, M. (1999) 'The Stability of the French Party System: The Enduring Impact of the Two-Ballot Electoral Rules' in Lewis-Beck, M. (ed.) *How France Votes*, London-New York: Chatham House, pp. 130–52.

Sedgwick, A. (1965) *The Ralliement in French Politics*, Cambridge, Mass.: Harvard UP.

Seiler, D. (1980) *Partis et familles politiques*, Paris: PUF.

Shipway, M. (1996) *The Road to War: France and Vietnam, 1944–47*, Oxford: Berghahn.

Siegfried, A. (1913) *Tableau politique de la France de l'Ouest sous la Troisième République*, Paris: Colin.

————. (1930) *Tableau des partis en France*, Paris: Grasset.

Simmons, H. (1970) *French Socialists in Search of a Role*, Ithaca, NY: Cornell UP.

————. (1996) *The French National Front: The Extremist Challenge to Democracy*, Boulder, Co: Westview Press.

Sirinelli, J.- F., (ed.) (1992a) *Histoire des droites en France*, 3 vols., Paris: Gallimard.

Smith, G. (1989) 'A system perspective on party system change', *Journal of Theoretical Politics* 1 (3): 349–63.

Sorlin, P. (1966) *Waldeck Rousseau*, Paris: Colin.

Soucy, R. (1986) *French Fascism: The First Wave, 1924-33*, New Haven: Yale UP.

————. (1995) *French Fascism: The Second Wave, 1933-39*, New Haven: Yale UP.

Sternhell, Z. (1978) *La Droite révolutionnaire, 1885-1914: les origines françaises du fascisme*, Paris: Seuil.

Stone, J. (1986) *The Search for Social Peace: Reform Legislation in France, 1890–1914*, New York: SUNY Press.

Tarde, A. de and Jouvenel, R. de (1924) *La Politique aujourd'hui: enquête parmi les groupements et les partis*. Paris: La Renaissance du Livre.

Therborn, G. (1977) 'The rule of capital and the rise of democracy', *New Left Review* 103: 3–41.

Thibaudet, A. (1927) *La République des professeurs*. Paris: Grasset.

Todd, E. (1988) *La nouvelle France*, Paris: Seuil.

Vinen, R. (1993) 'The Parti Républicain de la Liberté and the reconstruction of French conservatism, 1944-51', *French History* 7: 183–204.

————. (1995) *Bourgeois Politics in France, 1945-51*, Cambridge: CUP.

Waline, J. (1961) 'Les groupes politiques en France', *Revue du droit public et de la science politique en France et à l'étranger* 77: 1170–1237.

Ware, A. (1996) *Political Parties and Party Systems*, Oxford: OUP.

Weber, E. (1962) *L'Action française*, Paris: Stock.

————. (1977) *Peasants into Frenchmen: The Modernisation of Rural France, 1870-1914*, London: Chatto and Windus.

Wileman, D. (1990) 'P. – E. Flandin and the Alliance Républicaine Démocratique, 1929-39', *French History* 4: 139–73.

————. (1994) 'Not the Radical Republic: liberal ideology and central blandishment in France, 1900-1914', *Historical Journal* 37 (3): 593–614.

Willard, C. (1965) *Le Mouvement socialiste en France, 1893–1905: les guesdistes*, Paris: Editions Sociales.

Williams, P. (1964) *Crisis and Compromise: The Politics of the Fourth French Republic*, London: Longmans.

Wilson, F. (1982) *French Political Parties under the Fifth Republic*, New York: Praeger.

Winock, M. (ed.) (1995) *La droite depuis 1789*, Paris: Seuil.

Wolf, D. (1969) *Doriot: du communisme à la collaboration*, Paris: Fayard.

Wolinetz, S. (ed.)(1988) *Parties and Party Systems in Liberal Democracies*, London: Routledge.

Ysmal, C. (1989) *Les Partis politiques sous la Cinquième République*, Paris: Montchrestien.

Zeldin, T. (1958) *The Political System of Napoleon III*, Oxford: OUP.

————. (1973) *France, 1848-1945, vol. I, Ambition, Love and Politics*, Oxford: OUP.

Ziebura, G. (1967) *Léon Blum et le parti socialiste, 1872–1934*, Paris: FNSP.

INDEX

www.ingramcontent.com/pod-product-compliance
Lightning Source LLC
Chambersburg PA
CBHW060037030426
42334CB00019B/2362